GOLDEN WINGS AND NAVY BLUE

John Fay was born in Brazil and brought up in New
Zealand until the age of nine when he came to
England. From school in 1940 he joined the Fleet Air
Arm as a pilot and after a year's training joined 832
Squadron and spent two years in the aircraft carrier
HMS *Victorious*. After some months in the Service
Trials Unit he was appointed in 1944 to the first
helicopter course in the country. After the war he
joined the British European Airways Helicopter Unit,
subsequently becoming a test pilot at Westland
Aircraft. He is keen on ballroom and sequence
dancing, photography, gardening and music.
He lives near Chard in Somerset.

GOLDEN WINGS AND NAVY BLUE

John Fay

HALLMARK PRESS

Published by Hallmark Press International Ltd
34 Lambton Court,
Peterlee,
County Durham
SR8 1NG

Second impression

Typeset by TW Typesetting, Plymouth, Devon

Printed by CPI Antony Rowe, Eastbourne

Dedicated to all Fleet Air Arm personnel,
past, present and future.

'Yes, we do fly aeroplanes even though we wear naval uniform.'

'No, we don't have an RAF pilot sitting beside us.'

'During the first hour of an A/S Patrol we were looking for periscopes under every wave. During the second the pilot is bored, the observer indifferent and the TAG asleep. For the third hour both the observer and the TAG are asleep and the pilot is propping up his eyelids with matchsticks.'

Remark made to the author in 2006:

'You were in *19 Course*? You should be dead!'

CONTENTS

LIST OF ILLUSTRATIONS

FOREWORD

In the years since the war I have written several articles concerning some of my experiences in the Fleet Air Arm from 1940-1946. I have now collected these together and considerably expanded them, giving them more detail and, I hope, more interest. In particular I have added a section on my year as a rating and the training we underwent. As I have emphasised again and again, I was lucky, lucky with my appointments, lucky with the various dangerous situations that left me alive and untouched. And I should point out that most of the latter were not due to enemy action so much as to the day-to-day incidents that occurred with all aircrews while they were training or honing their skills.

I have several people and institutions to thank for their help. Outstanding among them is John Herbert, a fighter pilot in 896 Squadron aboard HMS *Victorious* during the 1943 Pacific trip. Using a camera he bought for $10 he took numerous photographs and sorted some 300 out to send to me, some of which are reproduced here.

Then David Gibbings whose eagle eye spotted many typing errors that other people missed, and who corrected some of my other mistakes and asked pertinent questions about things that landlubbers might not understand. And the following: John Barnes, Doug Briggs, John Burbidge and Bruce Petrie, all ex-members of 832 Squadron; and Mac Rutherford, formerly of 841 Squadron, all of whom helped in many different ways Also David Kinloch and R.D.Layman.

For permission to use quotations from their books I would also like to thank Ray Barker (*Victorious The World Over*) and Bob Fletcher (*Touch and Go*).

Selections from *High Flight* are produced with permission from the book *John Magee the Pilot Poet* published by This England Books, PO Box 52 Cheltenham, Glos. GL50 1YQ, UK.

Chris Wren's cartoons are reproduced by the kind permission of *Aeroplane Monthly*.

I should like to thank my editor Sheila Seacroft and all the Hallmark team for the help they have given me in the preparation of this book.

Finally I should like to thank my wife Dorothy for her patience and her help in many different ways.

1

INTRODUCTION: 1943 CORAL SEA

The SBD Dauntless dive-bomber roared down the deck of the USS *Saratoga*, watched keenly by members of 832 Squadron, Royal Navy, who were embarked aboard her. Suddenly the engine noise stopped followed by a squealing of rubber as the brakes were applied and the aircraft came to a standstill. We were amazed; we had never seen an aircraft stop like that during its take-off run, but then the *Saratoga* was a bit different from HMS *Victorious*, to which the squadron had been attached for nearly two years, for the flight deck of the *Saratoga* was considerably longer. This was not the only time we witnessed an SBD stop in mid take-off, it happened again and seemed to be a fairly normal occurrence.

Unfortunately this had an unforeseen result. Some days later I was due to carry out a dawn anti-submarine patrol. Our squadron was equipped with Avengers. At that time they were called Tarpons, but the name was changed to agree with the American name; and wisely too, surely one would want to go into battle in an Avenger rather than a Tarpon! For operational reasons our aircraft were taken on board the *Saratoga* while an American fighter squadron was embarked in the *Victorious*. The unusual, and perhaps amusing, events leading up to my take-off run are described later. Anyway, I started my acceleration down the deck, but after a very short interval I thought my engine was not pulling as it should. In this situation I could either continue the take-off run or try to stop. Had I been on board the *Victorious* I would have continued on ahead for certain, but on board this mighty ship I thought I could pull up, after all had I not seen this done quite easily by the SBDs? I don't remember making the decision to throttle back; I had only split seconds to decide what to do. Anyway my left hand pulled back on the throttle and I stood on the brakes and skidded down the deck.

I could see I was not going to make it! With the forward end of the flight deck approaching fast I steered slightly to starboard so that I would drop in the water from the overhang of the deck rather than be sliced in two by the bows of the ship. Just before I reached the end I released the brakes as I thought this would reduce the tipping action and the aircraft would not go in upside down. It went in upside down anyway, for the fuselage hit the deck as the aircraft started to fall and the aircraft was tipped into the Coral Sea.

During the war pilots used to shoot a line by saying, tongue in cheek, 'There I was old boy, upside down and nothing on the clock (i.e airspeed zero),' followed perhaps by something like, 'and my guns were still firing at the enemy ...!' I could better this by saying, 'There I was old boy, upside down, nothing on the clock, *and under water!*'

However at the time I was not thinking about this, I was holding my breath and trying to get out. I undid my parachute and then my safety harness and started to clear the cockpit, only to find my helmet lead holding me back. I remembered that instead of having a clip in the middle of it, this American-type lead had no easy disconnection. I thought that if I tried to find the cockpit connection I would lose precious seconds and might possibly panic so I carried out the more familiar action of taking off my helmet. All this was taking time and I was fast running out of breath. They say that when one is near to death one's past comes before one's eyes, but my own thoughts ran: 'You fool, so you thought you were going to get through the war alive,' and, 'What a shame I have to die so young.' I was also thinking of my parents and the effect it would have on them.

I pushed myself out of the cockpit, anticipating being able to get some precious air into my lungs in a few seconds' time. Had I been able to hyperventilate before going under water I would have been able to hold my breath fairly easily, but of course I had no time for such a thing and it was only with determination and a sense of self-preservation that I was able to hold my breath all this time: the urge to gasp was paramount. When I did extricate myself I found I was underneath a wing and some more seconds had to elapse before I came to the surface by the trailing aerial. The ship was about 150 yards away by this time. I took two or three gulps of air and then looked over what was normally the bottom of the fuselage, but which was now on the surface pointing up at the sky, and saw Bob Procter my Observer and the Air Gunner, Bob Kinghan, on the other side. The relief was enormous and I can well understand the feeling captains have of wanting to go down with the ship when there are people still on board. Apparently Bob Procter had got out quite easily, but the other Bob had had some trouble. In his position in the turret he had carried out a backward somersault with the aircraft as it dropped, his escape hatch had been broken and he had to crawl through a hole that was not nearly big enough to take him. He had hurt his eyes in getting through he also looked rather pale. He said that he felt all right.

Unlike British-built aircraft the Avenger did not have an automatically inflating dinghy and the aircraft sank before we could pull the internally stowed one from the side of the fuselage. Indeed, at that stage none of us even thought about it and I, certainly, would have been too exhausted to swim the few strokes to the aircraft to inflate it. I wonder how many American lives would have been saved if the dinghies had come out automatically like the British ones did?

When the aircraft sank there was no possibility of the depth charges exploding, because the observer controlled their safety. He had a control lever in the rear cockpit and he could keep the depth charges at SAFE until the pilot told him he was attacking a submarine.

I pulled the tag to inflate my life jacket and sat comfortably in the water beside two lights that the ship had dropped after we had fallen into in the sea, it being dawn and the sun was not yet up, and waited for a destroyer to rescue us. After a while I found myself getting lower in the water and realised that the mouthpiece of my life jacket was undone and most of the precious gas in the jacket had escaped! I was too breathless to blow the jacket up by mouth so remained where I was, a few inches lower in the water than I should have been, upheld by the kapok in the life jacket. We thought momentarily of sharks, but firmly believed that the small phials we carried were an efficient deterrent. Little did we know that they were absolutely useless!

After fifteen minutes in the warm waters of the Coral Sea we were picked up by the USS *Fanning*, aboard which we received unbounded hospitality, the *pièce de résistance* being the ice cream, which the ship had received the previous day for picking up the crew of a British aircraft that had had an engine failure. Later on we were returned by breeches buoy to the *Saratoga*. It was quite a coincidence to be picked up by the *Fanning* for I had had dinner aboard this destroyer when she was in Noumea.

I was lucky; but the thought remains: if I had not throttled back and tried to stop the aircraft would I have had enough power to become airborne at the end of the flight deck?

I was still at school in 1940 and after Dunkirk I felt I should enlist. My parents were in the Argentine and I had promised them I would not join up without their permission, so I sent a wire to them and they replied back immediately that it was all right. I was very fortunate for at about this time the headmaster put up a notice saying that young gentlemen were required for pilot or observer duties in the Fleet Air Arm. I had never heard of the Fleet Air Arm and I had originally wanted to go into the RAF. I think it was the *young gentlemen* bit that got me! Vague thoughts of being treated like a gentleman from day one appealed to me! This of course did not come to pass and almost everyone during the war had to be in the lower ranks before being commissioned. I was told later that Vice Admiral Bell Davies, VC, was the one who had been responsible for the notice, having written to the headmaster. I met him a few years later when I was in the Service Trials Unit; he had dropped a rank or two to become Captain of HMS *Pretoria Castle*. He became a pilot in World War I and was a Squadron Commander in the Royal Naval Air Service. He retired from the Navy with the rank of Vice Admiral, but was recalled as a commodore of convoys before becoming a ship's captain.

I went to a recruiting centre in Reading and was interviewed by a fatherly old Royal Marine. He was busy working on something and he looked up and said, 'How do you spell Haslemere?' I said, 'I suppose it is HAZELMERE. He said, 'Strangely, it is not, it is HASLEMERE'. I mention this because my very *last* appointment in the Navy was to Haslemere!

The school term finished a week or two after this and I went to my Aunt Dorothy and her fairly new husband at Chipstead, Surrey, where they were living in my grandmother's house and looking after her, for she had either Alzheimer's Disease or some kind of senile dementia. The next few weeks stick in my memory as a time I suffered from a lack of sleep. The Germans were coming over a lot and the air raid warnings were sounding. It was not too bad during the day, but at night we had to get up and go to the air raid shelter that was in the garden. This had extremely uncomfortable seats and sometimes I felt that it would be better to risk the bombing than to endure the discomfort. On 11th September the biggest barrage we had yet heard was put up and heralded my nineteenth birthday on the morrow. In my diary I record that a shell must have burst every second. This was the anti-aircraft gun putting up a box barrage; I don't think it caused many extra casualties among the enemy, but it certainly improved everyone's morale. I record that I went to bed at last at 2.30 a.m.

Since I did not hear from the Admiralty I wrote to them to see what was going on. I think this did the trick, for a pilot I met many years afterwards said that he had to wait ages before he was called for interview. A few weeks later I was sent a travel warrant and told to go to HMS *St Vincent* in Gosport for a medical and interview. Just prior to this I had been staying with the Lawrences who themselves were staying with some very kind people, the Yates, at Oxshott. Since Mr Yates had been in the navy he immediately told me that HMS *St Vincent*, despite being His Majesty's *Ship*, was a shore station, or stone frigate as it was often called in the navy. This probably saved me from having a red face and a fruitless search around Gosport looking for a ship called HMS *St Vincent*!

An Admiral, a Lieutenant-Commander and one other conducted my interview. The first question was, 'What is a barometer for?' 'For measuring the pressure of the air, Sir.' 'And what would happen if you took it up a mountain?' 'The reading would go down, Sir.'

I have often wondered whether if I had added, 'And of course the body of the barometer would go *up*, Sir!' I would have gained extra points! I had heard that in the old days one might be told to sit down. If one protested there were no chairs it was a black mark. If one immediately sat on the floor one gained a point. Other questions followed, in particular whether I had done any rowing and if so where? I said I had done rowing, but hesitated on the *where*. I did not want to say, 'On my grandfather's lake.' As I believed they might think I was showing off. I was asked what muscles hurt after rowing and I told them, 'The back muscles,' which satisfied them. Other questions followed about my gymnastic prowess, as they did not seem to think I had taken part in all the sports I had put down on the paper I had filled in. I was asked whether I could do a long arm balance. I told them yes, I could, but only on the low parallel bars. I suppose if I had said, 'Wot's er long arm balance, Surr?' they would have known I was trying to make out I could do more things than I had claimed.

Questions on Trigonometry followed. I did not do too well on these and this might have been a good thing because when they called me back into the room after the interview I was told I had passed for *pilot*. No mention was made of being passed for *observer* as well.

I took the medical an hour or two later. The most difficult test was to maintain a pressure of mercury while holding one's breath for a full minute. I carried out some hyperventilation and then utilising my chemistry knowledge (where while using a blowpipe one could keep a continuous pressure by puffing up one's cheeks) I managed to keep the mercury at the correct height using the cheek pressure alone. Anyway I passed and went home to await further developments.

Among the entrants that day was Tony Garland, often known as Judy for obvious reasons. We later arrived on the same course together and finished up on the same ship together, although being a fighter boy he was in a different squadron.

I was called up to join on 16 September 1940. It was only after I had been in the navy for a few months that I realised that FAA – The Fleet

Air Arm – was only one letter removed from my name – FAY! I had known that, when my three initials (JSF) were superimposed to make a monogram, an Admiralty pattern anchor could be created by the addition of a single stroke to make the right-hand fluke of the anchor. As well as forming an S, part of the anchor rope must he placed in such a manner to form the short crosspiece of the F. The creation of this monogram was mere coincidence, my family had no naval tradition; the only other military member of the family was my father who was in the Royal Engineers during World War I.

2

HMS *ST VINCENT*, GOSPORT

The train journey to Portsmouth was a bit fraught as it took two hours to get to Balham from Purley due to air raids. At Balham there was large crowd and I thought that if a bomb dropped now there would be absolute carnage. On the train I met one or two other entrants including Brilliant, Hunter, and Tony Garland. I noted that my joining instructions stated that I would receive 1/6d (15p) for any meals I had to pay for while travelling! How far would that go today?

At *St Vincent* the first thing we did was to sign various forms including one giving the names of our next of kin and headed rather ominously THIS IS NOT A WILL! At 2015 hours the sirens went and I spent my time in a shelter until 0115 hours feeling intensely bored. I was in a dormitory with about 15 others and they not only included youngsters like me, but one or two men who had been in the navy some time and had been selected for flying duties.

Our beds had palliasses on them. I had not come across the word before, they were in fact straw-filled mattresses, and were not at all comfortable. I was reliably informed that courses only a few months previously had to sleep in hammocks, which for my part I would have found even less comfortable. On re-reading my diary I am surprised that we ever spent any nights in the dormitories for the red alerts seemed to be frequent, although Portsmouth never had any heavy attacks when I was there. But the dormitories were a place of refuge and somewhere one could put one's feet up and talk to the others, and were the only bit of the establishment one could call one's own.

Next day our course, which was 19 Course St Vincent, was bussed to HMS *Victory*, the stone frigate (i.e. a shore station, not Nelson's flagship) and were kitted out. We were also given a circular metal box for keeping our caps in; I still have this, it has lasted well. I was now a sailor with bellbottom trousers and a suit of navy blue and earning 2/- (20p) a day. I found the uniform complicated as there were no pockets as such, only a couple in the most awkward places, and there was a money belt. Instead of fly buttons there was a large flap that came up and buttoned near the waist. The bellbottom trousers were normally ironed inside out and creases put on the outer and inner edges of the trouser legs. When the trousers were turned the right way round the creases were then concave on the inner and outer sides of the legs. Some keen Jack Tars would have extra flares put in the trousers so that they were more bell-like. Another practice by the keen ones was to iron the trousers so that the trouser legs had squares down the length of them. To me this made them look as if they had been folded and packed in a suitcase and left for some time; indeed, I seem to remember seeing a cartoon about this. Uniforms that had been altered in this sort of manner were called tiddley suits. At the time I joined we were given caps and some ribbons labelled HMS *St Vincent*, which had to be sewn on in the acceptable manner.

I was also given two pairs of boots. I was not accustomed to wearing shoes or boots that had leather soles as I found they were noisy and tended to slip, so I had rubber soles put on them. No RN types seemed to notice this fact so either this was legal or they were not concerned about them.

Early on 18 September I kept waking up to the sound of running water and thought it was rain. However, in the morning we found our dormitory was an inch deep in water caused by a tap left running on the landing outside the room. Later that day we were taught about shooting. No doubt this was given high priority in case of invasion. Having gained my shooting colours at Bradfield I did not learn much on this occasion! Next day we shot in earnest at targets and, including a sighting shot that unfortunately was included in the score, I still managed to be the top scorer as far as I could ascertain.

To go ashore in the navy one has to catch a 'Liberty Boat', which was available only at certain times, although, of course, on a shore station it is physically possible to walk out through the gateway. So, having lined up, those of us on this particular Liberty Boat were inspected by an officer and marched through the gate. Crossing to Portsmouth on the ferry I had a meal, saw a film, and then was an interested spectator watching a French sailor holding up another drunk one and trying to calm him. When he started being sick I faded from the scene.

A few days later we had one of the innumerable air raid warnings. This one occurred during a navigation class and by mistake I went down to the wrong air raid shelter. This one was full of rough matelots and after a quarter of an hour I got heartily sick of their language, which was not that of Shakespeare. Every sentence seemed to have the f-word in it

HMS *St Vincent*. 19th 'Rodney' Pilots' Course. 19.9.40–10.11.40.

– sometimes two or three of them. I almost wished they let loose a b-word just to add a bit of variety to their language. The present-day person reading this might wonder at the fact that I was shocked, for with television putting on more and more shows in which the f-word is used with considerable frequency one has almost become hardened to it. But in those far off days the word was comparatively new to me.

Thanks to knowing the Morse Code from an early age I did well in our first 'Buzz' practice. I owe my skill at Morse to my early enthusiasm for it. I owed my skill at knots to my Boy Scout training and I was good at drilling a squad thanks to OTC training at Bradfield. However, at navigation I seemed to be lagging behind. I don't know why this should be as my maths was normally fairly good.

One day I was informed that there was a parcel for 'Pay'. As this was the name I had been given erroneously in various other notices, I understood quite correctly it that the parcel was for me. Confusion was caused in the Regulating Office and a Petty Officer accused me of being deaf; this epithet being laced with a string of 'bloodys'. I suppose I would have been put on a charge if I had answered him back, so I kept mum!

Having said that, at no time did any of the Petty Officers use words that, if television shows are to be believed, appeared to be commonplace in other services at the time.

The world is full of coincidences. I met a chap called Holdsworth in 18 Course who was the occupant of the room I had when taking the Littlego exam at Cambridge. He had a photo of himself in that room, and being tall and blond was easily recognisable. I told him about the coincidence.

Also on the course ahead of me was Hugh Popham who was an author and who wrote the excellent book *Sea Flight* depicting his many adventures in the FAA. Since his father was a governor in the West Indies this was a news item in the Canadian newspapers when he arrived there. Quite an amazing character was Barry Lister. I remember him standing on a table and dishing out duties to members of his course in a way that made him stand out as a natural leader. He had been a member of the Bradford Repertory Company, which must have given him the advantage of being an experienced public speaker. Like Hugh Popham I thought he must be anything up to 30 years old and we were amazed to find that he was in fact only 19! His secret was divulged when he arrived in a midshipman's uniform after he was commissioned. A year or so later Barry was killed in one of those accidents pilots all fear – a collision in the air. This one was over Northern Ireland.

These two characters started on a course two or three months before mine and I would never have met them were it not for the fact that Barry became ill and Hugh Popham was wounded by shrapnel. They finished up in 18 Course, the one before mine.

Another coincidence, if one can call it that, occurred when I was standing by the edge of the parade ground. The seaman beside me looked familiar and we both realised we knew each other. He was P.R. Stevens who was at my prep school with me. He had been slightly senior to me and was not only good looking, but brainy and charming as well. Beyond wondering how he would get on in the seaman branch I did not think any more of the meeting. However, about the time of the end of the war I went to a dance at Cranleigh. The Lieutenant-Commander there looked familiar and he was also an FAA pilot. The penny suddenly dropped and I realised it was Stevens again. So he must have transferred to the FAA and done well, as he deserved.

On 10 October I noted in my diary: A day of blue sky and overcast sky alternately with air raids and all clears to go with them. In one of our classes the Yeoman of Signals told us about the letter **U** in International code. When signalled it meant, 'You are standing into danger!' He mentioned an incident when the submarine HMS *Thetis* was being salvaged and at which he had been present. Suddenly a large French oil tanker loomed out of the fog straight at them. They signalled 'U'. Luckily it was understood in time and a collision averted.

I was amazed and pleased to discover that we had the very first course of New Zealanders with us. These consisted of: Jock Bennett, Gordon Black, Geoff Burke, Denny Evans, Bruce Girdlestone, Eddie Hunt, Doug Harris, Ken Procter, Harold Hawken, Doug Hill, Pete Holthouse, Clive Hoosen, Arch Hugill, Frank Pennington (often known as Faj because of his initials), Ron Spackman, 'Sully' Sullivan, and Dale Wiren. This was another coincidence for me, after all I was part New Zealander at heart having spent five years of my childhood there. Of all the people on 19 Course only Arch Hugill, Ron Spackman, and Jock Landles joined me a year later in 832 Squadron. Tony Garland joined 809 Squadron in the *Victorious* on the same day as I joined 832. I encountered few of the 19 course members after the war. I met Linstead at Northolt, and I met most of the New Zealanders – those who survived – at the reunions of their Fleet Air Arm Association, which I flew out to join on two occasions.

No reference to HMS *St Vincent* during the war years could be complete without mentioning Chief Petty Officer Wilmot. Physically small, he had a tremendous voice and forceful personality. He dominated the parade ground. He even has a mention in Google, where he is called 'Famous and feared'! I don't know about 'feared', perhaps 'held in awe' would be more appropriate. He had his pleasant side so one is left with a feeling of admiration for him. I often wonder what a man like him would have achieved if he had had a good education; his lack of it is revealed in his most famous phrase: 'You lot get fell in at 0730 hours. Them's what's keen get fell in previous!'

While searching for Wilmot on Google I came across an interesting fact about the New Zealand volunteers. I quote, 'One draft was aboard the liner RANGITANE when it was intercepted by German raiders in the Pacific (Nov 1940). 13 accepted parole and were returned to non-combat duties in NZ; others became prisoners of war (it wasn't their choice, it depended on which raider, THOR or KOMET, they were captured by).'

A week or two later it was decreed that FAA potential officers should have white bands round their caps instead of the normal cap bands. I think this was a grave mistake: we stood out like sore thumbs; we could never hitch a lift from Petty Officers and the like; and railway booking clerks would mistake us for St John's Ambulance personnel! We were also forever explaining what we were. Of course to hitch a lift it was best to remove the white band and replace it with an HMS *St Vincent* ribbon. When I had the HMS *St Vincent* cap band on a lorry driver stopped without me even having to make the hitchhike sign with my thumb. I made one bad mistake in Portsmouth when I went into a large naval canteen with my cap displaying my white band. Everyone stopped talking and looked at me. I slunk off as rapidly as possible!

One of the tests we potential airmen had to do was prove that we could swim. To this end we had to swim one length of the outdoor baths at St Vincent. No one failed, least of all the New Zealanders; neither, of course did that pseudo-New Zealander (well, at least I had a brother who was a New Zealander!) – me! However, this was September, the water was fairly cold and I just wondered how the course that followed us would cope. Were they taken to warm swimming baths, or did they have to endure freezing water just to prove they could pass the test?

Portsmouth had been bombed before my arrival, but there was, in fact, little actual bombing of the area during my time, although I noted that the Germans set off some fires in Portsmouth during one raid. I see that on one night there was a heavy barrage going on as I returned to the gates of the barracks and I had to go to the wardroom cellar and used my gas mask as a pillow to enable me to sleep there. The wardroom cellar was my usual place of refuge during an air raid warning. At another time during daylight I could see about 40 German bombers circling around, which made everyone rush for the shelters.

One day we were marched down to a cutter in the harbour and looked forward to a row around the place. Unfortunately the sirens went off just as we set off and we had to return and take shelter. Another time we were able to push off, get in some boat-pulling time and row round the harbour. We saw the submarine HMS *Swordfish* at anchor and wondered how long she would last. In fact she was sunk by a mine off Brest only a few weeks later, none of the crew survived. We also saw a lovely clean British cruiser that was in stark contrast to the French units there.

A strange rumour swept around the place that Japan had declared war. At the time we gave little thought to Japan being an enemy so it was strange and prophetic that this story should circulate.

At payday I received the first money I had ever earned and was given 30 shillings (£1.50)!

On 7 October I saw in the newspaper that *The Highland Patriot* had been sunk. She was the ship in which my brother Dick and I travelled to the Argentine in 1939. In January she had had a two-hour fight with a U-boat, but had managed to drive it off with her guns. Five torpedoes were fired at her; I should think the U-boat Captain was pretty browned off at wasting five of his precious torpedoes! This time she was hit by one torpedo, which set her on fire. A second one, fired after a 20-minute interval, narrowly missed the lifeboats. Fortunately a British warship saw the smoke and picked up the passengers.

I paid a visit to the sick bay for the epidermathytonpedis on my left foot. The attendant said, 'What's the matter with you? I said, ' I have Athlete's Foot'. I then got a ticking off for knowing better than the doctors! I forbore to tell him that I had been to two doctors before who had diagnosed it. It really was amazing how some jumped-up little men can try to take it out on one, usually in full view of some insignificant spectators.

Petty Officer Oliver gave us a lecture on a machine gun, which I found interesting. Since I mentioned this in my diary it must have been the Vickers Armstrong machine gun that I had to know intimately at Bradfield. I remember that at school we had to be able to deal with various stoppages and also had to take some particular part to pieces blindfold and put it together again. At one time PO Oliver observed that he had been in the navy X number of years and had only reached the rank of PO. Here *we* were and after a year we would all be officers! I can't say I blamed him for his slight show of pique; on the other hand we were to be aircrew and the naval side was of secondary interest to us, although to have declared that at any time would be blasphemy! Later, when we were commissioned, we were told that we were naval officers first and members of the Fleet Air Arm second.

Some of the Petty Officers were good at making their lectures interesting. One told us about the senior officer being the last to get aboard any small boat and the first to disembark. He put it this way: 'The captain wants to stay in his quarters until the very last so that he can carry on drinking his gin. So he waits until all the other men are aboard the boat then he gets in last. When the boat reaches shore, the captain is in a hurry to get into the local wardroom so that he can carry on with his gin drinking. So he is the first out.'

On one particularly beautiful moonlit night I got out of bed three times with the various alarms and excursions. Then we were shaken by four bombs that were dropped on Whale Island.

Our knowledge of the Morse Code was tested with a buzzer test and I got 50 marks out of 50. Our class was Rodney B and we had 8 people with 50. The next best class was Rodney A with 4. I learnt that the general opinion among the POs was that we were the most efficient squad.

I came bottom of the class in a navigation test. Depressing! Whilst I did well at practical things I was not so good at the written work.

Back at *St Vincent* we went to the rifle range for a bit of shooting. For this we used Ross rifles, it was pity we were not doing groups, but were supposed to aim directly at the target. We were allowed one sighting shot, so when I found my first shot was a Magpie I adjusted my aim. My next shot was an Inner, then three Bulls and another Inner. Total score 17 out of 20. Not too bad and I did not hear of anyone doing better, but then as I had done quite a lot of shooting in my life I did have an advantage.

A few days later I was coming back to Portsmouth and had just got off the Gosport ferry when the sirens went and there was a good bombardment as I walked to *St Vincent*. I was let in and went down to the Wardroom cellar. The chaplain came in later on and presented us with some apples, at the same time asking if any of us suffered from night starvation!

I note that I had stomach ache on 23 September, and I thought it was due to eating 9d worth of coconut ice the night before! My duties that day included floor polishing and cleaning a night head. In the navy the loos are called *heads*. This gives rise to a joke, presumably apocryphal, telling how ratings write to their parents about a new position they have been given. The parents are glad their son is doing so well and proudly tell all their friends and relations that little Johnnie has been made Captain of the Heads.

There was a terrific barrage of AA in the afternoon as about 50 enemy raiders flew over, and then we had another red warning during instruction. After this I was put to washing dishes left outstanding because of the warnings. Then another warning was sounded and I was able to leave the washing up with a clear conscience. Perhaps this was the only time I have welcomed an air raid.

On 25 October there was another heavy barrage with searchlights flicking all over the sky. Again I went to the wardroom cellar and had a cold and uncomfortable time lying on the floor, but at least my gas mask made an excellent pillow, although it was a trifle hard and bumpy.

On a Saturday night I went ashore with Tony Garland and saw *North West Passage* at the Victoria Cinema. We ran into Tubby Higgs there and he joined us at Kimbells later. Another air raid warning sounded as we returned to *St Vincent* and we spent most of the night in the wardroom cellar once again.

We got in rather a mess at Divisions on 29 September. It was the Petty Officer's fault. We were trying to get sized and the PO gave an incorrect order. Lieutenant-Commander Martineau came down on him like a ton of bricks, and on us too, saying, 'Odd numbers in the front rank, even numbers in the rear rank ...' He repeated this several times, getting quicker and quicker as if we were children! I went ashore before lunch and had a meal in the Central Hotel. The food was good but there was not enough of it. I went to the cinema with Wallace, who was on an observers' course. Once again I spent the night in the wardroom cellar; it was stuffy down there and the floor was cold but I managed to sleep despite the snores from others. We had a long red alert next day and we got pretty hungry until we were allowed to go to tea in shifts.

Conan Doyle writes about the strange episode of the dog in the night. I had an occasion in Pompey (Portsmouth), where, after seeing the film *Naughty Marietta* and loving it, I was at peace with the world, the moon was shining and the stars were visible. On the way to the ferry I met a dog; or rather the dog met me. It followed me all the way to the ferry; twice I thought it had turned off but it came back despite my entreaties to make it 'go home!' I sat down in the ferry and gazed at the moon's reflection in the water. All of a sudden the dog arrived, but this time a sailor forcibly removed it. Just as I reached the wardroom cellar the Bosch started a fire in Pompey. I had a bad night in the cellar at one time imagining that the boy sleeping near my feet was a pillow and I tried to turn him over with my feet!

We did some arms drill for the first time, but having done it in the OTC, it was second nature to me. I did not go ashore as I had only 1/- in my pocket! I note that on my second payday I received £1.18, but had also written a cheque for £2 and I had no money in my pocket for a day.

Half way through our course of eight weeks the course ahead of us left and was replaced by the course behind us. In other words the courses overlapped. I heard a story about the very first course, how true it was I don't know: It started with 60 men, 46 received commissions and now only 2 were alive!

My place of duty when on watch was at one of the Fire Pumps. On the evening of 18 October we were practising in a mist. There was a sudden noise of a plane followed by machine gun fire and we ran for shelter. However nothing happened either then or in the air raid warning that followed, although during the afternoon an aircraft machine gunned HMS *Collingwood* (a training establishment not so far from us) and injured 35 men.

On 26 October I started weekend leave. I set off about noon, but owing to the crush outside the gates I was delayed for about 15 minutes waiting for a bus and missed the first Portsmouth train to Waterloo. The sirens sounded at about 1315 hours, but I managed to have an uneventful journey to Waterloo. I went across to the other station, which had been bombed and which had a single ten-minute train to Charing Cross. It was practically deserted. I saw many signs of bomb damage everywhere I went, especially at Clapham Junction. From Victoria I caught a train to Purley then bussed to Chipstead railway bridge and walked the rest of the way.

Next day I was awakened by the sirens at 8 a.m., and all through the day the raiders came and went, there being several loud crumps on occasions. I went to church on my pushbike and with a Fleet Air Arm cap band replacing the white band. The vicar, the Rev. Grigg-Smith, greeted me like a long-lost friend although he did not know me. He said that he would put my name down on the Roll of Remembrance. I thought this was a bit ominous and premature, but did not say anything! He was very good in the way he kept up with servicemen and wrote us letters; we also received a present from the parish later on.

My Aunt Betty, Uncle Robert Foulger's wife, arrived in the afternoon wearing her MTC uniform. Uncle Robert was my godfather, but not a very good one. I forget where he was during the war, probably in Africa. Later on he became. Commissioner of Police in Singapore and then Commissioner of Police in Tanganyika.

On the way back to Gosport the warnings went when I was at Waterloo. And AA went up overhead. Being under the glass of Waterloo Station was alarming! When the train arrived it took two hours crawling to get to Guildford, from there on speeding up, and I slept most of the way. The last Portsmouth to Gosport ferry had gone and I had to sleep as best I could in a freezing shelter nearby. At 0500 hours the ferry left and after walking to *St Vincent* I crawled thankfully into bed.

My future brother-in law, Jack Andrew, had some relatives who lived in Alverstoke and on 29 October they invited me to dinner. Mrs Stocker looked comparatively young and pretty whilst Mr Stocker turned out to be an engineering Rear Admiral and looked quite a bit older. For a Rear Admiral to be entertaining the lowest form of animal such as a Naval

Airman Second Class was incongruous to say the least. What they thought of entertaining a rating who looked about sixteen I can only guess. They gave me a sherry and after a talk gave me a delicious dinner of soup, chicken and a sweet that was a new one to me. After dinner we heard the news and they made me tinkle with the piano before I rushed to catch the bus at 2215 hours. While waiting for it a German aircraft flew overhead and I nearly jumped out of my skin when two AAs went off very close by. There was such a good blackout in Gosport that I thought I was still in the country as we went through the town.

We were issued with flying helmets on 30 October. This seemed a bit premature as we were not to fly for some time yet and anyway in a place miles from Gosport – Luton.

On 1 November we did some shooting and the Petty Officer said, 'I bet you're shooting left and right.' I have two target cut-out results in my diary. They are both 1" groups and all the shots were in the bull except for one inner!

I was able to snatch some hours away the following day and visited Awbridge, my favourite spot on this earth and my grandfather's family seat – big house and 200 acres, plus quite a large lake. My Aunt Clarrie was there as were old friends of the family, Major and Mrs Dewer. Among other things I had a luxury bath before Major Dewer drove me to Romsey station. I should have arrived at Portsmouth at 2055 hours, but we finally made it to there at 2340. Even worse, I missed the last ferry across to Gosport and spent the night in a crude air raid shelter with the rain and wind beating hard outside. I caught the first ferry next morning and crawled into bed at 6.30 a.m.

That day was not my best. At divisions a naval airman fell flat on his face in a faint. We were in the drill shed and had no band to divert our attention; we did a lot of standing while the Captain spoke to us. However in my case the worst thing I did was to forget to turn up for fire pump drill. Petty Officer Batten, an oldish man and a taxi driver in civil life reported me to Lieutenant Bach. He also said that I was always forgetting to turn up, which was not true. After seeing Lieutenant-Commander Ainger, my divisional CO, I was put on Commander's report! Unfortunately the Commander was having a blitz on the Fleet Air Arm recruits and I knew he would make an example of me. He said, 'What is your excuse?' I said, 'I have no excuse, Sir, I just forgot.' I received seven days No. 11 punishment. This was not too bad and my first day's punishment consisted of getting two buckets of coal; running round and round the parade ground (luckily this was broken by a red warning); cleaning knives, and I should have had something else, but I seem to have been missed out.

I was woken up on 6 November by a firewatcher and was given the job of putting up the chains between the posts on the large parade ground. This took me about five minutes. My No. 11 punishment at 1330 hours consisted of cleaning out the Instruction Air Office, which was little used and seemed pretty filthy. At 1730 I did some strenuous running with fifteen Collingwoods who had failed to get out of bed during a night air raid. The worst part was running with a rifle in the slope arms position. After this I sorted out Lieutenant Morton's shed for him. On reading this in my diary I am wondering what on earth was Lt Morton's shed, and what was kept there!?

Half the dormitory came back drunk or, in most cases, pretending to be drunk and made a row for about half an hour. We were just settling down when an air raid warning sounded and I had to go down to the wardroom cellar once again. However, I at last got to bed and got some sleep.

On 7 November I woke at 0730 – the very time I was supposed to report for work! I slipped on some overalls and ran to the front gate where all I had to do was wash out and rinse a bucket! Following that I had enough time to have a shower before breakfast. At 1320 hours I was sent collecting wood from the stables by the Petty Officer with whom I first had a row over a parcel. He was better tempered this time and gave me my work for the morrow: at 0710 I was to light the fire in the Regulating Office.

As from 7 November, we were to take no notice of daytime alerts unless we got the 'action stations' on the bells around the establishment. Following this announcement we had three double reds today just to start things off!

My No. 11 consisted of arms drill and I was able to give a little instruction just to keep my hand in. After this I was in the Petty Officers' mess and did washing up. The wash place had dozens of cockroaches in it, which made it look disgusting. The messman was very decent to me, as were most of the people who gave me No. 11 work to do. Like the others he let me go a bit early.

Early next morning I duly made the fire in the Regulating Office. There were two other men doing No. 11s, but they had no job and merely looked into all the papers they could find.

After much anxious waiting after divisions we were at last told the results of some recent exams. About seven people failed and the rest of us passed including me. The relief was great! The Port and Starboard watches did some route marching in the morning and afternoon respectively, but I, as I was on a No. 11 punishment, did none!

My hectic job for No. 11 in the evening was to move double beds from the top of C block to the POs' new sleeping quarters, and the single one back up there, which was quite a strain.

Due to a new ruling that states that no one may sleep above the ground floor I slept in G mess. Many people came back drunk and late which was perhaps to be expected after the exam results.

On 9 November I again had to make a fire in the Regulating Office; this time with a Regulating Petty Officer watching my every movement. Perhaps he thought naval airman could not make a fire!

The No. 11 punishment on a Saturday lasted 1½ hours. The fat PO air gunner of the Collingwoods made me type out some Morse buzzer tests for him. I put in several things like OICU RMTU BFXY which he would not actually recognise until he started to transmit. I hoped I would I be well away from the place before he realised what I had done!

3

ELEMENTARY FLYING TRAINING SCHOOL, LUTON

Our course was called at 0600 hours on 10 November. Part of the course was sent to Elmdon while my half was sent to Luton, Bedfordshire. The Elmdon party set off at 0700 amid parting cheers, whilst we in the Luton party had to wait until 1100 hours before being bussed to Pompey station. Arriving in London we had about two hours to wait and I phoned my Aunt Dorothy at Chipstead. Unfortunately she was out, but I gave my grandmother my new address. The fact that she was able to do this indicates that my grandmother must have been unaffected by the dementia that she suffered from only a year or two later.

After the *St Vincent* course we were promoted to the rank of Leading Naval Airman and we proudly wore an anchor symbol, or killick, on our arms to denote that rank.

We eventually arrived in Luton at about 1900 hours and the New Zealanders greeted the local inhabitants with a Maori haka. This is what New Zealanders are wont to demonstrate before the start of various sporting events. I reproduce the words here:

> Ka mate, ka mate, ka ora, ka ora.
> Ka mate, ka mate, ka ora, ka ora.
> Tenei te tangata puhuruhuru
> Nana I tiki mai whakawhiti te ra
> Hupane ! kaupane ! hupana ! kaupane !
> Whiti te ra !
> Ringa pakia, waewae takahia kia rite
> E kino nei hoki – Ringaringa i torona kei waho mau tonu,
> Tau ka tau, hei – Tauka tau, hei – Ki runga o Tamaki
> Whangala mai ra
> Nge-nge-nge ara-tu ara-ta, aratau.

There is nothing friendly about the word *mate* (pronounced *mah-tay*) in this context. It means death! After all it is a *war* dance!

We went to a pub where the inhabitants could not take their eyes off our white cap bands. At length we were taken to Luton Hoo about four miles away where we were to have digs. This is a historic country house and is set in 1000 acres of parkland designed by Capability Brown. James I visited there in 1611. However, lest the reader thinks that we were billeted in luxury in that house, let me disabuse you; we were put into the stables! The house itself was being used as a convalescent home. After a decent supper in the canteen we were given our rooms and I shared one with Reg Elliot and D.A. Davis. On the whole the place was quite comfortable, we even had sheets on the beds! So our status was improving!

We had to rise each morning at 0630 hours and leave at 0700 for the airfield, and since we did not get back until about 1900 each night there was little time to admire the countryside.

In those days Luton aerodrome was a very different place from the one we know today. It was a grass airfield, slightly sloping in places and our day accommodation and classrooms were in wooden huts adorned, in some cases, with Fougasse cartoons which gave some basic rules of safety to pilots.

Our first day at the airfield, 11 November, was spent in being introduced to the place and to the senior officers including the flight commanders of the four flights A, B, C. and D. We were also give tin hats, parachutes, earphones, etc. We received a little ground instruction; otherwise we spent the day doing very little. The next day the weather was awful, so instead of going up for our first flight, we had ground instruction all day. This included navigation and meteorology. In the evening I went to the cinema with D.A. Davis. We bought seats for 1/6. We thought we heard the cashier say that the 1/6 seats were upstairs, but on arriving there the usherette said there were no 1/6 seats upstairs. Davis muttered, 'Sorry, we thought the girl downstairs said the seats were upstairs.' She replied. 'It's all right, I'll put you in the 2/6 seats!' So there was some advantage in being in uniform!

We had our first flights next day. The aircraft we used were Miles Magisters. Designed as training aircraft for the RAF they had a DH Gipsy Major engine and a total of 1,293 of them were built. The instructor and pupil were seated fore and aft and communicated by a voice pipe called a Gosport tube. Unlike the Tiger Moth, a biplane, which trained so many pilots, the Magister was a monoplane. It also had flaps, which the Tiger Moth did not have. Because of this slight added complication Magister pilots generally took longer before their first solo than did the Tiger pilots. I was introduced to my instructor Pilot Officer Jack. Unfortunately

I felt no rapport with him and while flying with him I learnt a few new swearwords, so obviously he had no rapport with me either. All this was probably my fault; I see in his book *Sea Flight* that Hugh Popham got on well with him.

Tony Garland came back from his flight. He had been violently sick, poor man, and it was some days before he got over this problem. Then I went up. The first thing I saw was Luton Hoo! There was no sensation of speed and I felt I was in heaven, in fact I think I would have done a parachute jump if my instructor had suggested it. After a time I took over the rudder pedals; then the control column and then both together. Try as I might I could not prevent my port wing from dipping and at the same time allowing the plane to drift right. When I asked to be able to do what I liked I was OK and dived over Luton simulating a dive-bombing attack! PO Jack had to tell me to pull up as I was too low. After some more attempts at straight and level flying we headed for home and Jack landed. I felt slightly sick on the descent but this was probable due to the cream buns I had before the flight!

On 14 November I did a bit of taxiing, which I found rather difficult. In the air I was introduced to climbing, but we had to return early, as my earphones were not in properly in the helmet. Jack was not too pleased!

There was no flying on 15 November due to a low mist. I had a weekend off and was going to visit Bradfield. After ground instruction I went to Luton and caught a train to London. The worst air raid London had yet received was in progress, but luckily nothing came near me. After a long wait at Victoria Station I caught a train to Chipstead and arrived at 2230 hours. I slept in the hall all night. Next morning I caught a train to Reading. It was an extremely slow one and I did not arrive at Bradfield until 1530. As everyone was watching the football match against Charterhouse I went to the music schools and played the piano for a while! At Hillside all the boys seemed pleased to see me. I went to Grubs (the Bradfield school shop) with Gordon Cox, a contemporary of mine, and met Mr and Mrs Bax and Mr and Mrs Sopwith on the way. At Grubs I met Mr Price my former Science master and had a chat. I was about to get into the bus to return to Reading when I met Sergeant Major Dash. He said. 'God bless you Mr Fay!' I must pay tribute here to Sergeant Major Dash who took us for gym and boxing as well as assisting with the OTC. He was a veritable mine of information about gymnastics and military skills. He was also one of nature's gentlemen and I can't remember him ever raising his voice to anyone. When the history of a school is noted I think that people like him should have a section to themselves; their influence is great.

At Paddington Station I had just got into a taxi when there was a terrific bang nearby. The taxi driver said, 'That was a piece of shrapnel – wot comes down after it goes up'! After reaching Luton I spent the night shivering in the waiting room until 0630, when I walked to the airfield.

On 17 November I spent a 65-minute flight doing taxiing, climbing, straight and level flying, gliding, and stalling. It was cold and my fingers were frozen.

We were told that in the event of engine failure we should ease the stick forward and put the nose down; this is to prevent the aircraft stalling. Some years later when I was training helicopter pilots I started to tell some jet pilots that in the event of engine failure one should do the opposite to that which one did in a fixed-wing aircraft, i.e one should ease the stick back (this is to help to maintain, or even increase, the rotor rpm). I was promptly reminded that with fast jets one *should* ease the stick back and gain height; after all at 500 knots one should be able to gain a few thousand feet in altitude!

There was no flying for three days due to the weather being misty, cloudy, or with gale force winds, so we had ground instruction all day long. We managed to fire the Browning machine gun on the range and I was impressed with its rate of fire. On arriving back at Luton Hoo I found that our small dormitory had been made into a recreation room. The occupants of my dormitory were shifted into a loft where there is no light. It was a bit of a comedown after our snug little dorm.

On 21 November we had more machine gun practice, but with the Vickers this time. Its rate of fire is very much slower than that of the Browning. Due to the fact that the ammunition had to be used up some of us were able to fire as much as fifty rounds.

I have mentioned the coincidence of meeting Holdsworth. Another coincidence occurred at Luton. A chap from 20 Course came up to me and asked if I was the brother of Maryele Fay. I, of course, said yes, I was. It turned out that he was from Buenos Aires and that he knew my sister Maryele fairly well! This was Hugh Anson May who was later appointed to a squadron in HMS *Avenger*.

I note in my diary that I was Duty Petty Officer, as was Tony Garland. This seemed a strange title, as we were only Leading Airmen. The duties were not arduous: we had to check in people after they had come back from leave. We also had to watch the showers and hot water to prevent the tanks being emptied.

On 22 November PO Jack gave me medium turns to do – my first bit of flying for several days. I found them rather difficult to do as I could not keep the nose on the horizon. Next day I advanced to circuits and bumps (taking off and landing continuously). My take-offs were OK according to Jack, but my landings were poor. The trouble with Jack was that he never gave any encouragement and lost his temper too easily. I did hear, however, that he made good pilots; just as long as he did that I didn't mind. During the next few days I added recovery from spins to my repertoire. Then Jack showed me a loop, a flick roll and then a stalled turn. He must have been in a happy frame of mind for he did these without being asked. Then he showed me another loop and told me to do one by myself. This was quite successful. The loop is one of the easiest aerobatic manoeuvres to carry out and during it one is kept in one's seat by centrifugal force. In contrast the slow rolls need straps to keep one in. I felt slightly ill when we finished, but managed a few circuits and bumps. Later that week PO Holt, my flight commander, took me up while Jack took Bruce Girdlestone for a pre-solo check. Bruce was the first of our course to go solo. Holt gave me one or two tips that helped me later. My flying improved this week and I saw from my confidential report that Jack thought so too. The reports were intended to be confidential, but since we knew where they were we were able to get sneak views of them when the instructors were not about! Tubby Higgs was suspended this week, which meant he had failed the course. C. Smith and Dixie Dean were also suspended. I was very sorry about Dixie Dean, he was a good chap and a good friend.

Quite by chance I ran into him after the war. We recognised each other from across a street in Bournemouth. He told me that after leaving the Fleet Air Arm he joined the RAF and rose to the rank of Wing Commander! This rather points to the fact that the Fleet Air Arm dipped some people too readily.

Another really unfair case happened to a friend of mine, Doug Briggs, who was on 28 Course. He had ten hours flying training, but with the bad luck of the draw his instructor was the junior of all the instructors so whenever there was good flying weather the more senior instructors nabbed the available aircraft and took their pupils flying. The junior instructor never got a look in, so his pupil – Doug – never obtained sufficient flying hours and was dipped, as were that instructor's other two pupils. Doug reverted to becoming an observer and had to undergo another four weeks at HMS *St Vincent*. He later joined 832 Squadron.

No one had told us that using the rudder during a dive in a Magister could blank the elevators. I found this out the hard way when I tried to pull out of a dive with a fair degree of rudder on. The aircraft did not want to do it; instinctively I centred my pedals and all was well.

Bradfield had an Old Boys' day and I managed to get weekend leave on 29 November. The fact that my instructor was away helped too! I left with Tony Garland who was also on leave. I called at my aunt's place in Duke Street near Selfridges and found that some of the street had been hit by bombs; her shop was all right, but she was out. I caught a train from Paddington to Reading and had an egg in the café under the archway. At Bradfield it was like coming back to school again. I saw all the beaks (house prefects), Matron (Miss Hedges, who was always an excellent woman) and Mr Sopwith, my housemaster, and then was given a bed in the sick room – this was glorious after Luton Hoo! Next day I went into breakfast with the other boys in hall. Mr McCormick my old music teacher) took breakfast. He was now a housemaster. I also went to chapel, causing many astonished looks from some of the boys, for it is not often that a bell-bottomed sailor goes to chapel in Bradfield!

I went to hear boys declaim in Big School, this normally consisted of the boys learning by heart some famous speech or perhaps a piece of poetry and then having to recite it before the whole school.

After lunch Kenneth Slade turned up in battle dress, he was a house prefect with me in Hillside for my last year there. Then Kenneth Kemp, he was also in the army, arrived and we went to watch the Old Boys versus the school football match, but we were too busy talking to take much notice of it!

We had OBs' tea in Hall and I met Burton Brown and my old music teacher, Dr Woodham, who was on leave (now an officer I was glad to see); also Charles Neat who made the remark, 'The hat's too American.' I should explain that the white band around my sailor's cap was what he was complaining about. I also met old boys Wood, Hawthorn, Winsor and really too many people to mention here.

With a few speeches the portrait of Whitworth, the former headmaster, was unveiled. It was painted by a man called Speed and was a marvellous likeness. Apparently Speed had to get Whitworth to give him a history lecture before he could catch the correct expression.

Mrs Sopwith gave the two Kenneths and me a dinner before I returned to London. The city was in thick fog and taxi drivers had deserted their cabs. I took a tube to St Pancras and found that the only train was a goods train, which I was allowed to travel in. I slept the rest of the night in the Luton waiting room and then walked to the airfield in the morning.

Back at Luton Sergeant Johnson gave me a pre-solo check. I took him round for circuit and bumps three times. My first landing was not too good but the others were OK. I wished that Johnson were my instructor; he was a decent fellow, did not swear at anyone like Jack did, and was very encouraging. I was not a bit nervous for my first solo and enjoyed myself.

The senior course moved on and I shifted into new and better accommodation. Harrington and Dixie Dean are also in the dormitory with me, Dixie until he left.

Barry Lister was in the course that was leaving and I bought a motorcycle from him for £20. It was a Sunbeam 250 cc. It was in good condition, but I did not try it out until my return from Canada some six months later. In the meantime it was looked after by George's Garage in Luton for 2/- per week. In the event, however, they charged me considerably less than that! Barry had shown me how to work the beast, but after a lapse of months I had forgotten some of it and on trying to run the engine I kept applying the valve lifter instead of the clutch, so the engine stopped each time! Fortunately someone came along and told me what I was doing wrong. That bike took me many thousands of miles during my leaves and when I was flying helicopters in the south of England. I finally parted company with it 1944.

New pilots are apt to lose their bearings and I joined the serried ranks of those who get lost shortly after their first solo. I flew along railway lines trying to make sense of the map, all to no avail. I was lost!! I saw other planes but they were too far away to be of much use. It started to rain and for the first time I experienced rain coming at me horizontally instead of vertically. After an hour's flying plus half an hour being lost I decided to land. I found a likely looking field near some houses and with no obstructions. I made a dummy run and saw it was not wired over to prevent German gliders landing. I put the aircraft down quite well and then taxied back to windward where the gate was. Two men came along and I put one in charge of the plane while the other one led me to a telephone. The gateway was very muddy and I tripped when my boot got stuck and made my hands very muddy. I went to a farmer's house where there was his wife and daughter. This was not the first time they had entertained an airman as three week previously another aircraft had landed in the same field.

I could not get through to the telephone exchange for some time and Luton 3905 was engaged so I told them to ring me. In the meantime the farmer's wife gave me a cup of tea. Then an RAF corporal came along and told me that a pilot from Cranfield would come along and pick up the plane and take it there. While he, the corporal, would take me in his car. In fact, I had landed not far from Cranfield and had I used my eyes a bit more I might have seen the airfield!

I must explain that *ab initio* pilots were not permitted to take off again once they had made a forced landing. Clearly in the past some pilots had attempted this and crashed, so when I eventually spoke to Holt and told him that I had landed in a field and that the aircraft was now at

Cranfield, he said, 'So, you took off again, did you?' I'm sure he expected the answer, Yes' and must have thought there goes another pilot who will be kicked off the course. However, I was able to reassure him.

On arrival at Cranfield I reported to the Guardhouse and Watch Office and was fixed up with a bed with some RAF chaps. I had a meal with the RAF personnel in the cookhouse. It was the inevitable baked beans as usual. All the men were surprised to see a sailor, but were one and all very decent to me and lent me what I wanted.

Next morning I was in my flying kit and by my plane at 0830 hours. Tony Garland arrived with PO Jack in another Magister, and Tony took that aircraft back to Luton. After my aircraft had been refuelled the mechanic's efforts to start the engine were not successful. A snowstorm sprang up and the aircraft was put into a hangar. When the storm abated I swung the propeller myself and the engine started first time! The next minor incident was caused when the aircraft got stuck in the mud. Jack must have been sick of my face by the time we arrived back at Luton!

I had previously done some instrument flying in a Link Trainer. Although the Link Trainer was used primarily for practice in instrument flying it could be called the forerunner of the modern simulator. For the uninitiated I should explain that it consisted of a machine that looks like a stubby bit of fuselage. The wings and tail unit were merely cosmetic appendages. It was electrically powered and the pilot's controls enabled it to move around three axes on a fixed base. Once the hood was closed the pilot had to rely in his blind-flying instruments. An instructor (or occasionally a fellow pilot) outside could give instructions to the pilot and on his desk a 'crab' tracked the aircraft's progress on a chart. Apart from the valuable practice it gave one, it illustrated very forcibly how one's senses could be deceived, for if one did a turn and then straightened up there was a strong feeling that one was turning in the opposite direction. One *must* believe one's instruments. A few days later when airborne I did some real instrument flying under the hood. Later, Jack showed me some flick rolls, stalled turns and slow rolls. Then he descended over Barton, our satellite airfield, and beat up the neighbourhood. Was he feeling frustrated or just happy I wonder?

Just before Christmas PO Holt my flight commander told me to do some map reading. Well, after the fiasco of getting lost I certainly needed the practice! I went up to Bedford and back following the railway line all the way – a foretaste of many hours' doing the same thing over the years. Later, after an arrangement with D.A. Davis we met over Luton Hoo and tried some unofficial formation practice, being careful not to fly too close. Later I met Waller in another plane, but I could not recognise him as he would not put his goggles up and I did not want to compromise either

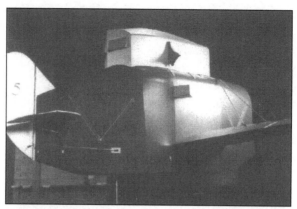

A Link Trainer viewed from the outside.

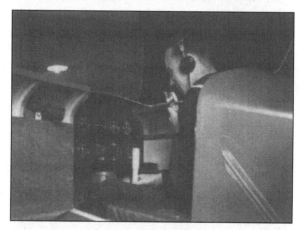

A view of the cockpit.

Sid Carpenter gives instruction from the outside. The object on the table is a 'crab', which moves over a map showing the pupil's progress as he flies a simulated cross-country flight.

him or myself. Then I caught up with Davis again and we did some simulated fighter tactics mostly over Harpenden. We were pretty stupid really for if our numbers had been taken we might have dipped the course.

Christmas leave started for me during the afternoon. In London I tried to stick to the Underground. Victoria had been bombed and I had to go by bus from there to Clapham Junction. I arrived at The Dial House, where my Aunt Dorothy was now living with her husband of about three years. I arrived there at 2100 hours just as Churchill was speaking on the radio. Unfortunately I was not expected as the telegram I had sent had not arrived.

Next day I went to church and during the service the vicar read out the names of all the people from Chipstead who were in the forces. All service personnel had been sent a Christmas gift and he read out some of the thank-you letters he had received. He did not know I was in the church and to my horror he then read out mine! It was the longest of the lot as I mentioned going on my first solo and how much happier I felt after doing so. Coming out of the church I met Ian Stoddard and Mrs Talbot Smith who invited me for cocktails. So there I was – almost the lowest form of naval life having drinks with a naval officer, a Major and about ten other people.

I cycled over to Oxshott to see the Yates and the Lawrences. But I could not stay long as I felt a chill coming over me and riding back I did not even have the energy to ride up small hills. I went to bed on my arrival and saw Dr Judge who gave me a Doctor's Certificate.

A few days later I was back at Luton. I was horrified when Jack said that it might have been a good thing for me to drop back to the last course as I was now a bit behind on flying hours. I don't think he realised that this would mean leaving all the good comrades I had met on my course and having to be absorbed by a different course. Fortunately no change of course came to pass; I stayed in 19 Course.

PO Jack took me on a cross-country flight to Maidenhead. Strangely we passed right over One Tree Cottage in Beaconsfield where my father's brother David lived. I managed to disgrace myself in the cockpit by dropping my map and I had to ask Jack to take over until I could retrieve it.

At the beginning of 1941 we were told that we were going to Canada for our advanced training. Thirty-five of us were to go; nine were not. We had to report to an airfield near Manchester on the Friday and it was quite likely we would sail next day.

In the meantime Jack gave me a cross-country to do to Beaconsfield. This was not too successful and on my return I was guided to the airfield by following another Magister. After landing I had to stand out in the cold for a Morse Code test using an Aldis lamp. In exams that were held the previous day I got 80% on Armaments and a pass in Aircraft Recognition. The worst exams lay ahead, namely Navigation and Airmanship.

We finished exams by 3 January and prepared to leave Luton. First, however, I had to fly around to get my flying hours up to 50. Prior to leaving, the Commander gave us a talk and said that we were the best course they had had at Luton so far! I just wondered whether he said that to all the courses!

4

EN ROUTE TO CANADA

On 4 January 1941 thirty-five of us crowded on to an RAF lorry and we were taken to Luton station. Our kit bags had the code words C/Peter/Bean marked on them. Someone said that the RAF airfield at Peterborough was providing a lot of ground crew, hence the 'Peter' bit. Another small coincidence was that when I was in the BEA Helicopter Unit shortly after the war we were stationed at Peterborough! From Luton the train took us to Manchester Central station. Then began a series of mishaps that made me remark in my diary that I didn't know how the RAF was not annihilated during the first week of the war! But, of course, this was RAF Training Command, not Fighter Command. There was no RAF lorry at the station to take us to Wilmslow. Then when we did arrive there they denied all knowledge of us so we had to go out and seek out own accommodation for the night. The first YMCA we tried was full; the next hotel was 16 shillings per night (a lot of money to us in those days); the next hotel we were told about did not exist due to being bombed. Eventually I went with Mike Langman and Jock Landles to the YMCA at London Road station and we got a bed for the night for a shilling each. We also had a rotten meal.

We had a restless night due to the light being on all the time and people coming and going. We also had to put up with noises issuing from soldiers who had nearby beds.

We walked to the other YMCA and had a good breakfast. I then went to the Central Post Office and sent a telegram to my 'guardian' in England (Aunt Dorothy) about my movements and also a cable to 'E.M.' Fay in the Argentine saying, 'Congratulations. Sailing Canada shortly.' The congratulations were for the anniversary of their wedding.

We eventually got on a train to Wilmslow. I was in a compartment with Bill Davis and Reg Elliot and a family taking two children away from the bombing.

At Wilmslow, which is a drafting station with no airfield, we found we still did not officially exist, but at least they gave us a meal. We got the food, but nothing to eat it with, it being a tradition in the RAF that everyone has his own 'eating irons' i.e. cutlery. The next half hour was rather amusing as we ate the food given us with things ranging from corkscrews to large soup ladles. I had the latter. We were then put in a hut, which we soon made like home with the help of fires and the little wireless I had brought with me. However, we found that the blankets were very damp.

That little wireless went with me to Canada and back and I was still using it in 1945. By that time the Bakelite case had been broken and it had a wooden one instead. Radio sets were in short supply so this one was invaluable.

At one time we were kept waiting for half an hour while mail was distributed. The RAF finally realised that we could not possibly have any mail and we were dismissed! Then we were told to report to receive subsistence pay at a certain time. We waited for three quarters of an hour while the RAF got theirs. Then were told, 'There is nothing for the Fleet Air Arm, you may go.'

We thought we should be leaving next day but instead were told to have breakfast on the morrow at 0200 hours and to be ready to leave by 0300 hours.

On 8 January we were marched to the station with our kit bags. Some of the New Zealanders found it difficult to carry their trunks as well as kit bags. We eventually arrived at Gourock and embarked on the *Duchess of York*. We were shown down to a deck on the waterline where we had to sling hammocks. But there were no hammocks! Eventually however they turned up and for the first time in my life I had to sleep in one. Hammocks are not too uncomfortable, but it is difficult to sleep on one's side.

No one owned us; the Navy thought the RAF was dealing with us and vice versa!

There were about 700 German prisoners of war on board, largely Luftwaffe, most of whom had first class cabins, but then I suppose they had a large contingent of officers. Their quarters were enclosed by barbed wire. Among these prisoners of war was the only German to escape and get back to Germany. More of that later.

The scramble for meals was terrible. But then there were about 2,000 troops and airmen on board plus our small naval contingent. There were at least two sittings for meals and we never seemed to have enough food.

On 9 January we did not sail. The crew were on strike!

The details I heard were as follows. The crew signed on for a round voyage and they completed this; however, on arriving back at Gourock they found that the Government, by a new law, had commandeered the ship for troop carrying. Result: crew not paid; for paying means paying *off*. So the crew had no money and were obviously discontented.

Later on the crew were paid, but naval ratings were required to run the ship. Not us, I was glad to say!

The notes about the ship were written in my diary whilst I was in my hammock so my writing was even worse than usual!

On the 10 January there was a little less rush and fewer queues for breakfast. However, washing facilities were limited and the fresh water was turned on for only an hour each day

It was a beautiful morning and the sunrise over the Scottish hills threw a glorious panorama of colour on to the soft comfortable-looking clouds, which moved across an otherwise blue sky. We weighed anchor at 0930 and so silent were the engines that I did not realise that we had moved until some time had elapsed. We passed the *Franconia* and the *Orontes*.

We negotiated the boom defences, which, I was told, consisted of a row of mines in threes. Gradually the ships anchored in the Clyde disappeared from view.

There were three destroyers in line ahead and soon a battleship passed us and signalled, 'What is your maximum speed?' and then, 'Take up position astern of us!'

We felt very bucked to find that we had the following ships to escort us:

    1 Battleship: HMS *Ramillies*
    5 Destroyers
    1 Submarine

Soon, however, the submarine and one destroyer dropped astern of us. Clearly they had nothing to do with us.

We passed out of the Clyde into the open sea. Scotland became a few islands and there was Ireland on our port side. I thought to myself, 'We are definitely on our way to Canada. What adventures lie ahead?'

At 1630 hours we turned back for the Clyde!

We had previously sighted a convoy and all of a sudden the battleship started signalling 12.12.12, plus some more, to us and turned to starboard and eventually back on her own track. The destroyers continued in line ahead whereas previously they had spread out all around us.

We could not understand what was going on and we thought to ourselves. 'Invasion?' 'A Naval battle?!' Or 'A concentration of U-boats ahead?' I never did discover what the flap was all about.

I achieved a miracle and got to the bar to purchase 6 shillings worth of chocolates and two bottles of ginger beer. It took me half an hour's waiting in a queue.

After a day waiting in the Clyde we moved out at about 1300 hours in a convoy of big ships. I counted three three-funnelled vessels and most of the ships were over 10,000 tons in my estimation. The names I was able to read were; *Franconia, Empress of Japan, Arundle Castle, Orontes* and *Cameronia*. Our escort was one battleship, three cruisers and about seven destroyers. Most of the day we had some sort of aircraft with us: a Blenheim, six Hurricanes and a Sunderland, while a Whitley came and went at various times. I don't suppose the Hurricanes were actually guarding us, they just happened to be there. However, if I thought that this sort of escort was going to escort us across the Atlantic I was soon disillusioned!

Next day a Squadron Leader, who we now knew was going to be in charge of us, gave us a talk. He was sorry we had not got better accommodation, but nothing could be done about it and we would have to make the best of what we had. He took a list of our complaints and said he would try to sort them out. The one complaint that the entire ship's compliment made was the question of the canteen. There was chocolate in plenty in the hold, but it was not brought up to the canteen. Moreover the canteen was open for very limited times and to purchase anything at all one had to join a long queue. The men behind the canteen did not appear to want to co-operate at all. We understood that the CO had the matter in hand. The trouble was that with limited food at meal times we felt the need for more sustenance.

Next morning the canteen was open for only five minutes. This so infuriated Jock Bennett, one of the New Zealanders, that he broke the door down. He was put under open arrest and I though matters would be serious for him, but in the end he was told to write an essay entitled, 'The Qualities Required for a Fleet Air Arm Officer.' This he wrote with the help of Sid Carpenter.

Sid had only just come down from university when he joined the FAA. During a class at St Vincent I remember him telling one of the officers that he had applied to join a considerable time ago, but had heard nothing from the Admiralty. I wondered what would have happened to me if I had not jogged the Admiralty's memory.

I read a message flashed by Aldis from the convoy leader. Among other things it said, 'Cease Zig-zag!' So we were now steering a straight course.

I had to do a two-hour anti-submarine watch. It was a very long two hours, I was bored and cold and, considering the terrific escort we had, rather useless.

There was a so-called 'talent contest' in the evening in our mess. The various voluntary items included songs, imitations and instrument playing punctuated by jokes and stories by a few officers. A man played the spoons – something I had not experienced before. There were not too many entries so a Wing Commander with a jutting jaw said that if there were six more entries he would sing a song. Unfortunately there *were* six and the Wing Commander sang a Purcell song – the wrong thing for a concert I thought – he made faces while singing and had no sort of voice. In short he made a complete fool of himself! I understood that he made a habit of doubling around the deck in shorts and falling over when jumping obstacles! One of the six entries said he would do Napoleon's farewell to his troops. He stood up, folded one arm across his chest and said, 'Mes amis, adieux!'

A soldier sang a song in which nothing vulgar was actually said and would be in the mind of the listener only. It was probably one I heard later when I was in the squadron and which started off:

> Let's sit down
> Drinks all round.
> Let's have a jolly good supper,
> For a man who sleeps with another man's wife
> Is a fool if he doesn't
> Send his girls to school . . .
> And the rest!

By now no entry for the concert had come from the navy, but I almost walked out in shame when one of our number got up and sang an absolutely disgusting song. He stopped after the second verse, but it was enough to give the FAA a bad name All our chaps were appalled.

After the concert I walked up to the bows and sang a few songs with some airmen. It was rather a nice moonlight night with the moon reflecting on the water and with all the convoy visible.

It must have been next morning that we left the convoy at 0300 hours. So the magnificent escort we had was no longer with us. However, we had the *Ramillies*! I could only assume that the superior speed of the two ships was supposed to elude any U-boats that might be around.

Years later I read that the German prisoners were planning to take over the ship! They saw the escorts disappear and wanted to seize their chance. They rose early looked all around the horizon, thought there were no other ships and then – lo and behold – there was the *Ramillies*! That ship came in quite close to us and we were able to have a good look at her. What an impressive sight she made! Enormous; strong; invulnerable. Although, of course, she was not invulnerable, torpedoes in the right places could have sunk her.

It was only very recently that I learned, in conversation with Dr Peter Liddle of The Second World War Experience Centre who had been talking to one of the guards only a few weeks previously, that one of the weapons the Germans were going to use was the tops of the taps. But how were they going to cut the barbed wire that closed all the entrances to the part of the superstructure they were in? When walking around the ship I often wondered what plans had been made to release the prisoners in the event of the ship being torpedoed.

It was during the night swinging in my hammock that I started dreaming in German. It could not have been a very erudite dream as my German was limited; however, I found myself yelling out some words in German and woke myself up doing so. Fortunately the other guys swinging in their hammocks must have all been asleep. Had they been awake they might have surmised that they had a German in disguise in their midst and asked a few pertinent questions! I know I would have been absolved but things might have been nasty for a while.

I played 'Foxy' Hunter at chess. I won once and he won three times. It's a good way to pass the time, but I do not play very often. The last time I saw 'Foxy' was after we had left Canada and returned home. I never saw him again; I often wonder what happened to him as he was full of life and enthusiasm and would have made a good officer.

On 18 January we were making only eight knots. Rumour had it that the engines of the *Ramilles* had broken down.

Next day there was quite a rumpus with the RAF, ending with several people being put under close arrest! What happened was that four people were put up to do anti-submarine watch from 0630 to 1000 hours. We usually got up at 0700 so no one woke us. The four people were not awake to carry out the anti-submarine watch, consequently there were strong words between us and an RAF sergeant who made the gross remark that he would see that things were made hot for us at our Flying Training School. Later a sergeant came down with some orders from an officer and he said, 'Anyone who is late for submarine watch in future will be put in the cells.' 'Foxy' Hunter was asleep at the time, but woke up on hearing this and said, 'Ha!' The sergeant promptly put him under arrest for 'Insubordination to a Senior NCO' and 'Indirect insubordination to an officer.' Hunter, of course, had not even realised there was a sergeant there.

He went up before the Wing Commander who said he would propose that he was not recommended for a commission and he also gave him fatigues for the rest of the voyage. All this was very unfair and Hunter was not allowed to say a word in his defence.

I don't remember whether it was during this fracas or another time that an airman called Fisher, who was on our course, was had up before the Captain on some charge or other. Now, Fisher's father was RN and in rather an important position. The captain seemed to have no idea that we were not ordinary seamen being transported, but semi-trained men going for more flying training, so when Fisher happened to mention that his father was a captain in the Navy, *The Duchess of York's* captain said, 'What, of a trawler or something?' Fisher replied, 'No sir, of HMS *Warspite!*' The *Warspite* being, of course, one of our battleships!

However, the finale to all our troubles came in the afternoon when Squadron Leader Fryer came down and had a chat with us. He said the Wing Commander had his back up that morning and the 'No commission' business was bunk. Fryer was our future Chief Flying Instructor, he helped us a lot during the voyage and I was hoping we would remain on the right side of him.

We had a concert in the evening and very good it was. The best item won a prize and was by two RAF men who imitated the Western Brothers. I should explain that The Western Brothers were a well-known pair who were popular on the radio. They were very la di da laconic types, one of whom wore the inevitable stage monocle. They picked on contemporary items of news and made jokes about them. In this case the jokes were all topical, and there was plenty of material available in this ship!

On 21 January it was rough and cold all day. I walked about two miles in all around the decks for exercise. Next day, when we rose in the morning, we were impatient to see land after a week at sea and hoped we would catch a glimpse of Canada, but it was not yet visible. It was a lovely day with blue sky and the sea fairly calm. I remarked in my diary that I didn't know how Columbus stuck it for three months! By midday we did sight land and glided into Halifax harbour. Some Hudsons had sighted us previously and they now flew over the ship. I expected Halifax to be a big place, but I was disappointed to see how small it was, and trees hid most of it.

Directly we tied up the Germans were taken off. They went ashore and walked away between two ranks of Canadian guards. I seem to remember they had fixed bayonets, which was just as well as an organised rush could have seen the escape of several of them

I have some cuttings in my diary from Canadian newspapers that show that two Germans escaped shortly afterwards. One was recaptured fairly quickly having been found in a restaurant with false identification papers in English. Another cutting reveals that one of the Germans' most successful fighter pilots was among the prisoners. He shot down 56 Spanish aircraft in the Spanish Civil War, and subsequently fought in France, The Netherlands, Belgium and Britain. He was shot down over

Halifax, Nova Scotia. A group of pilots wearing various types of uniform prior to returning to Britain. Commissions were not received until their arrival. Some of the pilots have removed the unpopular white cap bands.

the English Channel. Another pilot carried as a memento a huge cane on which were carved bombs and aeroplanes. One bomb was labelled London and had five notches in it.

As for us, we had to sit tight and were paid $10 after a long and tedious process that we now associated with everything the RAF did.

Next day we had breakfast at 0700 hours and went ashore an hour later where, with great RAF efficiency, the Fleet Air Arm was soaked with rain and then put in the wrong carriage!

The train set off with the German prisoners on board plus a large contingent of RAF and us sailors. It stopped for quite a time in Truro, Nova Scotia, and we all got out to stretch our legs. The train started moving without any warning and there was a terrific rush to get on board again, however, it was only moving up a few yards!

The food was good on the train and a great relief after the ship's terrible rations. The night was not too bad and we slept on a combined bed-luggage rack. We travelled all day, the route taking us through Montreal.

It was during this journey that Oberleutnant Fritz Von Werra escaped. I did not mention it in my diary, as it seemed a sort of run-of-the-mill sort of thing. But this man had already tried to escape from England by bluffing his way into the cockpit of a fighter aircraft. Having left our train he crossed the frozen waters to get to America, which was neutral at that time, managed to get down to the Argentine and from there get back to

Germany. He was the only German airman to escape and get back to the Fatherland. One has to admire him, but after all his efforts he was shot down later on! His story is given in Paul Brickhill's book *The One That Got Away*, which was also made into a film of the same name.

Late at night we arrived at Collins Bay, near Kingston, where we were put on buses – after an RAF wait!

5

7 COURSE, 4 GROUP, AT 31 SFTS, KINGSTON, ONTARIO

We debussed at the airfield and were mustered in a very large shed and then taken to our dormitory. It was lovely: we had sheets! It also had a large oil heater, which kept us warm in the extreme Canadian winter. We went for a meal but, as ever, the food was there, but the cutlery was not!

We saw the Lieutenant-Commander in charge of us next morning and he gave us the afternoon off. I tried to see the dentist for I had had toothache all the way across the Atlantic but, as luck would have it, he was on weekend leave. I went with two others to Kingston, sent off some cables and saw a film. I also bought some oil of cloves for my tooth. It was marvellous to see a town that was not blacked out; I had almost forgotten what a lighted street looked like. We had two very good meals at reasonable prices. We ran into 'Tiny' Foulkes who was RAF and was one of the few RAF men on our Kingston course. Foulkes was a pianist and during our course he seemed to have a part-time job with the local radio station (CFRC Kingston). Barry Lister and Hugh Popham managed to persuade the station to give them a Fleet Air Arm Half Hour and they managed to fill half a dozen half hours. Hugh said that he never heard of any criticism or praise so he never knew how their programme was received.

Next day we did little, just received some books and maps and had the afternoon off.

It was not until two days later that I was able to see a dentist, who took an X-ray of my tooth. Next day he had not made up his mind what to do. He did, however, feel my forehead and said I had a fever. He took my temperature and it was 102° Fahrenheit, which is quite high. I had intended to see the doctor anyway after the dentist as I had a sore throat. I was put to bed straight away. Next day Ginger Davis and Reg Elliot brought some things down for me. I was fed on slops only, but as it happened I did not feel like eating anything else.

I was in the sickbay for five days and on coming out I had the tooth extracted. It had an abscess on it and was the largest tooth in my head. No wonder it hurt!

Shortly after leaving the sickbay I received a letter from my mother giving details of my sister Maryele and Jack's civil wedding, which is the only marriage that counts in Argentine law. It is worth quoting her letter verbatim:

> You never saw such a farce! Dad, Dick, Gerald Gower and Trevor Barber were present. The registrar turned to Maryele and asked her a question. He gabbled so hard one couldn't understand what he said. She turned to Jack to interpret and the registrar said, 'That won't do, if you can't answer by yourself I'll annul the whole thing.' Then he asked Dad something he couldn't hear. Jack explained that he was deaf. Dad approached nearer, the registrar repeated his question and Dad said, 'Si,' hoping it was the right answer. Meanwhile a most disagreeable woman was standing by with papers to sign and in the middle another woman entered and talked to her in a loud voice. All I gathered from the whole service was that Maryele and Jack were expected to live in the same house! I certainly would not feel married after that.

I should point out that Maryele and Jack had a proper wedding later!

I started walking into Kingston during a terrific snowstorm and was picked up by Lister and Holdsworth in a ramshackle old car they had bought for $15. Apart from the fact that there was the occasional, 'Hold tight!', getting out to push, and skidding a lot, the journey was uneventful! Coming out of the cinema I ran into Gordon Black, Doug Harris, Ken Proctor and George Merriot. We had supper together at McCalls which seemed a better place that the others I had tried so far. To get back to the airfield we had to take a bus following a snowplough and the journey took two hours. On the way I helped to push some cars out of the way! How the snow whipped through me! Even the run from the gates to the hut was torture; but after a shower and crawling into bed I felt better.

Next morning I stayed in bed rather than having breakfast. On reading this in my diary I realise how our discipline was on a fairly loose rein. I cannot see army recruits in training being allowed to do such things. The main thing was that it worked. Strict discipline was not necessary.

Having got up I was in time for some cockpit drill, which lasted most of the morning. Our vital actions for the Fairey Battle before take off could be remembered by the word PRAFTS. The P stood for 'Petrol on Port Tank' I recall. After sixty of so years the rest of the mnemonic escapes me!

Next day, 10 February, I met my instructor, a Sergeant Balchin. I had much more rapport with him than I had with my previous instructor and we got on well; he was a good bloke.

The aircraft we used in Kingston were Fairey Battles of which 2,185 were built. The Battle was a two-seater medium day bomber. According to one source it was obsolete by the start of the war, and was a disaster as it was too slow vulnerable and undergunned for warfare in the Second World War. In France shortly after the German breakthrough in 1940 an attempt was made to halt the German advance towards Brussels by bombing two road bridges over the Albert Canal near Maastricht. Six Battle aircraft were to be sent by No.12 Squadron. Split into two groups of three the Battles attacked through a withering barrage of anti-aircraft and small arms fire. All six aircraft were shot down.

I flew four other types of Fairey aircraft during the war and I once had the privilege of meeting Sir Richard Fairey at his house when I was training his son, also called Richard, to fly helicopters.

On my first flight in a Battle it seemed to me that I was on top of a huge bus, and flying over the countryside it seemed to me that I, little me, could not possibly have any effect on the plane if I touched the controls. I made my first few medium turns rather gingerly, eyeing my instruments and almost flying blind at times. When I stepped out of the aircraft at the end of the flight it was like disembarking from a ship at the end of a voyage.

I must insert here that the airfield was one large skating rink and the countryside was white. It was to remain like this for some weeks until the thaw arrived. Landing and taking off was not too difficult under these circumstances, but taxi-ing could be a bit fraught, especially in a wind.

On 12 February I went up for my second flight with Sergeant Balchin and did circuits and landings. I still did not have the feel of the machine; it felt like driving a bus after riding a pushbike. But three days later I had a solo test from Flying Officer Knowles. Due to the ice I skidded all over the place when I was taxi-ing. I failed the test because there was another aircraft outside me in the circuit and I did the wrong thing, in F/O Knowles' view. However, after another circuit with Sgt Balchin I was sent off solo.

On Sunday I went to church, which is a good way of meeting people. After the service there was a singsong and eats. Then everyone was asked where they came from. I said 'Buenos Aires!' which created quite

RAF Kingston, Ontario. 7 Course, 4 Group. 31 SFTS. January 1941–May 1941.

1941. Some happy Leading Naval Airmen during a visit to Niagara Falls.
Left to right: 'Foxy' Hunter, Tony Garland, Sid Carpenter, Jeff Aggleton, Reg Elliot,
'Hutch' Hutchins, 'Ginger' Davies.

a stir as was my intention – it was my parents' home, not mine. Denny Evans said Paekakarike which sounded most exotic. That was why he said it, although he lived in Wellington!

Maryele should have been married on the 12 February, but as Jack was ill the wedding took place on the 14th.

We had our mid term exams and I did not do too badly. Some of the Canadians received only 15% in navigation, which meant they were worse then I was!

We circulated among the Canadians and met one or two girls. One rather pleasant one always showed the men to whom she talked a picture of her boy friend who was in Bermuda. A sort of Keep Off the Grass notice I reckoned!

I was down at the Guardhouse waiting for some means of conveyance to go into Kingston when I learnt that the CO of the station, Group Captain Shackleton, had died of a heart attack. I was sorry to hear this, although he had spoken to our course only once, I had been impressed by his obvious warm-heartedness. He seemed to have an interest in everyone and everything and he came into the mess while we were eating to see things for himself. I once saw him playing ice hockey with some of the airmen in the rink here.

I bought some gramophone records in Kingston. No one told me that Canadian records have not been tested at source. Perhaps I should have paid attention to the sales girl who appeared worried that I had not tested them. Anyhow they were pretty useless as they turned out to be very faint. I only hoped that if I was ever flying a Canadian-built aircraft they were produced to a higher standard!

I went up on a height test and climbed to 15,000 feet. The day was good and the view was marvellous. We had not got oxygen fitted to the aircraft and I remark in my diary that I was not affected by the altitude.

Another day I went on a navigation flight to Perth and Sherbot Lake with Sgt Balchin. He was a good chap and only got annoyed when I deserved it, which was so different from PO Jack, at the sound of whose name I still trembled!

Highly illegal! I flew over America at Grindstone Island. I could now say I have flown over the USA! I also went on a little private navigation exercise of my own to Picton and Trent. It was simple stuff as I could see the next apex of the triangle each time I got to the end of a leg. I also dived the aircraft and reached 260 mph, but Battles can do more than that if required.

Later on after not flying for a week I found I had almost forgotten how to fly. It is amazing how a beginner can lose the touch if he doesn't keep it up. I did not make a note of why I had not been flying, but it was probably due to the lack of airscrews. Apparently there were only about ten for the hundred or so aircraft we had there!

Marks, an American volunteer in the Royal Canadian Air Force and who was on our course, was suspended on account of his ground subjects not being too good. He had worked hard lately and was a fine fellow. The American volunteers deserved the highest praise fighting a war that was not their own (yet!).

The New Zealanders were, of course, good swimmers, so when I came last in a 50-yard race of five people I was not too abashed. Then, to find out who would be among those representing the airfield in a swimming competition, I had to race against Arch Hugill and I won! I then played around with a polo ball, which, as usual, left me exhausted. It really is a most tiring sport and since I lacked stamina I was never any good at it.

I had to get up early one morning and taxi five aircraft out of the hangar. This was more tiring than it might seem. After that I had to do a navigation test with a Flight Lieutenant Rendle, a fine chap and a real gentleman. On entering the aircraft I found that my right arm was tired after holding the control column back on the five aircraft I had taxied. I had to alter course on the first leg of the exercise quite a lot. The last leg I did under the hood. After several minutes Flight Lieutenant Rendle said, 'You're doing fine, how much longer do you think you have?' I glibly said, 'About four minutes, Sir,' not having the vaguest notion. Sure enough four minutes later I pinpointed right over the aerodrome!

As the Fairey Battle could not do aerobatics we had short trips in an aircraft called a Yale, which is very much like a Harvard. It was a queer aircraft as everything was in French, thus we had metres and kilometres per hour. These Yales were part of a batch that had been ordered by the French. Some of them had already been delivered to the French and when France was overrun the Germans accepted them gratefully! I was told that before the war all French aircraft had a reverse movement of the throttle compared with other nations, i.e. to throttle back one pushed the throttle *forward*! Fortunately for everyone's safety the Yale had a throttle that operated normally, otherwise I could see people throttling back for landing and finding they had applied full power!

Sgt Balchin and I did a few slow rolls, loops and a spin. I felt a little sick on coming down, but not as much as some other people I thought. Flying was suspended after I landed as two planes had had their engines cutting out due to snow in the air intake. After suffering an engine failure one Flying Officer turned his aircraft back and landed. We were given dire warnings about never doing this. The reason is fairly obvious: one might collide with another aircraft. And one would be landing down wind so that one's groundspeed on touchdown could be very high: the false impression given by looking at the ground and judging one's airspeed by this could result in a stall.

Having said that, one of our course, Hedley Archer, did land downwind after an engine failure on the climb. I think he wanted to avoid landing in Lake Ontario. He was furious when an officer went up to the plane and started berating him without asking him if he was all right.

After another of the seemingly endless exams we were told we had passed. I was disappointed to find I received only 21 marks out of 50 in Maintenance as I could have sworn that I had done well.

It was in April of 1941 that the first *Tee Emm* was published. TM stood for Training Memoranda and treated air training in a light-hearted manner. It was mainly an RAF magazine and was amusing and instructive particularly where it concerned Pilot Officer Prune who was a dim-witted pilot prone to making all sorts of mistakes, generally referred to as 'putting up a black'. There were degrees of 'blacks', one might 'put up a bit of a black', or one might 'put up a colossal black', for example if one made a landing with the undercarriage up. It was issued to the Fleet Air Arm and we looked forward to reading it every month.

In August 1944 the FAA came up with its own magazine *Flight Deck* with equally humorous articles and it had its own particularly gormless pilot who was a Sub-Lieutenant (A) RNVR. I might add that he could equally well have been RN! In particular the magazine had some outstanding cartoons by Glyn. Who can ever forget his cartoon of someone putting up a frightful black? In this case a young officer was depicted entertaining a large native in the wardroom who was dressed in all the hideous refinery of a witch doctor complete with shrunken heads, skulls, etc. Another speciality of Glyn's was to depict in his own inimitable way the *CW List Illustrated*, the *CW List* being a register of new appointments. When Commander So and So had been appointed to 'Victory .addl. (not to join)' for instance, the commander was depicted outside the main gates of *Victory* with his own tent and camp fire. Another was 'Miss ____3/O WRNS *Eaglet* for plotting duties'. I leave it to the reader's imagination the drawing of this one.

However, back in Canada in 1941 spring seemed to have arrived at last and with the clearance of the snow we were able to undertake other activities. I went riding with Reg Elliot, Bill Davies and Gordon Black. I was fortunate in having a good horse, Danny Boy, which unlike the others' horses was obedient. Having come to a good open patch Reg and I tried a gallop. When I had gone some 300 yards I looked back and saw no Reg. I galloped back and found that his horse had decided to go up a side turning. Reg had determined otherwise and the stirrup had 'fallen off'. With Reg doing a steep turn to the right he had no hope of staying on. The horse, Birdie, halted for a moment and I followed it across a garden, which still had snow on it. But Gordon and Bill had caught it and I led it back across the garden only to meet two irate females who said the horse had come across their 'lawn'. I apologised in polite naval fashion and beat it.

Next day we went riding again, this time with the addition of Hutchins. I nearly came off as Danny Boy wanted to repeat the performance that Birdie had done the previous day. We passed some convicts on the way out and one said to me, 'If you have any cigarettes drop them on the road further on.' I told him I had not got any. Convicts wear blue uniforms out here and some workmen do too. I should think it would not have been too impossible to make a preliminary getaway using the workmen as a sort of screen.

At the end of March 1941 we started night flying. It was during our training for this that we had our first casualty. There were a few RAF men attached to our course while in Canada and one of these was A.C. Reardon. I have newspaper cuttings in my diary explaining what had happened. The cockpit was seen to be in flames and the engine was backfiring. The instructor tried to get back to the airfield, but could not make it and the aircraft struck the ground. Reardon was killed instantly while the instructor was taken to hospital suffering from burns, bruises and shock. It was the luck of the draw as to who was flying that plane that night and it could have been any one of us who was killed. Unfortunately Reardon was not the last one of our course to be killed during training.

I had previously observed glows in the northern sky when in the south of England caused by the Aurora Borealis. Here in Canada I was privileged to see the real thing: great masses of coloured curtains weaving and rolling across the northern sky in a most impressive display.

Squadron Leader Fryer, to whom I made reference writing about the trip across the Atlantic, was the Chief Flying Instructor. He was an excellent man and a hands-on one at that. He could often be seen riding around on one of the airfield's tractors, chivvying someone up or putting something right. Years later I was in an office at Westland and a man was sitting there. When I was introduced to him I discovered his name was Fryer. I said, 'Oh, there was a Fryer in Canada.' He replied, 'Yes, that was me!' Unfortunately at the time I had forgotten that he was in the *Duchess of York* with us otherwise we could have reminisced a bit more.

A notable event for me was that my mother sailed up from the Argentine in an American ship to see me! The voyage took two weeks each way and as America was neutral at the time there was little danger of being sunk by a U-boat. I was on tenterhooks in case I put up a black and found myself confined to the airfield for some misdemeanour. I hitchhiked part of the way to Montreal to meet her and then had to take a bus when drivers willing to stop became thin on the ground. We had time to look around before going back to Kingston together and even found 'Toothbrush Steps' which I so named because my father had to clean them with a toothbrush as part of his freshman's initiation when he attended McGill University. My mother stayed in a hotel in Kingston and I was able to see her on many occasions. I had not been with her since 1939; not a long period compared with other service men perhaps. I was not to see her again until 1945, by which time I was a Lieutenant (A) RNVR.

Apart from that another highlight was a visit to Niagara Falls. Several of us hired a taxi, or perhaps it was two taxis as I have a photograph showing that eight of us were at the Falls together. With me there were Tony Garland. Foxy Hunter, Sid Carpenter, Jeff Aggleton, Reg Elliot, 'Hutch' Hutchins and Ginger Davis. We spent the night in Toronto and then carried on to the Falls. They were, of course, a magnificent sight and one of the places that one should visit before shuffling off this mortal coil. Others I have managed to achieve are The Grand Canyon, Rio de Janeiro, Table Mountain, and The Empire State Building. I should like to visit Macchu Picchu, but I fear I shall not make this one.

6

RETURNING TO BRITAIN VIA ICELAND

We finally finished our course in May 1941 and departed from Kingston taking a train to Halifax where we were put up in an RCAF camp. We left Kingston with spring well advanced so Halifax was a bit of a shock with cold and depressing weather. I managed to cash a cheque for £15 in the town, which brought my balance down to almost nil. Later I discovered that the cheque went down with the ship taking it back to the UK, however, the bank had other means of finding out what cheques had been written and my account was duly debited.

While waiting in the camp we were on occasions more or less confined to barracks. We overcame this little problem by forming up as a squad and being marched out of the camp by Harold Hawken, who seemed to be the one with the best leadership qualities among us. The guards at the gate were fooled and did not stop us. I wonder whether the CO ever discovered our deception?

We eventually embarked aboard HMS *Ausonia*, which was a converted merchant ship. Unfortunately we were attached to a very slow convoy and were going to Iceland. We had no duties on board despite being naval ratings or, to quote the words of one of the ship's officers who visited us, 'Naval officers in disguise.'

There was little excitement apart from the time we launched a boat to go to investigate a suspicious Portuguese ship. In the event, however, that little mission was aborted so I suppose our captain was satisfied that she was bona fide.

In Iceland we were sent to an RAF camp where we remained for some days. We were not permitted to go into Reykjavik as apparently the natives were a bit hostile after the allies had taken over their island on a temporary basis. Whilst one can't blame them, I wonder what life would have been like for them if the Germans had taken them over instead.

I cannot remember what our accommodation was like, but I have photographs of us carrying out our morning ablutions in a nearby stream so I guess we did not have many facilities. It was fortunate it was summer; I dread to think what it would be like in an Icelandic winter!

Strangely, one of the best things about Iceland was the bathing. The pools we swam in were heated by the thermal springs that abound and it was delightful to swim around in such warm water. The Icelanders were there as well and I was ashamed at the way some of the RAF men leered at the girls and tried to get to their changing rooms. It was only the presence of some Icelandic men that prevented things going from bad to worse.

An Icelandic girl in the water allowed one ample bosom to come out of her swimsuit, which intrigued the men. She pretended she did not know it had happened, but I think she was quite happy to be ogled by everyone.

The CO tried to keep strict discipline, as he knew we would be happier with things like that. With a mixture of nationalities it could not have been easy, but the NCOs coped well.

A man whose lowly job was to keep the toilets clean impressed me. He said that whatever the job one should always do one's best and he would do his best for the toilets despite it being a menial job! I hope he did well in life.

At last we were put on board a ship and transported back to the UK. Having reached there we were told to go down to Plymouth. After another long train journey we reached our destination only to find that they knew nothing about us. Having left our names and addresses we were told to go on leave, so back we all went to London to split up and go our various ways.

After that leave we went on our next course.

7

GREENWICH NAVAL COLLEGE

The course at Greenwich Naval College was generally known as The Knife and Fork Course. I do not remember actually learning anything there and any teaching of etiquette as to which cutlery to use at table was notably absent. However, it gave me a chance to see a naval college at its best.

The college was originally Greenwich Hospital and was established in 1694 by Royal Charter for the relief and support of seamen and their dependants and for the improvement of navigation. It is set in landscaped grounds by the River Thames and UNESCO recognises it now as being of outstanding universal value, for it comprises the finest and most dramatically sited architectural ensemble in the British Isles. The site was planned by Sir Christopher Wren, and his grand design was completed by noted architects such as Hawksmoor and Vanburgh. The famous painted hall, executed by Sir James Thornhill between 1707 and 1726, was our dining room, and I felt very humble that I, a mere midshipman, should be eating in such a famous hall.

In 1869 the hospital was closed and it became the Royal Naval College where naval sciences were taught to officers from all over the world. The Royal Navy finally left in 1998 and handed it over to the Greenwich Foundation.

By this time I was a Probationary Temporary Midshipman (A) RNVR, appointed 'By Command of their Lordships', although I was unable to actually wear my uniform until it had been ordered and made for me by The Army and Navy Stores. I remember telling the tailor that I wanted wings on my sleeve and he looked a little shocked. He must have thought I was mistaken, no doubt he looked at this young bloke who looked about 16 and thought I could not possible be a pilot. Anyway, when the uniform eventually arrived – no wings! I suppose I should have said to him, 'What do you think I have been doing for the past year?'

I said that I do not remember learning anything at Greenwich. I might have learnt something if the course had run its normal length, but it was curtailed due to the Petsamo-Kirkenes raid where the FAA lost 16 aircraft. This was a raid apparently intended to show the Russians that we were in full support of them, and was ordered by the cabinet. Swordfish and Albacores of 827 and 828 Squadrons flew from HMS *Victorious* and HMS *Furious*; Fulmars being the fighter escort. The targets were German warships, troop transports, docks, etc. Unfortunately things went wrong when the striking force was spotted by a Heinkel 111, which was able to give warning of the approach. Targets were few at Petsamo with not many ships about. Flak was light but one aircraft was shot down. Things were different at Kirkenes where there was stiff opposition. Apparently there were all sorts of German planes about, including Ju-87s, Me-110 and 109s. Nigel Ball managed to shoot down a Ju-87. One enemy fighter did a steep turn into the sea. A minor raid on Tromso followed and three Fulmars went in with 20 lb bombs. One aircraft was lost on this little mission.

The effect of losing 16 aircraft and their crews on a fairly small service, as the Fleet Air Arm was at the time, meant that the courses were accelerated to try to restore the status quo. Since I was designated as a Torpedo Bomber pilot rather than a fighter boy my next course was a TSR (Torpedo Spotter Reconnaissance) course at Crail.

8

TORPEDO COURSE, CRAIL

Crail is a small village sticking out into the North Sea in Fife and it was here that HMS *Jackdaw* was located. At this Royal Naval Air Station we were to carry out our torpedo training using Fairey Swordfish and Fairey Albacore aircraft. When I say 'our' I mean 19 Course St Vincent, but in fact we were no longer that, for we were joined by other pilots, some of them were from the course behind us (20 Course), since we took so long getting back from Canada that they caught us up.

We flew the Swordfish first. This obsolete but remarkable aircraft, affectionately known as the 'Stringbag', was in service from the start of the war until the end. In 1941, when I first encountered it, the aircraft was supposed to carry a torpedo, or mines, or bombs. Later on in the war it was to be fitted with rocket projectiles, RATOG (rocket assisted take-off gear), and Glow Worm, a bright light for illuminating surfaced U-boats at night. The Stringbag was slow and quiet, not so quiet as the Albacore perhaps, but it certainly was not a noisy aircraft. More Swordfish were operational at the end of the war than at the start.

I quote from *Alone on a Wild, Wild Sea* by E.E. Barringer which tells the remarkable story of 835 Squadron:

> The Stringbags flew more hours than any other type of allied aircraft and sank a greater tonnage of enemy shipping – substantially over a million tons. And what is perhaps more pertinent, they undoubtedly saved a large number of merchant seamen and merchant vessels from a watery grave. They were, above all else, protectors of convoys. Once the war at sea had been fully joined, most of the Air Arm's twenty-odd Swordfish squadrons were employed on convoy escort duty and it was the contribution of these archaic-looking but robust and dependable biplanes which, at a critical moment in the Atlantic, turned the possibility of defeat into the certainty of victory.

Until my uniform arrived I was in civvies. But it arrived at last, complete with maroon-coloured lapels to indicate I was an RNVR midshipman; RNR would have had blue ones, RN midshipman would have white. A lonely looking 'A' (for Air Branch) was on my sleeve. When I became a Sub-Lieutenant in September the 'A' would be in the middle of the curl of the stripes. There were several tales of what we were mistaken for by the general public. One midshipman was asked by an old lady in a hotel to get her a drink. He did so and when she tried to tip him he said, 'The Royal Navy is always ready to oblige, madam!' At a railway station I was once mistaken for a porter.

The training unit was officially 785 Squadron under the command of Captain Patch RM whose claim to fame was that he was the leader of a sub-flight that sank three ships and a submarine in a single attack.

However, R.D. Layman, who was an eminent American naval historian and whose business was Aeronaval Research, found that this was incorrect.

He states that there were three, not four, vessels present: the submarine *Iride,* submarine depot ship *Monte Gargano* and torpedo boat *Calipso.* The submarine was preparing to transport four underwater assault craft for an attack on British warships at Alexandria. It and the depot ship were sunk; *Calipso* was unscathed. In the confusion, the Swordfish crews received the impression they had sunk four ships, for they thought there was another submarine alongside *Monte Gargano,* and *Calipso* disappeared in a welter of spray and smoke when the depot ship blew up. They reported this in all honesty and good faith.

The attack received wide publicity in the wartime press and as a result has been presented as fact in repeated publications. The crews' error in no way detracts from the skill and courage of their attack, or its success, which prevented what might have been a damaging blow against the British Mediterranean Fleet.

Other instructors were Lieutenants Whitfield, Ball, Tivy and Slater. Now, Ransford Slater was a sort of relation of mine in that his sister had married my uncle. It was some weeks after meeting him at Crail that I realised I had met him before at Cookham where his parents lived (his father, Sir Ransford Slater, had been governor of the Gold Coast). I vaguely remember my Aunt Dorothy getting excited at the thought of meeting him again and certainly he made quite an impression when he arrived in the garden at the gathering. He was charming and smiling, put everyone at his or her ease and was obviously quite a character.

Many months after my course at Crail my Aunt told me that Ransford had done something that no one had done before, she did not know what it was but apparently it was important. It transpired that in April 1943 he had carried out the first landing in a Swordfish on a Merchant Aircraft Carrier, the MV *Empire MacAlpine*. This ship was the forerunner of the dozens of these Escort Carriers, often referred to as 'Woolworth Carriers' or 'Banana Boats' that made such a major contribution to the war effort. Not only that but he was chosen to be CO of 836 Squadron because of his exceptional qualities. He was just the sort of man to get on with the captains and men of the Merchant Navy and it must have required a considerable amount of tact for the navy personnel to liaise with their opposite numbers. Among other matters he arranged was for the air party on the ships to sign ship's articles and hence placed themselves under the orders of the Ship's Master.

I had my first flight in a Swordfish as a passenger with Lieutenant Tivy. I must say I had forgotten this until I checked my logbook, and just wonder what the purpose of the flight was. When flying in the open cockpit at the rear of the aircraft it is advisable to hitch up oneself to the G string. This will prevent one from being thrown out of the aircraft in the event of violent manoeuvres or negative g. There was a sad case of someone who did not hitch himself up and he was thrown out of the aircraft to a nasty death.

I at last climbed into the cockpit of this famous biplane, feeling as if I was about to fly something from the Great War. The view from the cockpit was not good, indeed for deck landing one had to cock one's head at a peculiar angle in order to see forward. It was a simple aircraft to fly. The most intriguing thing was watching the poppet valves of the engine going in and out! Surely this must be the last military aircraft in the world in which this would be possible. After carrying out some local flying to get the feel of the aircraft, I followed this with *Low Flying Over The Sea*; an exercise obviously intended to get us used to the height at which we would drop torpedoes. It was not at all difficult when there is enough wind to ruffle the sea, but when the sea is like glass it can be difficult and dangerous.

This was followed by some formation flying and it was during one of these practices with Paul Whitfield leading, that I found myself dropping back. Naturally I increased the throttle setting, but to no avail. I checked my engine instruments and found the oil pressure was zero. Fortunately we were near the airfield and I peeled off and made a landing before my turn hoping that no one would baulk me. When I stepped out I found that oil was coming out of the bottom of the plane at a fast rate. I was really lucky that I had the engine trouble where I did; I could have been over the sea. I found out later that the oil pressure pipe had burst. A day or two later that same aircraft carried out another forced landing!

Next day I did a spot of Link Training. The instructor said that I was doing flat turns and that next time he would make me fly using the Turn and Bank Indicator only!

Later I flew with Paul Whitfield as leader and Mike Langman as No. 3. We carried out ALTs on the ship *The Isle of Thanet*, ALT standing for Attack with Light Torpedo (i.e. an 18-inch one as opposed to ones used by surface vessels which were 21-inch the measurement being the diameter of the weapon). I could not use the camera mounted on the wing due to the poor visibility. Normally these cameras recorded everything about the moment one drops the torpedo or, in our case and at this stage, a smoke float. When parameters are recorded on a chart it is possible to see the result of the 'attack', the Sighting Error, Range from Target, Height in Feet, and the Attitude of the Nose, and whether the Wings are Level being recorded by the camera. Also on one's chart are written the speed of the target, the side (port or starboard) of the attacking aircraft and the result of the shot (hit, or miss by how much forward or aft of the target).

We did some practice firing with revolvers. This was the first time I had used a revolver and I was fairly successful.

I was glad to receive £40 for my uniform allowance and £1/14/6d for my travelling expenses to Crail.

After more simulated torpedo attacks we flew with a heavy cylindrical piece of metal to simulate the weight of a torpedo. The aircraft was very heavy in consequence and for take-offs the mixture control, which acted the same way as a boost cut out, was needed to give extra power. One young pilot who did not know about this, or had forgotten about it, came careering off the runway straight at us and the old car we used as a shelter. We scattered and ran like hell. Fortunately he got off the ground with about 30 yards to spare. Eventually we carried real torpedoes with dummy warheads (what else!) and dropped these 'runners'. It was very satisfying to do this and to watch the torpedo go under the target – or miss it as the case may be. These items were, or course recovered; after all, the torpedo cost about £1,800.

The torpedo was a complicated piece of machinery: it not only had to be propelled using the energy stored in compressed air, but it must steer a course, stay at the correct depth, compensate for the rotation of the earth, and explode on hitting the target. The explosion was caused either by a magnetic Duplex pistol or by a contact head. To ensure the torpedoes hit the water nose first there were also some rather Heath Robinson attachments made of wood and attached to the tail that were supposed to ensure the torpedo flew through the air at the correct angle before hitting the water. These broke off on hitting the water.

It was during one of our various training flights that I landed my Swordfish, turned off the runway and found to my horror that my brakes were not working. My starboard wing was going straight for the propeller of another aircraft. I could do absolutely nothing about it and my starboard wing was shattered at the tip. An investigation found that, indeed, my brakes were faulty. Nevertheless I was hauled up by my flight commander, Captain Patch, Royal Marines, before the Captain of the Air Station. Why he did this I did not know and I was highly nervous. Patch pointed out that the brakes were found to be faulty, but some probing by the Captain made me believe that he, the Captain, thought that it was all my fault. He said, 'All right, Fay, we will just put it down to an error of judgement on your part and say no more about it.' At this I railed and said, 'No Sir, my brakes were faulty and I could not do a thing to prevent the accident.' I gathered later that this remark by the Captain was an old trick, had I said, 'All right, Sir, thank you very much.' He would have known I was not telling the truth.

In making out my report on the accident I was ably assisted by Lt Temple-West RN and was very grateful to him. He witnessed the accident, being in the first plane on the left of the runway. He spoke in my defence and was extremely encouraging and helpful in advising me, and was very sympathetic. He was a very cheerful man and had learnt to fly at his own expense. He was on floatplanes but was doing a torpedo course with us.

After a few flights in the Fairey Swordfish we were introduced to the Fairey Albacore. Eight hundred and three Albacores were built and they

1941. Albacores on the deck of HMS *Victorious*, with a lone Fairey Fulmar on the stern. The windshields are raised on the forward end of the flight deck.

1941. A Fairey Albacore. This one belongs to 817 Squadron, one of the two torpedo bomber squadrons aboard HMS *Victorious*, the other being 832 Squadron.

served in many parts of the world. It first flew in 1938 and was intended as a replacement for the Swordfish. It entered squadron service in the spring of 1940 and was first used in carriers in 1941. Its performance was only slightly better than the Swordfish and one would be hard pushed to attain 100 knots indicated airspeed when fully loaded. Semi-official documents stating that its maximum speed was 169 mph are misleading and are probably based on the corrected airspeed at the most favourable altitude and temperature – plus some wishful thinking. It was more expensive to build than the Swordfish and for that reason in the middle of the war the Admiralty decided to concentrate production on that aircraft. The production was undertaken by Blackburn and officially these later aircraft should have been called Blackfish.

As a pilot my own decision would have been in favour of the Albacore by reason of the better performance, better forward view and the fact that it had a closed cockpit and cabin. Anyone who flew a Swordfish in winter would have gladly exchanged it for an Albacore. The Albacore had an unusual advantage over most aircraft – it was exceedingly quiet due to its sleeve valve engine, thus making it excellent for night work.

My first few minutes in an Albacore were also rather strange because for the first time in my limited experience I was sitting in front of the wings and I felt I had no datum with which to check my lateral attitude. I soon settled down, however, and began to enjoy the view, which was vastly superior to that of the Swordfish. Digressing slightly, flying in a Walrus felt even stranger: not only was there a wheel instead of a control column, but the propeller was not visible to the pilot! Once familiar with the aircraft, the training continued using the two types of aircraft more or less alternately. Whereas the Swordfish had only a fixed-pitch propeller the Albacore had a constant-speed one, the rpm being selected by a long lever situated on the left of the throttle. We used 3,200 rpm for take-off and 2,800 rpm for cruise. In a dive the pilot had to select coarse pitch; woe betide him if he forgot to do this for he would overspeed the engine. In a steep dive the hydraulically-operated flaps were placed fully down for use as dive brakes and the aircraft could descend at a steep angle without airspeed limits being exceeded. The Albacore also had slats – an aerofoil on the leading edge of the wing. These would extend automatically when the airspeed became low and enabled the aircraft to fly at a slower speed without stalling. When practising ALTs some months later with my squadron I was very thankful for this bit of equipment for the slats came out suddenly with a loud bang. I was climbing much too steeply at the time while trying to take avoiding action. Had I continued, the aircraft would have stalled and possibly gone into a spin.

Prior to arriving at Crail most of us had carried out only two hours' solo night flying, so we had to gain more experience. The schedule consisted mainly of conventional circuits and landings, as would normally done in daylight. There were no ground lights anywhere because of the blackout and the lights marking the runway were very dim, in fact one could not see the surface of the ground prior to touchdown, but had to judge where it was by the position of the lights on either side of the runway. While in the circuit one had to concentrate on the blind-flying instruments otherwise it was possible to become disorientated. Simple things like faulty cockpit drill before take-off could be deadly and it was not unknown for pilots to forget to uncage the artifical horizon and the direction indicator with fatal results.

We did the night flying at Dunino airfield and were taken there by lorry. As far as I remember this was a grass field and the smoothest part had been marked out as a runway. We started with three serviceable Swordfish, but Casey put the first one unserviceable by wiping off the three starboard pillar lights with his main plane; we counted them as they went over, 'Crash! One. Two. Three!' Costly did the same thing with a port pillar light. Then I went up. My first landing was a good one, but on the second approach I was too high so I throttled back. I swung to the left but did not have enough airspeed for the controls to respond properly. I found myself heading down on number 2 port pillar light so

I applied full throttle and went round again. This time I landed too high and came down with a bump. Brown then went up and made an 'into the ground' landing wiping off the starboard wheel. He managed to get airborne again but of course on his next arrival the aircraft swung right round after touching down.

A few nights' later I managed to get in one dusk landing. These sort of landings were useful in that one could orientate oneself and get an idea of the general layout of the location and could imagine what things would look like when it became completely dark. Unfortunately Bell did the same thing as Brown had done and wiped off the starboard oleo and wing. With a crashed aircraft sitting on the runway there was not enough space left to carry on flying so we had to pack up.

On the next occasion it was third time lucky and things went better. Lt Wathall, who was responsible for the flare path, remarked that no aircraft had been pranged while he was in charge. The fact that no aircraft went unserviceable this time proved his point. However, Jack Cramp nearly ploughed into the ground on making an approach similar to the one I had made on the first night. Like me he applied full power and went round again.

We were lucky that no one was hurt during these episodes. Unfortunately the course behind us was not so fortunate. When we were at Arbroath we heard that Hedley Archer, who was on 19 Course St Vincent with me, had been killed while night flying.

At this stage of the war propellers were called airscrews. The term was altered later by the Air Ministry after twelve airscrews were ordered and twelve aircrews arrived instead!

9

DECK LANDING TRAINING, ARBROATH

Our next appointment was to Arbroath in Angus for a deck landing course, the CO of the squadron being Lieutenant-Commander D.M. Russell. During the course I see from my log book that we also continued with instrument flying practice, formation flying, etc. and an exercise I had forgotten about called depth charge dropping, presumably we used smoke floats or some other indication to see whether our simulated drops were on target. We also did more ALTs, some dive bombing, night flying – and wind finding. The latter, so far as the pilot was concerned, merely consisted in flying a perfect rate one turn using the Turn and Slip indicator (the equivalent American instrument is the Needle and Ball). It was the observer's job to take accurate sighting of a smoke float that we had dropped and from his calculations work out what the wind was at that altitude.

I see that in all I carried out 56 ADDLS during the course, which included 8 at night. ADDLS stands for Aerodrome Dummy Deck Landings. The runway was marked out with an area the size of a flight deck and it was onto this space that we made our approach, guided by a batsman. The approach was like that of a precautionary landing, i.e. the airspeed was slightly lower than that used for the usual type of powered approach; the nose was held higher and to adhere to both of these parameters more power than normal was used.

The instructor, the batsman, would stand on the port side at the aft end of the 'deck' as if in a real aircraft carrier holding his bats with which to give instructions to the pilot. The senior pilot was Lieutenant R.N. Everett, RN. He was what was known as a 'personality batsman' in that he would be wiggling his bats all the time making little movements to 'control' the aircraft. Indeed he was quite a character in himself and a strong one. This method of batting could be irritating at times and to a

Back row, L to R: Fay, Spackman, Cramp, Laurie.
Middle row: Costley, Casey, Langman, Holthouse, Brown, Mudd.
Front row: Newton, Lawrence, Bell, Hawken, Holme.
Some of the pilots on the deck-landing course at Arbroath.

large extent was unnecessary, calm signals did just as well, but who were we to complain?

Everett had taken quite a lot of photographs during his career and had sent them to the Admiralty, which, if they deemed them suitable, would publish them with the appropriate publicity. Later in my career I tried to emulate him in this respect, but none of my efforts were considered suitable. Prior to being appointed to Arbroath Everett had seen some action with 810 Squadron in Norway. Later on in his career he was Captain of a destroyer. If I remember correctly, when he was below decks his ship hit a sandbank or rock (I forget which) and in accordance with naval tradition this rather blotted his copybook.

I do not know whether the instructors who did the batting for us at Arbroath ever had a batting course. With the Fleet Air Arm being so small at the time courses probably did not exist. Later, however, with the expansion of the FAA and the existence of the Escort Carriers it was necessary to have a definite course for batsmen. The people on course had to have a steady supply of pilots doing circuits and bumps for them. I never came in contact with the scheme, but the term 'Clockwork mice' came into being, referring to the pilots who did this job.

Lt Everett gave us an interesting lecture, which he called *Swordfish Blitzkrieg* and concerned the two and a half years he spent in HMS *Ark Royal*. He kept us in fits of laughter most of the time with his laconic way of expressing things. He described an Italian aircraft that had met him 'by accident' as 'an elderly aeroplane looking like two Swordfish tied together and with an enormous great propeller having a chain drive.' He added, 'It *was* airborne when I saw it.'

It was while we were at Arbroath that a distressing accident occurred. We had one or two Swordfish that had dual control and one day Roger Black, a New Zealander, and Sid Carpenter were sent up to do instrument flying, one pilot acting as safety pilot while the other flew on instruments. In cases like this it was always most important that each pilot knew who was the temporary captain and in charge of the aircraft. In those days the instructor would say, 'You have her.' and the pupil would reply, 'I have her.' The present-day routine is to say, 'You have control.' And the pupil answers, 'I have control.' It appears that each pilot thought the other had control and the aircraft hit the ground and burst into flames. Both pilots died from their injuries. The funeral for Sid was held in Arbroath and what was particularly painful and sad was the presence of Sid's mother. When the guard fired their rifles over the grave in salute she was so visibly shattered that an officer there stopped any further firing. As mentioned before, Sid was a university graduate, he was quiet and intelligent and the most pleasant chap you could wish to know.

10

771 SQUADRON, FLEET REQUIREMENTS UNIT, RNAS HATSTON (TEMPORARY APPOINTMENT)

After the Arbroath course I had a spot of leave and during it I received notification that I had been appointed to 832 Squadron in HMS *Victorious*. This was a great feeling, having read so many tales of pilots joining squadrons during the Great War it felt almost unbelievable that I should be taking part in what felt like a great adventure.

I see from my log book that two attempts were made to fly me to the Royal Naval Air Station at Hatston in the Orkneys in a Proctor piloted by a Lieutenant Creighton, but bad weather forced us back. However, I eventually arrived by train at Thurso in the extreme north of Scotland. While waiting for a ferry I went to a nearby hotel and to my surprise and pleasure there was Tony Garland! I have mentioned before that Tony and I went to St Vincent on the same day for our interviews and medicals, joined the same course (19) at St Vincent and trained together at Luton and in Canada. On returning to Britain our paths divided as he was a fighter pilot and I was a TSB pilot.

To have an old friend joining the *Victorious* at the same time was an added delight. I was so overcome that I blurted out that I was joining that ship, forgetting that we were in a public place and could be overheard by all the old ladies sitting around the lounge! If any of them were a spy no doubt the news would have been in Berlin by that evening! Had a senior officer been there no doubt I would have been for the high jump.

On reaching RNAS Hatston, which was a small aerodrome on the outskirts of Kirkwall, the capital of the Orkneys, I found that the *Victorious* was not in Scapa. So any information beamed to Berlin by the little old ladies would have been false! She was, in fact, in Iceland. To find work for me I was attached to 771 Squadron which was a FRU (Fleet Requirements Unit). While there I had to take part in the normal duties of officers who were appointed to the Air Station. The Lieutenant Commander who normally took divisions informed me one day that he would be away on a particular day and that I was to take his place. Naturally I was a bit worried about it, not so much as having to give the commands to the whole ship's company, but hoping that I would give the correct ones! In the event, however, as I walked towards the hall I found that the officer concerned had arrived back in time to take the divisions himself.

I was not so lucky another time when in charge of a small group, the details of which I have long forgotten. The rating would, in the particular circumstances, come up to me and report the men present and correct, I in my turn would go up to the RN Lieutenant Commander salute and report the same. We had, in fact, practised this as ratings. In this particular instance, the rating came up to me a saluted and to my horror said that the squad was *not* correct and that one or two men were absent! Frankly, thinking that the whole drill was a bit of naval bull, which in civilian life would be settled in a conversation, I then reported the squad present and correct to the officer, intending to sort things out with the rating when this bit of ceremony was over. Unfortunately the officer had heard the rating's words and he promptly ticked me off in front of the men (something that my training in the OTC rightly said was frowned upon). He then did what I should have done – asked the rating who was missing and why!

The aircraft used by 771 Squadron were Rocs and Skuas and years later my experience, limited as it was, of these aircraft prompted me to write an article 'On The Rocs' for one of the FAA magazines. The following few paragraphs are based on this article.

About forty years after the war, when seeing the remains of a Skua lying on the floor of the Fleet Air Arm Museum, I was reminded of the fact that this type of aircraft was considered by the pilots who flew it to be a heap anyway! In fact the Blackburn Skua and the Blackburn Roc were the worst aircraft I ever flew!

Hitherto, misled by the drawings of some over-enthusiastic artists and the exaggerated newspaper descriptions of their achievements, I was under the impression that Rocs and Skuas were rather sophisticated types by Fleet Air Arm standards and that they had quite a reasonable performance. I was soon disillusioned! One of the first things told me, incorrectly, was that one dictionary gave the description of a Skua as being a seabird that folded its wings and dived steeply into the sea. It was added that the Blackburn Skua tended to resemble its namesake closely in this respect!

Despite my remarks Skuas did achieve a remarkable success during the Norwegian campaign in 1940. Flying at their extreme range aircraft of 800 and 803 Squadrons flew from Hatston to Bergen and dive bombed the Germans' light cruiser *Königsberg*. All 15 of the 500 lb bombs were either hits or near misses and the ship turned over and sank.

The Fleet Requirements Unit was commanded by Lieutenant-Commander N.E. Goddard. Goddard was the man, then a Lieutenant, who piloted the Maryland when on 2 May 1941 with Commander G.A. Rotherham, LA J.D. Milne and LA J.W. Armstrong as his crew spotted that the German battleship *Bismarck* was missing from its anchorage in Norway. The break-out of this ship sparked the dramatic hunt that resulted in its ultimate sinking in the Atlantic.

There were about half a dozen pilots in 771 Squadron and I remember the names Davies, Green, Treece, Treen and John Randall – enough for a poker school anyway. When the wind howled around the airfield we would get down to many a game. Surprisingly it never appeared to be too cold in the Orkneys, the influence of the Gulf Stream tended to keep the frosts at bay.

John Randall later joined 832 Squadron, became Senior Pilot and, after I had left the squadron, the Commanding Officer. We kept in touch until his death in 2004.

The duties of the squadron consisted mainly of target towing, general Naval co-operation and flying round the Orkneys beating up various establishments – Army as well as Navy – in order to give bearing practice to guns' crews. There was also the odd spot of simulated dive-bombing to be carried out on the fleet at anchor.

My experience of flying Rocs and Skuas was limited to a mere ten hours and my remarks should, therefore, be read with this in mind. Pilots with more experience on the type and those with some front line experience with new aircraft might have more favourable recollections than I have and, too, I am relying on memory for it seems that I must have had a rest from diary writing during that period.

The Skua differed from the Roc in appearance by having turned up wing tips and by having no rear gun turret. The cockpits were basically similar. The aircraft had originally been designed for Taurus engines, and what a difference these might have made! Owing to the lack of these engines the only type available, the 890 hp. Bristol Perseus XI was fitted instead. This lighter engine had to be mounted on a longer nose to maintain the canter of gravity in the original position.

The astounding feature I found when flying these aircraft was the time-lag, which seemed to be built into them. Whether or not this was due to the fact that the aircraft we used were fairly well teased out I never actually discovered, but I shall never forget sitting at the end of the runway ready for take-off, opening the throttle and finding that nothing had happened!

Eventually, after a delay, which was probably only a few seconds, but which seemed many more, the engine rpm rose and crept up to the correct figure for take off. Again, on approaching the airfield for landing, it took a full circuit for the undercarriage to go down and lock! However, the time-lag was not the major worry for a new pilot; the worst feature was the serious lack of power and the attendant lack of manoeuvrability in anything but descending flight or when speed had been built up in a dive. I once heard of a pilot who had carried out a slow roll in a Roc at sea level. Brave man? Fool? Skilled pilot? I do not know; among any group of pilots there would be different opinions. I do know that after becoming airborne the pilot had to take care to maintain the correct airspeed during the climb, for the best (and possibly only!) climbing speed was but only a few knots greater than the stalling speed. Because of this, it was only after several flights that I could persuade myself to carry out anything but the gentlest of gentle turns during the climb for fear of a stall or spin. Upon gaining a few thousand feet of altitude and placing the aircraft in a dive, the aged and dying creature that it appeared to be suddenly seemed rejuvenated and quite lively and capable of a few manoeuvres.

It was fitting that my last flight in a Roc was a series of dummy dive bombing attacks upon HMS *Trinidad* and HMS *Victorious* while they were anchored in Scapa Flow, for the 'Vic' was to be my home, on and off, for the next two years.

I see from my logbook that while in 771 Squadron I had to ferry an Albacore from Hatston to the Royal Naval air station at Twatt, which was also in the Orkneys. The name was unfortunate as it had several meanings, and in particular one which, in my innocence, I had not heard before, although it has one less 't'. I understood that when it was mooted that the name should be used the Admiralty was approached in order to try to change it. Back came the reply with a query as to why this should be desirable. Perhaps the Admiralty was as naive as I was!

The pilot who ferried me back to Hatston was Colin Nias, who had been in the St Vincent course ahead of me. I remember him as a tall lanky man. Later on, I am not sure whether it was weeks or months, he tried to fly between The Old Man Of Hoy, a narrow vertical rock just offshore, and the mainland. I fear he did not make it. It must have been around this time that Clive Hoosen, a New Zealander on my course, carried out some unauthorised low flying and hit some power cables. I remember him as an intelligent man, full of fun. Of all the things that were drummed into us during training, low flying was one of the taboos. But I suppose pilots will always want to do this and I must admit I was not guiltless. Occasionally tragedy will strike.

I heard the news of the attack on Pearl Harbor when I was walking near a cabin at Hatston. The radio could be heard through the walls. I must say I was astonished, but then I was not *au fait* with the situation out east. When the news of the sinking of the *Prince of Wales* and *Repulse* came over the radio in the wardroom some RN commanders were present and the shocked look on their faces impressed me; if I did not know how serious this loss would be their attitude alone would have told me. However, being old hands they probably knew fellow officers on board so they suffered in two ways.

11

832 SQUADRON IN HMS *VICTORIOUS*

HMS *Victorious* came back to Scapa at last and I was able to join my squadron. This ship, which was part of the Home Fleet, was of the *Illustrious* class and had a displacement of approximately 23,000 tons. A few facts: her top speed was required to be 30 knots, although I feel sure she was able to exceed this, it certainly felt like it when she was going flat out. She could carry 36 aircraft in her hangar. The ship's complement was designed for 840 officers and other ranks. This figure was swelled when squadrons were aboard. The petrol stowage for aircraft was for 50,000 gallons. The final cost of the ship after fitting out in 1941 came to about £6,500,000. The calculations were that the 3-inch armoured deck would protect it from a 1,000 lb bomb dropped from 4,500 feet; fortunately I never had to verify that figure! However, many months later the crew had reason to be grateful for the armoured deck when they were aboard for the ship's second trip to the Pacific. When Kamikazes crashed on deck they merely had to be swept over the side. The American carriers on the other hand were often badly damaged because, for some extraordinary reason, the armour was on the hangar deck and not the flight deck. The *Victorious* was the only warship in World War II to sail completely round the world; to do this she went through both the Panama Canal and The Suez Canal.

When I joined the ship she had two Albacore squadrons 817 and 832, and one fighter squadron – 809, flying Fairey Fulmars. The Fulmar design was based on the Fairey Battle, but was a separate entity. It was *not* a Battle converted for Naval use. It was a two-seater and its performance was inferior to any other fighters, British or German. Its armament was eight machine guns.

The one greatest concern of the Home Fleet at the time was the looming presence of the German battleship *Tirpitz*. Like her sister ship, the *Bismarck*, the *Tirpitz* was a powerful adversary and equalled in power only by the allies' battleships. The *Tirpitz* dominated our thoughts: if she left her base in Norway and got among our convoys to Russia she could decimate them. The fact that she sat there doing nothing was of almost equal importance for it meant that we had to retain sufficient forces to deal with her just in case she did come out. This tied up valuable warships that could have been used elsewhere.

Captain Bovell was the Captain of the *Victorious* from late 1940 until November 1942. The first squadrons came aboard in February 1941. 832 Squadron was formed on 1 April 1941, but did not come aboard until August of that year.

I was met at the top of the gangway by Sub-Lieutenant Brian Shaw, an observer, who took me to the wardroom to introduce me to other members of the squadron. Brian was the squadron staff officer and in civil life he was a solicitor, so that made him supremely qualified to take care of the administrative side of the squadron. He was extremely efficient and always the right hand man of the Commanding Officer; the squadron was fortunate indeed to have him.

Our CO was Lieutenant-Commander Plugge, and he was that rare bird for a CO, an observer. The fact that the observer was often senior to the pilot occasionally gave rise to altercations. I forget the details but on one particular flight an observer ordered the pilot to carry on when the pilot did not consider it safe to do so. After a bit of a row the pilot said, 'Well my half of the aircraft is going back to the ship, your half can do what it likes.'

There was a shortage of cabins so I had to make do in a dormitory, which was normally the ADC (Admiral's Day Cabin). However, as the cabins were below or on the waterline one did not sleep in them when at sea. Whilst I might have felt myself hard done by I was fortunate when I compared myself with the ratings, who slept in hammocks. The squadron maintenance crews had to work in appalling conditions: not only was the hangar cold, but also of course the ship was pitching and rolling. It was great credit to them that they did as well as they did, the aircrews owed them a great debt.

When moving around the area of the Captain's quarters I was intrigued to find hanging on the wall a framed poem by Admiral Ronald A. Hopwood RN which comes from the anthology *The Old Way* (1918)

I do not think the entire poem was included – indeed there are thirteen verses. The following are the first and fifth verses:

> Now these are laws of the Navy,
> Unwritten and varied they be;
> And he that is wise will observe them,
> Going down in his ship to the sea;

As naught may outrun the destroyer,
Even so with the law and its grip,
For the strength of the ship is the Service,
And the strength of the Service, the ship.

When the ship that is tired returneth,
With the signs of the sea showing plain,
Men place her in dock for a season,
And her speed she reneweth again.
So shall thou, lest perchance thou grow weary
In the uttermost parts of the sea,
Pray for leave, for the good of the Service,
As much and as oft as may be.

Pertinent to our present situation is an extract from verse six:

If ye win through an Arctic ice flow,
Unmentioned at home in the Press,
Heed it not, no man seeth the piston,
But it driveth the ship none the less.

As I moved up the seniority table I did get a cabin. Unfortunately the navy system was that if an officer senior to you, even by a day, came on board and there were no spare cabins he would be given yours. This was galling when you had to clear out your things to make room for someone who was in a course later to you but was senior to you merely because of his age.

The dining room section of the wardroom was separate from the anteroom section in which we relaxed and talked and where the bar was situated. We were surprised and disappointed some eighteen months later when we were in the USS *Saratoga* to find that there was only one room; consequently if we were playing cards, or having a quiet drink together, we would be disturbed by a steward who would come along and tell us he wanted to make up the tables and we had to move.

One section of our wardroom seemed to be unofficially reserved for senior officers and we never dared enter its invisible portals. Most of the officers there seemed to smoke pipes, and the acrid smell permanently pervaded to whole wardroom.

Most of the squadron disappeared ashore leaving me to carry out my first take-off from an aircraft carrier. It was 15 December 1941 and I did it while the ship was at anchor. Strangely, some reporter or other was on board filming. I never found out for what purpose and neither did I ever see the film.

I stood beside my Albacore as it went up from the hangar deck in one of the two ship's lifts, and when it had been pushed forward I climbed in and tried to start up. The engine started momentarily and then stopped. Rather surprised, I started it again and ran it until it ran smoothly. The starting system for the Albacore was by Coffman cartridge; one fired a cartridge and the power of the cartridge turned the engine. It was not the best of systems, but the starting system of the Swordfish was even worse for a heavy inertia wheel had to be turned by hand by one or two burly ground crew and the engine was then engaged and turned over. I tried to do it by myself on one occasion when no strong men were in sight, but being a nine stone seven weakling I could not get up enough speed on the inertia wheel!

The wings of my Albacore were spread and I waited for the ship to swing on its anchor until it was into wind then at the drop of a flag off I went. My stomach experienced a sinking feeling as we went over the bows, but this was natural. I left the flight deck feeling that at last I was becoming operational. Some lazy-looking barrage balloons came in sight ahead of me and I realised I had temporarily forgotten about them and did a hasty climb. I glanced at my instruments and found that the oil pressure was 60 lbs per square inch instead of 80. I rather expected to hear the engine go pop pop at any moment and climbed to give myself time to prepare for a forced landing if the engine did fail. By the time I reached Hatston the indicated oil pressure had dropped to 30, but at least the oil temperature had not risen. I touched down with thankfulness in my heart and my heart in my mouth. I found out later that the gauge was at fault so, of course, the actual pressure would have been all right all the time.

A few days later I flew down to Arbroath to pick up an aircraft that had had an engine change. The first Albacores had Taurus II engines, but these proved unreliable and pilots had experienced engine trouble. All the Albacore engines were to be replaced by the Taurus XII engines. The Taurus engines were unusual in that they had sleeve valve engines; this made them extremely quiet. I had Sub-Lieutenant Bill Browne, an observer, in the back. As the aircraft was not ready I, at least, managed to get a few days unexpected leave, I cannot remember what Bill was going to Arbroath for, possibly to meet his wife for he was one of the few of us who were married. I caught the London train in the evening, I tried to get a sleeper, but there were none available; however, when we reached Edinburgh the attendant came along and said that one prospective customer had not arrived and would I like his? I certainly would, and I handed over £1/4/6d and in the morning a further a 9/6d tip for his trouble and also due to the fact that it was Christmas. So, after a reasonable night I arrived at Kings Cross in a more or less respectable state.

After a night at Chipstead with my Aunt Dorothy and her husband Harold I went to London next day and visited my Aunt Clarrie who had a hat shop in Duke Street near Selfridges. The notice outside said MISS FAY. HATS, but the family always called it MISS HAY. FATS.

I went to the cinema and saw *Ships With Wings,* which was about the Fleet Air Arm. The film was shown on board the Vic later on and the Commander Flying put up a humorous notice about it, picking up the many faults in the film.

I cannot remember his notice verbatim, but the gist of some of his remarks was: 'All aircraft are to land downwind! No one is to take any notice of the fire raging on deck!'

A reviewer also picked on that fact that, despite the fact that an officer had been dismissed from his squadron many months ago no one had taken his place in his sub flight!

I packed three busy days into my leave, which included a trip to Coulsdon on my motorbike. Unexpectedly I met a boy called Stanway who was still at Bradfield and in my house. He was a very pleasant lad and a good friend of Derrick Lawrence. I'm sure he had a bright future ahead of him, but tragically he was killed in a train accident shortly after the war.

I left Chipstead by train in dense fog. At Kings Cross station I found it packed with service personnel of both sexes. I managed to get a 3rd class sleeper and slept in company with a CPO, a lady and a gentleman.

At Arbroath I found that my plane would not be ready until the next day so as I had some time to spare I walked to the cemetery and tried to find Sid Carpenter's grave; perhaps it was too early for a headstone to be mounted and I could not locate it.

Next day I watched from the side of the cockpit while a fitter ran up the new engine on the aircraft. I remember registering the fact that the cylinder head temperature advanced rather rapidly, but thought that the fitter was an experienced man and as he did not make any remark that this was a bit strange I forgot about it.

My take-off was normal, but on reaching about eight hundred feet the engine started popping and I lost power. I put the flaps down and looked for a suitable field into which to make a forced landing. I was not too worried as I was over open country. However, I found one but discovered that it had poles put across it to prevent the Jerries using it as a landing ground. I visualised landing, hitting a pole and being turned over. So I decided to land on the other side of them. This complicated matters, as there were haystacks and a house there. I knew that I would be safer doing a high stall and smashing the fixed undercarriage than trying to make a nice landing and overrun the field into a hedge. Everything went according to plan: I had to swishtail and sideslip to knock off height, but I was perfectly positioned to make a landing about twenty feet up. The aircraft then descended almost vertically and the undercarriage was smashed as I had wished. It then had a very short run on its belly before coming to a halt. I must say I would probably never have thought of doing a 'pancake' landing if I had not read novels about aircraft in the First World War for we were certainly never taught anything about them. I pushed the fire button with no visible difference to the forlorn look of the Albacore. I completely forgot to turn off the fuel and put the switches off, as I should have done!

I climbed out of the cockpit and was momentarily startled to find that the ground was only two or three feet below me but of course with the undercarriage satisfactorily smashed it would be. Having got clear and seen that the machine had not blown up I realized that the people at the aerodrome would be in a flap so having assured a local farmer that I was all right I walked half a mile to a farm in which there was a telephone. Having dialled 0 for the exchange I realised that it was the number for police, fire, etc. and I looked up the number in the directory, at the same time assuring a harassed housewife that I was all right. Having got through and made my report I went back to the aircraft to find a reception committee consisting of the Surgeon Commander, two Surgeon Lieutenants and various other people awaiting me. Having shown them a cut on the back of my right hand, which they called an abrasion, I went back to the Air Station in the ambulance.

Subsequent investigation revealed the fact that the engine failure in my Albacore was due to the clearances on the spark plugs being incorrect. On such infinitesimal distances lives can depend!

Next day Bill Browne and I were passengers in a Proctor and were flown to Donibristle. There I ran into 'Faj' Pennington, a New Zealander on my course. He was called 'Faj' because of his initials, although his name was Frank. He was a striking cheerful chap, tall and athletic looking; indeed, he was in the New Zealand swimming team. He told me that Bruce Girdlestone, also a New Zealander, who was on our course, had taken off from Machrihanish, got lost and arrived in Ireland where he was interned. This must have been awfully frustrating for him, especially as I understood that even if you escaped from Ireland the British authorities would send you back again. I have heard of pilots who met sympathetic Irish people who aided them to escape back to British territory, so Bruce was unlucky. Many years later when in New Zealand I asked Bruce to tell me about his time in Ireland. He appeared very reluctant to do this, so I reckon he was embarrassed about it all.

At Donibristle I picked up another Albacore and flew it to Crail. I have no record as to why I did this, but I spent the night there and that evening I ran into Francis Baring, also a pilot, who was at Bradfield with me. He told me that there were now 50 new names on the Bradfield Roll of Honour.

On Christmas day I took off for Hatston and I note in my diary that I was informed that there were enemy aircraft in the vicinity of Arbroath! I took 2 hours 40 minutes to complete the trip and ate a cold Christmas dinner on my arrival.

On 30 December I carried out my first deck landing. The ship steamed outside Scapa to the west of the Orkneys. As far as I could tell it was for my benefit only! I was the new boy who had carried out only one deck landing and I was required to do more. It was an odd thing, but I had never seen a deck landing from the ship before I carried out mine. I had the sky to myself. If that little effort could be costed I wonder what the tab would have been for the taxpayer to pick up?

Since I had not seen anyone else do circuits and landings from a carrier I did not know whether to do split-arse turns and get back to the approach as quickly as possible, or carry out the more staid sort of circuit we had been taught during training. I opted for the latter. I climbed up ahead of the carrier to about 700 feet and then turned. On the downwind leg I was careful to turn on the crosswind leg well before I reached the ship for there was not only a wind blowing, but also the ship was steaming away into wind at a fair speed. This gained me good points with Commander Ranald, but he said that my circuits were rather large! In all I carried out five deck landings that day, which was the last day of the year of 1941.

Ranald was the Commander Flying, a status known as 'Wings'. The Commander Flying is part of the ship's company and not attached to any squadron, but of course he is in overall charge of the flying and the Fleet Air Arm personnel that were aboard. Among some of the aircrew he was known as 'Daddy' because of his ruddy complexion and fatherly appearance.

Whenever the ship put to sea there was inevitably the call on the Tannoy, 'Out Pee Vees' (Out PVs), which mystified me at first. However, PV stood for *paravane* and these were knife-bearing torpedo-like devices for cutting mines adrift, they were on the end of long cables that were deployed on each side of the ship.

At sea the pilots and observers would take their turn as Air Officer of the Watch on the compass platform. The duties were not onerous and it gave us a chance to see how the ship was controlled. The officer on watch would give his orders on the blower to the helmsman who was below.

The signals expert would be on the port side of the platform. A senior officer or the captain would generally be in attendance except when things were quiet.

There was sometimes a call from a lookout, 'Monkey starboard' (or port). Monkey was code word for 'M' and in this case the 'M' stood for mine. Occasionally senior officers would take pot shots at these drifting mines, but they always missed!

These code words underwent several changes during my career in the navy and in aviation. Now at last the final version seems to have been reached. In the WWI the letter 'T' was 'Toc' (most of the older generation have heard of Toc H which stood for Talbot House, a recreation establishment for servicemen). I have seen the letter 'T' vary since then from 'Tommy' to 'Tare' to 'Tango'.

I was aboard ship at anchor for New Year's Eve, which was celebrated by the order, 'Splice the main brace!' I forget whether the officers had their rum free, I suspect not. However, I know I did drink rather more rum than I intended, and I have not liked rum too much ever since! Shortly after midnight when I was well asleep we had, 'Actions Stations!' sounded. I'm not sure whether this was to make sure we were ready for any emergency or whether it was a genuine alert. Anyway we crawled back to bed sometime later thankful to get our heads down.

Initially my deck-landing ability did not show much improvement as I see from my log book that on one occasion I caught my hook in the barrier while it was down, the man in charge lowering it smartly when he saw that I was travelling slowly enough to allow him to do this without endangering aircraft up forward. On another occasion I caught my hook in the last wire. However, I improved thereafter as my confidence and experience grew. The trouble with the Albacore was the weak undercarriage; in any sort of heavy landing it would collapse. Contrast this with the Avenger which we could drop from a height and the undercarriage could take it.

The ship and the squadrons carried out drills, ALTs in particular, and worked up for the next week or two. On 2 January 1942 we combined with 817 Squadron, which was the other TSR squadron on board the Victorious and with 809 Squadron, the fighter squadron, to have 25 aircraft over Scapa flow – the greatest number that had been there for months. Our practice attacks were against the battleships *King George V* (generally known as the *KGV* – Kay Gee Five – in the navy), *Rodney*, and the cruiser *Trinidad*. The fighter boys in their Fulmars came in and when they had created a diversion the TSR boys went in to make practice torpedo attacks. After that we went away and then returned to dive bomb them.

In my diary I see that I missed death or injury twice! In the 'attack' on the *KGV*, planes were coming in from all directions and I had to lift my aircraft over another one to 'drop' my torpedo and then get away. On these dummy attacks we usually dropped a smoke float so that experts could see the exact moment we dropped and assess the attack accordingly. A few minutes later another plane nearly flew slap into my starboard side. He came up from behind from the right and we both saw each other simultaneously and did the quickest steep turns that had been seen for many a day. If either of us had not seen the other we would have all been mincemeat. During the turn there were only a few a few yards between us.

Coming back from the dive-bombing and having formed up into a V formation of the three aircraft, Harold Willott, my sub flight leader, signalled us into echelon starboard. As I was on his port side I was the only one who needed to move, so I moved over to the number three position on the right of number two. Arch Hugill in that number two position did not realise that we were now in echelon and when we broke for the bombing attack he turned *right*! I only just managed to miss him.

When joining the others to land back on the ship we had to separate the landings more than usual as one pilot had smashed the barrier.

Next day, while the fleet was still at anchor some of us visited Flotta, an island in the middle of Scapa Flow, to see a play put on by crew members of the *KGV*. It was *Sweeny Todd, The Demon Barber of Fleet Street*. It was an excellent show and I understood that the principal actor was a professional who had made the part his speciality. Looking back I wonder whether this was Tod Slaughter, I see he was in the services during the war.

Whilst in harbour in Scapa Capt. Bovell ordered a 'tilt test'. If the ship was ever damaged on one side it was possible for damage control to transfer fuel from one side of the ship to the other to keep the ship upright. In this case all he was doing was transferring the fuel so that the ship took on a list. It was really amazing how a 10° list affects things. It does not sound much but it made walking very difficult and in fact the ship eventually reached 15°. Of course the inevitable happened: pilots seeing the ship heeling over to port in harbour reported that she had been damaged!

We would also do a stint on watch when in harbour and I had not been in the ship many days while she was at anchor at Scapa when I found myself on the compass platform at night. I was Air Officer of the Watch in harbour. I was all alone and wondering what the hell I was supposed to do, for no one had briefed me. Nobody else was anywhere near me. After a few minutes, salvation in the shape of Sub-Lieutenant John Barnes arrived and asked me if I knew what to do. He took me down

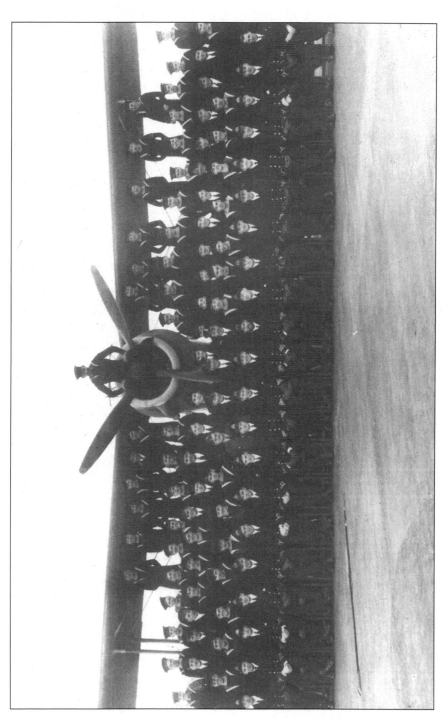

832 Squadron. Early 1942.

one deck just below the platform and started to tell me what the equipment did. We had not been there many minutes when an anxious Petty Officer arrived and said he had been trying to contact the compass platform as an unidentified aircraft was approaching. John said I should get on the blower and say, 'Alarm to Arms'. I did this twice, the ship was roused and things started to move; in particular the captain arrived on the compass platform.

I just wonder what I would have done if John had not arrived at that moment! Here was I, a newly promoted Sub-Lieutenant and looking about seventeen, in apparent charge of a rather expensive fleet aircraft carrier of the Royal Navy with about 1,400 men relying on me to do the right thing!

It was a false alarm and I soon found myself on the compass platform with just the captain for company. Since no one else was there I tried to engage him in conversation, thinking that his dignity would not be affected. But when he did not answer my question, even after prompting with a plaintive 'Sir?', I gave up; obviously I was committing *lèse majesté*. Thanks to John Barnes, however, I hoped that my impression on him was not unfavourable.

I thought Captain Bovell was the right man in the right place. I also thought that Commander Surtees was excellent as the Commander or executive officer. He was small, intense, completely on the ball and a strong disciplinarian. I'm afraid that Fleet Air Arm personnel who had him as their captain of an Escort Carrier later on did not think highly of him and the remark made was that he was mad!

12

ARCTIC WATERS

At last I was operational, even if it was just to the extent of carrying out a few A/S. (anti-submarine) patrols. My crew at this time consisted of Sub-Lieutenant David Johnson and Leading Airman Hollowood, and it was they who, later on, were my crew during the most daunting and scary four hours of my life. My first patrol got very boring after the first hour, the monotony being broken when I tried unsuccessfully to use the pilot's urinal! My deck landing was all right, but a bit far down the deck.

Shortly after this Arch Hugill and Gerry Child, his observer, had a bit of a tale to tell: they were doing an A/S Patrol when they received a message telling them to locate a crashed Hudson on a beach in Iceland. They found it and while circling around it had engine trouble and had to land beside it on the beach. A destroyer put out to pick them up, but its whaler got stuck near to them so, instead of decreasing, the number of stranded men was increased. However, Arch was eventually taken off with his TAG (Telegraphist Air Gunner), leaving Gerry to look after the aircraft. He had a dreadful time for his clothes and those of the other castaways got wet and froze on them. Being the only officer he had to take charge and tried to prevent them getting frostbite. During the night he pulled his parachute to use the silk as a blanket. In the morning he apparently had to walk eight miles in his flying boots to get back to any sort of settlement. He and Arch went on leave shortly after this presumably to let them recover from their ordeal. I didn't hear the details, but Arch managed to get his plane to Reykjavik; so I can only assume that repairs were made and he was able to fly it away.

On 16 January 1942, the squadron should have flown off to Hatston, but the weather was too bad to embark the non-flying members of the squadron and probably too rough for the squadron to fly off anyway. We would have done this on the 17th, but Hitler intervened and we landed-on the other TSR Squadron, 817, in a hurry and sailed out of Scapa at about 1700 hours. *Victorious* was in company with the battleship

HMS *King George V*, the cruiser HMS *Berwick*, and seven destroyers. When we were clear the tannoys began a, 'D'ye hear there . . .' and it was explained that a German force probably consisted of the *Tirpitz* and two cruisers was preparing to leave harbour. The *Victorious. KGV, Rodney, Kenya, Sheffield* and about 11 destroyers were going to Iceland.

On the 18th I went up on deck to watch the two A/S patrol aircraft land. Jerry Conolley came in and then Arch Hugill followed. The ship was pitching a bit and his approach was quite good, but then he found he was too high and also started to drift towards the 'island' (the superstructure on the starboard side of the ship). He could have touched down and caught the last wire, but he decided to go round again. He tried to open up but the aircraft swung to port and sank on to the deck and started moving towards the port side. His undercarriage hit a projection on the edge of the deck and there was a sickening crunch as his wing hit the deck and the aircraft disappeared sideways over the edge.

I was numb for a few seconds. Then I rushed to the side with many others who were watching. Blessed relief! Arch and his observer Gerry Child and the Air Gunner were on top of the plane, which they must have evacuated pretty quickly. The ship made a loud noise and blew off steam as a signal to a destroyer. One of them dashed along and picked the crew up. I remembered later that the plane was carrying depth charges, which, if they had been torn off, would have blown the plane and its occupants to pieces.

In another accident the previous day Sub-Lieutenant Mathias tried to go round again, but hit the barrier; his plane was swung round and it hit a pompom gunner on the head. There was little hope of the man's recovery. Sub-Lieutenant Shepherd was also unfortunate. Twice in successive landings he smashed his undercarriage.

On 19 January we arrived in Hvalfjord, Iceland, which looked a bit different from the time I was there in July 1941 on the way back from Canada. It was now covered in ice; whereas in July I was swimming in a hot pool.

Arch Hugill and Gerry Child came aboard from the destroyer that picked them up. They said that after their crash into the sea they had got into the dinghy and, remembering the depth charges, they had tried to paddle away from the sinking plane, but only managed to go around in circles! They then opened some chewing gum and were chewing contentedly when the destroyer picked them up. The first people Gerry saw were two 'dipped' observers from his course who were now doing time as ratings. The motion of the destroyer did not agree with them very much.

On the 20th HMS *Renown* joined us. My thoughts went back to that far off time in the late 1920s in Wellington, New Zealand when I had gone

Following a crash on deck the aircraft would often be temporarily suspended over the side of the ship by a crane to enable other aircraft to be landed.

aboard her. How could I have possibly guessed then that one day I would be in the navy, flying aeroplanes and be in company with that fine ship!

I went ashore with Jock Landles and David Johnson and climbed a small mountain. We walked along the top for a while and had a magnificent view of the fjord. The ships looked just like toys and one felt it would be possible to put out a hand and pick them up

I attended a debate by some of the crew. I only mention this because the motion has some relevance to the present day Navy. It was about having Wrens aboard sea-going ships. They favoured *not* having them aboard by 25 to 20.

Another walk ashore found us going along a road at the foot of the mountains. We inspected an invasion barge, which for some reason was lying on the beach. We saw some blackbirds and we thought they must be tough to survive conditions in Iceland. On another walk we took the hard way up and it was steep enough for us to slide down during the descent. On returning to the ship I found seven letters, two parcels and two papers awaiting me as the mail had arrived. One from my mother reported that there was a rumour out there in the Argentine that the *KGV* had been sunk together with *The Prince of Wales* and *Repulse*. The *KGV* was our flagship and was with us at the moment so that knocked that tale on the head! I fear that the rest was true.

American aircraft were, on occasions, flying up and down the fjord making a terrible noise. A Walrus flying around was quiet in comparison and at times looked quite fast for the elderly biplane that it was; it also seemed very manoeuvrable as befitting a biplane.

Up until then I was merely a spare pilot and not a full member of the squadron. However, with the departure of Lieutenant King to fresh fields I was now a proper member of the squadron.

We were stuck in Iceland and getting a little bored so I went for a trip down to the engine room. I would not have had a job down there for all the tea in China. I would have been the first to run if there was any thought of a torpedo hitting us. The engine room crew must have nerves of steel and deserved all the praise they could get.

We didn't get much entertainment on board ship, but occasionally in harbour we had a film show. The 'theatre' being the aft lift-well! The lift-well is the space at hangar deck level that was left when the lift is up flush with the flight deck. We saw a priceless film, *The Reluctant Dragon*. I almost bust my stomach laughing, it positively ached. I now understood the expression, 'I could have died laughing'!

The captain decided to have a march past on the flight deck with

HMS *Victorious*, 1942. Captain Bovell taking the salute. Officers from left to right: Sub-Lieutenants Shaw, Landles, Fay and Willott.

everyone saluting him. He did not like our salutes, although I can find nothing wrong with mine in the photograph reproduced on the previous page. He ordered us to do some with Commander Flying who took us into the hangar where we duly marched past him saluting. For some reason everyone thought this was very amusing, presumably because we looked so odd. In my case I made it even funnier by marching past with my chest out and trying to look proud and giving a smart dignified salute – I then nearly fell on the slippery deck.

On 7 February I recorded that there had been fog over us for the last two days and that it was not too cold, whereas in England it was freezing!

My parents sent me a tin of Dulce De Leche from the Argentine. This is a national delicacy although it can be made quite simply at home by boiling an unopened tin of sweetened condensed milk for about two hours in a saucepan of water. (I once found to my cost what happens if you let the water boil dry – the tin exploded and spread boiling condensed milk all over the place; fortunately no one was near.) Anyway, in the wardroom everyone was curious as to what it was; I tried to fool some people that it was bull's spunk, but they were loath to believe me. But at least it put them off trying to cadge some from me!

On one of out training flights I was in the air for 3 hours 20 minutes doing ALTs and air firing. My front gun, which fired through the propeller disc, jammed while I was doing this. Firing through the propeller was possible due to the interrupter gear, more properly (and correctly) known as a synchronisation gear, and was a triggering device

HMS *Victorious*, 1942. Guest night in the wardroom. A singsong is in progress.

invented by Anthony Fokker during the Great War. We did an ALT on the *Renown* and she put on 30 knots as we descended -a grand sight. She foxed us completely with her turns and I for one ended up close to the bow, an almost impossible place from which to drop a torpedo. This just showed how it was possible for the target to outmanoeuvre the torpedo pilots and how difficult it might be for just a few aircraft to be in the right place at the right time.

We put to sea at 0300 hours on 19 February. Our apparent aim was to escort or screen a Russian convoy, and after that we would bomb shipping in Tromso. 832 Squadron aircraft would go in first followed by 817 Squadron. The Albacores were to be armed with six 250 lb bombs and eight 40 lb incendiaries. If we could not find shipping we had an alternative target of oil tanks, etc. We were to bomb at dawn and make our way back in semi-darkness. Apparently the nearest enemy aerodrome was 30 miles away from Tromso and had Junkers 87s and 88s, but I expected there would be some enemy fighters knocking about somewhere.

The operation was cancelled! It was reported that the battle cruiser *Admiral Sheer* and the heavy cruiser *Hipper* or possibly the battle cruisers *Scharnhorst* and *Gneisenau* had been sighted. This is what I heard at the time; it turned out that the two ships were the *Admiral Sheer* and the heavy cruiser *Prinz Eugen*. The two TSR squadrons were to carry out a night sweep down the Norwegian coast to search for them and make an attack if they were found. We and the cruiser HMS *Berwick* with escorting destroyers were to go in close to Norway before we flew off. The Vic would then move away at high speed before the enemy bombers appeared, while we would land at Sumburgh, an RAF aerodrome in the Shetlands.

For the operation one of our aircraft had ASV (Air to Surface Vessel), which was an early form of radar. I did not hear the term 'radar' until 1943, in fact Plugge had to describe what the ASV was capable of during his briefing. He said that radio waves would reflect back from anything, even a bit of cotton wool and the reflected wave could be picked up and objects shown on a screen.

If we did make an attack some of the Albacores would drop flares on the far side of the target while the torpedo aircraft would attack the illuminated ships from the other side.

The Paymaster Commander, Commander Tucker, who always seemed to be in touch with MI9, gave us a short briefing. He made a point of saying that information about the movements of the *Tirpitz* and other ships came from a Norwegian source – some little man with a radio. Whilst this was true in certain cases I suspect that for the most part our gen came from Bletchley Park.

Whilst having a meal before the operation I had a good chat with De Longueuil. He was temporarily the Senior Pilot while Lieutenant John Stenning was on leave, so would be flying with the CO and with the chief TAG Petty Officer Dryden.

Unreported elsewhere in any book I have read, my diary records that just before we started the operation we received an O/U signal. That signal (pronounced 'Oh Break You') was the highest category (*Most Immediate*) and most important of all the radio signals that could be received. In this case it read, '*Believe you are being shadowed by surface vessels.*' I never found out who sent it.

Some de-icing gunge was smeared on our propellers. I felt it must have enormous adhesive powers to withstand the centrifugal force of the spinning propeller.

I put a hacksaw blade, two razor blades, needle and thread and matches down the side of my flying boots in case I was shot down over Norway. I also wanted to obtain a map of Norway, but could not get one. These precautions were rather simple compared with the more sophisticated equipment that we were provided with a few months later.

We climbed into our aircraft at midnight with Sub-Lieutenant David Johnson as my observer and Leading Airman Hollowood as my TAG. The weather got worse with strong winds and heavy snow, the deck was moving up and down about thirty feet at the bows. We were cold enough sitting in the cockpit but the ground crews when they had to venture on deck must have been frozen. We waited an hour on the flight deck for our eyes to become adapted to the dark, for we had not yet received the goggles that we could wear in a lighted room. At 0100 hours on the 23rd the ship turned into wind and one of my ground crew – either a fitter or a rigger – climbed up to the cockpit, grabbed my shoulder and said, 'Good luck, Sir'. I appreciated that. One by one we took off, each of us flying a course on leaving the deck so that we could pick up the aircraft ahead in the darkness. After leaving the flight deck I followed the aircraft directly in front of me. I had trouble finding my own particular sub flight leader, but formated on someone who apparently had no objection to my doing so. We maintained radio silence and in my diary I note that I identified myself several times during the flight, but I cannot now remember how I did this and I read that on no occasion did I see anyone else try to do so.

John Barnes recorded that the only aircraft in the squadron fitted with ASV was 4H, Peter O'Shea was the pilot and he was the observer. He went on,

> I think that the reason for giving me the job of using the ASV equipment was that I had had experience of working with ASV before

joining 832. I had been in 701 Squadron whose Walrus flying boats were among the first naval aircraft to get the new equipment. I think I was the only observer in 832 with this experience.

On 23rd February 1942, when we were thirty miles from the Norwegian coast, I started to get echoes, showing that the equipment was working. My recollection is that most of the echoes came from land, but in my report written on the next day, I say that I got three echoes, distant 8 miles and 18 miles off shore, which were 'with clear outline' and which 'were presumed to be ships'. The aircraft altered course in order to pass over these presumed vessels but nothing was seen.

Before reaching the coast the aircraft on which I was formating changed position and, not wishing to tag on to anyone who was not expecting me, I flew to starboard and slightly lower than the nearest aircraft. After all I was the new boy of the squadron and was virtually arse-end Charlie.

Keeping in formation was the hardest part of the operation and a great strain. One's life depends on keeping formation and not colliding with other aircraft. Any mistake on the pilot's part would mean not only the death of his crew, but the innocent parties in the other aircraft – a great responsibility indeed! It was bad enough in the daytime, concentrating on the other aircraft; at night it was infinitely worse. The only illumination we had was the formation lights, tiny things that could not be seen very far as obviously they would be a giveaway to any enemy searching for us, and they are not to be confused with navigation lights which can be seen for miles. To avoid collision one had to have one's eyes glued on the sub flight leader's aircraft, he in turn would be watching his leader. Occasionally we could afford a quick glance at the cockpit instruments. Any lack of concentration, when the leader carried out an unexpected turn for example, could be fatal for all concerned. Indeed, 817 Squadron lost two aircraft in a collision as we found out later.

I was able to count eight aircraft in the formation. The missing one was that piloted by Jock Landles. He did not find the formation after take-off and flew round the circuit by himself. This was something we would all have wished to do as it avoided the strain and dangers of formation flying at night.

It was during one of my quick glances at my instruments that I noticed that my ASI. (Airspeed Indicator) showed zero! Obviously the pitot head, the instrument mounted on the wing and measuring the speed of the air, had become iced up. I quickly switched on the pitot heater and all was well. We were still tooling along at about 70 to 80 knots.

After about 45 minutes flying in ragged formation we turned down the coast, crossing either bits of Norway or islands. Narrow escape number one occurred when an aircraft on my port suddenly turned sharply to starboard across my bows, missing me by a few yards. David Johnson, my observer, saw it and got the shock of his life, and no wonder! Many years later someone admitted to me that he had got fed up and decided to leave the formation! Number two narrow squeak occurred when the formation got lower and lower without my knowing it (mine was the lowest aircraft) and I suddenly looked to the right where the moon was appearing through the clouds and saw the water close to my wheels. The altimeter indicated minus 10 feet, but then I had set it to zero on the flight deck. Phew! Stick back and throttle open.

Eventually we steered west towards Sumburgh, but turned back and circled around before reverting back on to a course of 270°. The weather got progressively worse and a short time before our ETA at Sumburgh we ran into a severe rainstorm and the formation broke up. I carried out a lot of the flight on instruments alone and put 2 hours of INST/CLOUD FLYING in the appropriate space in the log book, but this instrument flying was infinitely preferable to flying in close formation.

On emerging into clearer weather the formation was scattered and I believe other pilots thought that I was the leader for they all flew towards me! I avoided them as quickly as possible! It must have been about this time that the CO Lieutenant-Commander Plugge, his pilot Lieutenant De Longeuil, and the TAG Petty Officer Dryden disappeared.

We dropped two flame floats in order to find a wind, but they both went out within a few seconds. We were luckier with the third, which stayed alight. However, about this time we obtained a D/F bearing to Sumburgh.

The flare path was lit up like daylight. So a night landing was fairly simple. I had flown for four hours ten minutes and I still had some fuel in my tank despite flying with the engine in rich mixture all the way, but then I knew that the engine of this aircraft operated slightly lean. I still had my torpedo although many pilots, including Jock Landles on his navex, had jettisoned theirs, as did all the pilots of 817.

Some pilots had less fuel remaining than I had and Gerry Conolley ran out of fuel at the end of the runway after landing!

Sub-Lieutenant. Wallis (817 Squadron) dropped his 'fish' (torpedo) on an E-boat, he thought. Otherwise none of the enemy was sighted.

So ended the worst fours hours ten minutes of my life! I say elsewhere in this book that millions of people across Europe and the world would have given their right arms to change places with me during the war. However, not for the night of 23 February 1942, I am quite sure!

John Burbidge, an observer, recounts the fact that he looked on that trip as a great adventure. It was only afterwards that he realised what difficulties and responsibilities the pilots had. He was uncertain of his position for a while and was very glad to see the lighthouse on Fair Isle ahead and to port; at last he was able to get some idea of his location.

In the officers' mess we had not heard about 817's losses and were all making jokes about the CO being late, but as time went by we realised that he was not going to appear and the mood grew sombre It was not until some years later that one of the pilots told me that he had seen the CO's flares go off. He made the assumption that that the pilot had dropped the flares by mistake instead of jettisoning his torpedo and had become temporarily blinded. However, anything could have happened, for instance he might have had an engine failure and used the flares to help him ditch in the sea. Unfortunately we shall never know the answer.

We heard that this was the first time that any Fleet Air Arm squadrons had taken off from a carrier, flown over enemy territory, and landed at a shore base.

To lose the Commanding Officer, the Acting Senior Pilot and the senior Telegraphist Air Gunner in one fell swoop was a bitter blow to the squadron. All three had wives and De Longueuil had been married only a few weeks before.

Next day we flew to Hatston in the morning and landed on the Vic while she was in the Flow. I still had my torpedo of course and thus saved the country some £1,800! There was a very strong wind blowing and the Vic was making only a few knots – just enough to be able to manoeuvre and keep into wind.

Jock Landles and I went ashore to the island of Flotta shortly after this. In complete contrast to the recent events it was a beautiful day.

Admiral Tovey, The Commander in Chief Home Fleet, came aboard a day or two later and shook hands with all the aircrews involved in the recent operation. The admiral's name was pronounced 'Tuvvy', a fact obviously not known to those doing recent (2005) TV programmes as his name was pronounced, 'Toe-vee' throughout.

The squadron was given a new CO and Lieutenant-Commander Lucas, RN, joined us. Somewhere during his time in the navy he had received the unfortunate nickname of 'Pig', although I should not think that anyone would call him that to his face. He was rather unapproachable and was not popular; if he had a sense of humour it was not apparent. This is not to decry his merits of being an experienced pilot and being strong willed. We did not know it at the time, but he was an alcoholic and about a year later, as I will reveal, he was dismissed from his post by the then captain of the *Victorious*.

Whenever we were in Hatston we would seize the chance to swing the compasses on the aircraft. This was to check for the deviation and other compass faults such as an incorrect lubber line. The procedure involved putting the aircraft on a piece of ground specially marked out with a compass rose (North, South, East and West, etc.) and turning the aircraft on to these points, noting the error and putting it on the deviation card. This was quite a tedious business. This card was then placed in the aircraft in view of the pilot and observer. I am mentioning this so that the reader can fully appreciate the next paragraph.

Around this time thought was given to all aircrews, RAF as well as FAA, as regards escaping from occupied territories. To this end various pieces of equipment were issued. The RAF had coloured handkerchiefs with maps printed on them; flexible saws could be fitted inside belts; compasses could be hidden in buttons. We ourselves were issued with special collar studs: a little piece of paper could be scraped off to reveal the miniature compass. On these being issued to us aboard ship our senior observer, Lieutenant George, RNR, was heard to remark, 'Now, I suppose we shall all have to go ashore to swing collar studs!'

There were also flying boots from which the top half could be removed to leave just a pair of walking shoes.

To brighten our grey days the ship would circulate amusing items from time to time and one of these was a letter that required a minimum effort on the part of the sender as he only had to underline the parts that applied. I have a feeling that this system originated from previous wars, but I reproduce two parts of the document:

	(dear	(father)	(offspring)	(sister)	(sweet)
My	(darling)	(mother)	(brother)	(friend)	(honey)
	(dearest)	(sweetheart)	(Butch)	(sugar)	(sweet pea)

It finished:

Keep (smiling) (chin up) (chest out) (neck in) (fingers crossed) (legs crossed) (tail over the dashboard) and think of me.

love and kisses) (as always) (yours) (sincerely yours)

Another humorous page that was circulated bears all the signs of having been around for many years and even nowadays I often see similar documents.

These are taken from letters written to HM Pensions Office:

1. I cannot get my sick pay. I have six children, can you tell me why this is?

2. I am glad to say my husband, who was reported missing, is now dead.
3. Sir, I am forwarding my marriage certificate and two children, one of which is a mistake, as you will see.
4. Re your dental enquiry. The teeth on the top are all right, but the ones in my bottom hurt terribly.
5. Unless I get my husband's money I shall be forced to lead an immortal life.
6. Please send my money at once as I have fallen into errors with the landlord.

It was while at Hatston during one of our periods of working up that a rather bizarre incident occurred. In a local shop I discovered a book published around 1895 and which described the etiquette of that era; it gave advice on the correct way to behave during those Victorian times and how to write letters on various subjects. My sleeping accommodation at the time was a small dormitory with Arch Hugill and Gerry Child, and to amuse them I started quoting from the book, not realising that our walls were pretty thin – certainly not thick enough anyway. I read out how to propose to a girl by letter. It was incredible, the alleged swain did not even address her by her first name and in flowery language he declared his undying love and his wish to plight his troth! We were all chuckling at this when the door opened and a Wren burst in and in ringing tones accused us of what today might be called porn! Perhaps a rather dirty laugh belonging to one of our number gave her the wrong impression, but there were we three innocent young officers sitting in bed in our pyjamas and being falsely accused! We were too flabbergasted to say anything before she swept out again. Had I had time I would have presented her with the book so that she could see for herself how innocent it was.

On 4 March we put to sea again to be the covering force for a Russian convoy. This does not mean that we accompanied the convoy but that we were between them and the Norwegian coast in case any German warships came out to attack it. We had a message piped to the effect that we would rendezvous with HMS *Duke of York* and HMS *Renown*. The day after we were the east of Iceland and steering 030°, but after meeting the two capital ships we steered 210°. Next day I had to rise at 0530 hours to carry out some shadowing practice on an 'opposing' battle fleet, but rough weather was against us and there was no flying.

During the night of 7–8 March the two TSR Squadrons were standing by as a report said that the *Tirpitz* was out and after the convoy. In fact the *Tirpitz* had somehow sailed to a position north of us, which Admiral Tovey did not know about for some time; and she was now steaming back towards Narvik. The squadrons were armed with torpedoes using contact heads and set for a depth of 25 feet, except for three aircraft of each squadron that were going to search for the *Tirpitz* and send back a sighting report if she were found.

I was unlucky, as being the newest and most junior of the squadron I was not going with the striking force, the only plane available being one with an old Taurus II engine, and anyway there was no observer for me. On reading my diary I just wonder why this was and concluded that Gerry Child was on leave after his ordeal and perhaps others were too. Probably because of this situation I had to do an extra lot of A/S patrols. On one occasion I was sent to investigate some black smoke but found nothing, although I did see one mine.

During the night I slept in the *Pilots' and Observers' Waiting Room*. What a cumbersome label for it! The Americans were better; they called their equivalent *The Ready Room*. I was called at 0500 and went up to the Compass Platform for a spell as Air Officer of the Watch.

On 7 March we sent out three aircraft from each squadron on a search for the *Tirpitz*. It was almost with disbelief that we heard that Tommy Millar, the pilot, and Bill Browne, the observer had found the ship and sent out a sighting report: '1BS 1DR course ... position ...' (i.e. One battleship, one destroyer course ... position ...). This was another occasion when the Most Immediate signal O break U was used, and Bill Browne said afterwards that he found it most surreal. After all, during our training one never expected that one day you would be sending out that rare and important signal. I recall reading that the signal was repeated to the Admiralty by one of our submarines, just in case they did not receive the one from the aircraft.

Reading my diary I was surprised that the *Tirpitz* had only one destroyer, but apparently she set off with three. Two of them had to return to base because they were running out of fuel, this left her with just the one – the *Fredrich Ihn*.

One of the three 817 Squadron aircraft with the crew Birch and Dunworth spotted the ship shortly afterwards. Unfortunately the *Tirpitz* had launched an Arado aircraft, which attacked them. Dunworth was wounded in the leg and one of the aircraft's ailerons was shot away. Dunworth managed to give his pilot a course to steer for the ship before passing out and the aircraft arrived back safely.

The story of the torpedo attack is well recorded in other books. It was a failure as no hits were obtained. During my training I was told that with twelve aircraft only one hit might be expected and that is the precise number of aircraft from 832 and 817 squadrons that made the attack, unfortunately that one hit was not obtained.

One or two things stand out: the strong wind that made it difficult for the slow-flying Albacores to catch up with the *Tirpitz* which was doing 30 knots into wind; and, to my mind, the clever manoeuvres made by the Captain of the *Tirpitz*. His action was to make an initial turn, which fooled the pilots into thinking that he would continue the turn and they started to position themselves accordingly – and then he turned the other way! Also one must not forget that the *Tirpitz* and its escorting destroyer were firing at the aircraft with everything possible; in fact they had eighty-eight guns firing in all.

Some people were inclined to blame Lieutenant-Commander Lucas. I didn't, for the squadrons were well drilled. They were just unlucky, also the immense size of the ship made some pilots misjudge their distance and drop their torpedoes too far away. On the other hand the Germans reported that some torpedoes were dropped at a distance of 400 yards and that one torpedo missed by a mere 30 feet.

I have read two books that said that the squadrons had had insufficient training, but I think one author was copying the other. Anyway the implication is nonsense; we were as well trained as any other squadron in the Fleet Air Arm. On all our training flights we did ALTs, with differing success depending on the weather, the type of ship and its speed and manoeuvrability, and sheer luck. Even in practice, with no one firing at them, sub-flight leaders were often caught wrong-footed by the manoeuvres of the ship, as I have previously shown. In the final analysis the fact that there were only twelve aircraft in the attack and that the pilots were flying slow and obsolete aircraft must be the principal causes of failure. Had we several squadrons of torpedo bombers like the Japanese had when they attacked the *Prince of Wales* and the *Repulse* the result would have been very different.

Unfortunately two of our aircraft were shot down and we lost Dick Shepherd and his observer L. Brown of 832 and Sub-Lieutenant Jones and his crew of 817.

The TAG, Leading Airman Hollowood, with whom I had been flying recently, was in the aircraft flown by Dick Shepherd so was lost. I thought highly of him, he was a strong-looking fine figure of a man and obviously intelligent. The fact that I was a pilot and he was a TAG can only be put down to the difference in our educations. It could have easily been the other way round – except I don't think I would ever have volunteered to be a TAG!

By a quirk of fate Hollowood missed changing positions with Leading Airman Robertson at the last minute.

Various books overestimate the speed of the Albacores and one gives them a cruising speed of 130 knots. I wish! In fact the speed with a torpedo would have been about 80 knots. 130 knots could only be obtained in a dive!

For general consumption Captain Bovell stated that no one was more disappointed than the crews of the aircraft who took part in the attack; it was a chance they had dreamed and prayed for. In fact he was furious and on the strength of one photograph assumed that the crews had all dropped their torpedoes too far away. He summoned all the officers to the wardroom, dismissed all the stewards and other wardroom staff and had the doors shut. He then lambasted the crews in front of everyone, which left us all pretty shaken. Fifty years later I was talking to one of the crewmembers that took part in the attack and Captain Bovell's words still rankled.

After the return of our Albacores my diary records that a Blom and Voss aircraft then flew towards the ship and was chased by our fighters, which scored several hits. The ship was beetling along at maximum speed and the stern was vibrating like hell in consequence. Later I was in the wardroom having a cup of tea at 1530 hours when the anti-aircraft guns and the multiple pom-poms started firing. Suddenly there was a loud bang, the lights jumped a foot or two on their cables and, surprisingly, one of my plates broke in two. I learnt subsequently that a Junkers 88 dived bombed us from 6,000 feet and the bomb fell just 20 yards off our starboard quarter. We were unfortunate to be landing-on aircraft at the time so the fighters could not get cracking.

The *Tirpitz* continued on to Narvik, but a few days later left there and headed south for Trondheim. On Hitler's orders she was not to put to sea if there were any aircraft carriers known to be in the vicinity. So our attack did do some good at least.

Two days later Jock Landles and I spent some time going through Dick Shepherd's things. He had left a note as to what to do with his kit if he did not return.

We set course for Scapa and had a fighter patrol of Beaufighters overhead during the daytime.

On the 11th we heard about the *Tirpitz* action on the 9 o'clock news. The pill was sugared for the public, instead of, 'No hits were observed', the report said, 'Results are not known'. It also said that the ship was last seen retiring under a heavy smoke screen, which was not true. They say that in war truth is the first casualty and this appeared to be an example.

Back in Scapa I went for a walk on Flotta with Jock Landles, a new doctor, and a new pilot called Mills. It was cold and windy and we had a welcome plate of bacon and eggs in the Officers' Club before catching the boat back to the ship. It was quite a rough ride back due to the high wind.

Tony Garland arrived back from leave and I had a chat with him and 'Steve' Stevenson. Tony was as cheery as ever, he was very popular and could get on with anyone. It was always very pleasant to have a natter with him.

I received the news of the birth of my first nephew, Christopher Andrew. In my diary I wondered whether I would ever see the lad. He is now a doctor and a strapping fellow aged over 60 and a grandfather. So I did!

Alan Lawrence of 817 Squadron received a letter from Harold Hawken in Malta who was on my St Vincent course. He told of the death of Michael Holdsworth. The reader might remember that this was the man whose room at Cambridge I occupied when I was taking the Littlego exam and whom I subsequently met at St Vincent. Harold Hawken, a New Zealander, was in a night-flying squadron and he said that they still got air raids every day.

Arch Hugill arrived back on the ship quite unexpectedly. He had flown to Iceland in a Liberator and then to Scotland by another aircraft. I met him with mixed feelings for I had been using his cabin while he was away, but now he had returned and seniority demanded that he have his cabin back.

The KGV players put on another show in the theatre on Flotta called 'Hullo Flotta' which was very enjoyable.

We were off again on 26 March for another Russian Convoy (PQ13).

A morning or two later we were all asleep in the Admiral's Day Cabin in that dreamlike stage of hearing stewards rattling tea cups and cleaning shoes and wondering whether remaining in bed any longer would be profitable. Suddenly there was a terrific bang and the ship felt as if it had been lifted by a giant hand and shaken. Everyone sat up, but being sleepy lay down again when nothing further occurred. On reflection this was rather amazing as we might have been torpedoed and also the Tannoy system might have been put out of action. I rose and went to the heads and for that reason missed an announcement on the Tannoy.

It transpired that the 817 Squadron Albacore carrying out the dawn A/S patrol had hit its starboard wing on the island and this had swung the aircraft into the sea. The depth charges had gone off a few seconds later. The crew were killed of course. Lieutenant Beer was the pilot, and he was that fairly rare beast, an RNR pilot. Sub-Lieutenant Davis was the observer and I had been chatting to him the night before. His body was the only one picked up by HMS Icarus; his neck was broken, otherwise there was scarcely a mark on him. It says something for the toughness of the Vic that no damage was caused to her; plates could have sprung or the propellers could have been damaged, but she carried on just as usual.

I wrote in my diary: 'Every flight might be a person's last and this has been brought home more to me since joining this ship than ever before. We are beginning to realise just how much chance we stand of coming out alive at the end of the war. The prospects seem slender at the moment.'

25 March. In the early hours of the morning the ship took up a protesting attitude; it bucked and kicked and shook and shuddered. The wind was about 60 knots or more. The steel wind shields on the flight deck were broken, the bows were bent, the fo'c'sle damaged and water poured down ventilator shafts and in some case up hatchways as in the case of our dormitory the ADC where water shot into there and also into the captain's quarters. It was very tough on the destroyers and my heart went out to the crews. The *Tartar* was damaged and had to go back to Scapa.

A special watch had to be put in the hangar, as the planes were prone to fly into the air with the up and down movements of the ship. In view of the weather and the subsequent requirements of the ship it was some three weeks before I got airborne again.

The 26th March saw the waves still terrific but it started to snow and the temperature plummeted and by the 27th the ship started to get encrusted with ice. This required extreme measures and these consisted mostly of elbow grease on the part of the crew who used brooms and shovels and steam jets to clear it away.

On the 27th I had the last half of the first watch to do on the compass platform. All the windows except the revolving ones (centrifugal force keeps them clear) were iced up. It was not very dark and the horizon was visible, but I could see no destroyers as they merged into the sea too well. The Captain was up there, as indeed he was most of the time while we were at sea. Captains rarely get any sleep; any final responsibility is theirs and the strain must be tremendous.

Before midnight we were steering 200° and were informed that we were going back to Scapa. The rolling of the ship was now much less.

On the following day we were told that in fact we would be putting into Rosyth for a week and there would be leave for practically everyone.

Before breakfast the next day we were opposite the Isle of May and Crail where I did my torpedo training. Before long we were in the river Forth and through the mist we could see the massive structure of the Forth Bridge. Many of the ship's company were up on the forward end of the flight deck and speculation was rife as to whether the Vic would pass under without taking a bit of the bridge along with it. In the event we cleared the bridge by about 12 feet. It was a curious sight seeing the Vic dwarfed for a change, normally she made everything else look minute. I changed my mind about this when we were in company with the USS *Saratoga*, it was the Vic's turn to look miniscule!

Next day I started some leave and lugged my suitcase about a mile to the bus stop. On reaching Edinburgh I ran into Jock Landles, Doc Mumford and a fighter boy from 809 Squadron called Godfrey. Godfrey and I bore some resemblance to each other and this caused occasional confusion. After the war he emigrated to New Zealand and I met him there during a FAA reunion many years later.

We walked together down sunny Princes Street and enjoyed a look at civilisation for the first time for weeks. I felt like wanting to dance in the middle of the pavement and holding my arms up to the sun. No wonder some people were sun worshippers; after the grey ship, grey skies, grey sea, to feel the warmth of the sun on one's face was stimulating. I had a lousy meal for 4 shillings before boarding a train to London.

I spent ten hours trying to sleep sitting upright in a compartment that I shared with two RAF Kiwis (i.e. non-flying types), a lady, a gentleman and a Sub-Lieutenant, RNVR. Of all the boring things, sitting in a train for 500 miles was not my idea of fun. However, the journey finished at last and from Kings Cross I took a tube across London and thence a train to Chipstead.

Service men on leave could get coupons for petrol and I had to go to Croydon on my motorbike to obtain them. Riding back I was stopped by two policemen and to my surprise they told me my licence had expired. I must say I had not checked, which was careless of me; however they let me go when they discovered I was a poor sailor on leave!

I have previously mentioned staying with some friends of the Lawrences at Oxshott. When I contacted them these kind people, the Yates, immediately invited me over for the day and I rode over on my motorbike. Mrs Yates was there with daughter Mary. Mr Yates was fire watching in London but arrived later. Fire watching could be a pretty anxious job, no doubt 99 times out of 100 there is nothing to report, but to be at the centre of a raid could be perilous.

Mary worked at the Admiralty so was pretty genned up about things naval, especially as her father was in the Navy in the Great War. She and I walked to the village for provisions and went to The Bear where we met Mary's married sister Brenda, who has two small boys. Someone asked me whether I actually flew aeroplanes, and I had to explain that people wearing light blue uniforms are not the only people to fly. Indeed, in similar situations some FAA pilots are wont to quip, 'Yes, but of course we always have an RAF pilot sitting beside us!'

I was persuaded to stay the night and in the evening Mr Yates used his basic petrol ration to take us to the cinema. I could not help

HMS *Victorious*, 1942. During the covering operations for the Arctic convoys snow and ice would often cover the superstructure. Much of it had to be removed manually.

contrasting things: there I was warm and comfortable sitting next to Mary and yet only a week or two prior to this I was over the North Sea in a cold black night in a single-engined aircraft carrying a torpedo.

I asked Mary next morning whether she could do with some silk stockings. She said, 'Are they black market?' I replied, 'No'. 'Well you know the answer then.' In fact I could obtain stockings in Iceland and would occasionally send her some. On one occasion she received only the wrapping, which was burnt – and no stockings! We assumed that the Post Office had been bombed and we were lucky to have some sort of clue as to what had happened.

Riding home to Chipstead on my motorbike I was going too fast and went off on to the grass going round a right-hand bend and fell on to my side. Apart from my pride I was not hurt although the bike suffered some damage to its lamp. Some kind motorist stopped to help me up. I remember that in those days RAF officers had to pay an increased insurance premium and this must be because being used to high speeds they are inclined to underestimate their speed when back on terra firma.

Back up north in The Orkneys again the squadron had several weeks of working up. On one Navex my observer David Johnson did well and we were within a few feet of our destination after flying for 250 miles! When at sea there were several crashes on deck, two Albacores came down too heavily and smashed their undercarriages. One Fulmar caught an arrester wire, but then went over the side and was aquaplaning along pulled by the ship and with the air gunner still on board until the ship stopped; a destroyer picked up the pilot. Another Fulmar pilot, Sub-Lieutenant Collins, was drowned when he crashed over the side after landing.

The 1st of May 1942 found us north of Iceland and covering two Russian convoys: one east bound, the other west bound (PQ15). Part of the covering force consisted of the battleship USS *Washington*, and the cruisers USS *Wichita* and USS *Tuscaloosa*. We were sighted and shadowed by enemy aircraft, as was the convoy, but we went into thick fog, which was an advantage to us.

I had a cabin at last, but of course during the night we slept above the waterline in the ADC. In view of the normal drab surroundings of the grey ship, grey sky, and grey sea, I decorated my cabin with as many colourful pictures of trees, flowers and the English countryside that I could find.

Unfortunately the existence of the fog had disastrous consequences. I was having tea when there were several loud explosions. No one knew what was happening so action stations were sounded as a precaution. In fact the *KGV* had rammed the destroyer HMS *Punjabi* in the fog. The

HMS *Victorious*, 1942. An Albacore has just landed. Others, with wings folded, wait to be taken down to the hangar deck by the forward lift.

explosions were her depth charges going off. The *Punjabi* drifted past the Vic and was sinking. Capt. Bovell called out, 'Good luck boys.' Some of our Carley floats were cut loose from the stern to help, and it was probably these that helped save several lives. The *Punjabi* sank, but the *KGV* was badly damaged and I drew a sketch in my diary showing just what the damage looked like: there was a long gash in her bows rather like a shark with its mouth slightly open, and this was on the waterline. In my diary I noted that 4 officers and 186 ratings were picked up by the *Marne* and *Martin*.

According to a newspaper cutting I have the *KGV* put into Liverpool for some temporary repairs and then went to America to be refitted properly.

Later that day it was announced that the westbound convoy (QP11) had been attacked by three destroyers. One merchant ship was sunk. HMS *Amazon* was damaged but able to move under its own steam.

The next day three destroyers attacked the convoy again and HMS *Edinburgh* was torpedoed by U456. She was apparently in a sinking condition.

The *Edinburgh* sank later. Unknown to us at the time it must have been a bitter blow to the British Government for she was carrying 45 million pounds worth of gold bullion.

I had the Air Officer of the Watch duty from 0600–0800. The *KGV* suddenly flung up a signal, 'One aircraft to be presumed hostile in sight bearing 180°'. I sounded off 'Fighters Stand To', and 'Alarm to Arms' was also sounded. However, the excitement was caused by the *KGV* mistaking a meteorological balloon for an aircraft!

Later the Tannoy announced that the eastbound convoy had been attacked by Ju-88s; they did no damage and one was shot down. It also said that we were going as far east as Longitude 6° East. A further announcement said that that the *KGV* would be replaced by the her sister ship the *Duke of York* at midnight and that on completion of our covering duties we would return to Scapa and the American ships to Hvalfjord.

I did two A/S patrols of three hours each on the way back to Scapa and noted that I was very cold. I sighted one mine!

Here I should mention that apart from dead reckoning navigation the aircrews had another piece of equipment to assist them in finding the ship if they ever got lost. This was a beacon on the ship. It consisted of a radio beam that swept a horizontal circle once every minute. The aircraft radio picked up the signal received a blip as it passed them. If they were going directly towards or away from the ship they would receive the blip at exactly one minute intervals; if they were going with the rotation of the blip they would get the blip at a longer interval and conversely if they were flying in the opposite direct they would receive the blip at shorter intervals. If one received the blip exactly on the minute it was impossible to tell whether one was going away or towards the ship so a turn had to be made to make an assessment. Fortunately I never had to use the system in an emergency. The only time I heard that it was urgently wanted was during the Bismarck search – and then it had broken down! As far as I remember we were never told about the construction of the system, but if one thinks about it must have had a device that allowed the ship to turn without affecting the timing of the beam; perhaps gyros were used. The Americans had a better system: the ship transmitted different letters of the alphabet in sectors so stopwatches were not needed.

We arrived back at Scapa on 5 May and most of us went on leave. My train passed through York on the way south and I noticed some bomb damage at the station.

Using my Aunt's house at Chipstead as a base I made visits to various friends. It was good to walk in the English countryside with them. Of note was a visit to the Axworthy family in Iver Heath, especially as they took me to the film studios at Denham and Pinewood where I saw what was to become a famous film, *In Which We Serve*, being made. The scene they were doing was the bridge of a destroyer that was being rocked to and fro in the 'rain'. Michael Wilding and Noel Coward were the two actors involved. I also saw Carla Lehman acting a scene from *Secret Mission*.

When I visited the Yates they had a lady friend there who worked at the Admiralty. Mary told me later that her friend had informed her that when I went back to the *Victorious* in Scapa I would find she was not there. Of course she could not tell me, it might have got the lady into trouble.

The much-needed leave was over at last and I went up to the Orkneys and indeed the Vic was not there and I was sent to Lyness for a week. Whilst there I met an officer and I said to him, 'You look very like another man who is stationed here'. He replied, 'Yes, and this caused me a hell of a lot of trouble!' He went on to explain that he was accused of giving away secret information to someone in the wardroom; in vain he said that at the time of the alleged crime he was on a ferry. Unfortunately the ferryman could not remember him and nor could others who could have given him an alibi. It was not until the accuser happened to see the look-alike in the mess that he was no longer under suspicion.

After a week, sixteen of us were sent to RNAS Hatston where we stayed for two weeks until we were at last embarked on a drifter. We were going to be transported to Iceland aboard the USS *Washington*.

The *Washington* was of the Indiana class of battleship. She had a displacement of 36,600 tons and fully operational it was 44,800 tons. Her top speed was 28 knots. She covered the Russian convoys with our Home Fleet from March 1942 for four months as the flagship of Task Force 39. She and our *KGV* were comparable in size armament and speed although the *Washington* had 16in guns and the *KGV* had 14in guns.

When she was on her way to join the Home Fleet what must surely be a unique circumstance occurred when the Admiral was washed overboard and drowned. The ship's history after leaving the Home Fleet was very impressive: at one time she was the only US battleship in the Pacific and she damaged three enemy cruisers and a destroyer, sank a battleship, a destroyer, an oil tanker and several transports, and sank more combat tonnage than any US Battleship.

We were taken to the *Dunluce Castle*. This was a ship due to be scrapped in 1939, but was purchased by the Admiralty and used as an accommodation vessel. After a few hours' wait we were put aboard the mighty USS *Washington*. The only British battleship I had ever set foot on until then was the *KGV* and this was for a short period whilst being transported from shore to the Vic. As a small boy I had been aboard the battle cruiser HMS *Renown* when she visited New Zealand.

We trooped into the wardroom which, unlike the Vic, had its wardroom and anteroom combined. We dumped our things on tables and drank coffee while people rushed around getting things organised. The wardroom was large as it extended from one side of the ship to the other. It was well lit in modern style, with small tables here and there which were extended for meals. The stewards were Negroes and were very slack compared with ours who were usually very busy.

I was sitting with Ken Smith on a sofa discussing Douglas Fairbanks who was an officer on board the ship when all of a sudden he came in! He came up to Ken and me and said, 'Good evening, my name's Fairbanks,' and extended a hand. I said, 'Good evening, Sir, my name's Fay'. I introduced him to one or two others of the squadron who around us. We had a few words about the war and the weather and he went on his way. Ken and I were rather bashful and found it difficult to say very much. I think he was glad we did not say, 'Oo, not Douglas Fairbanks the actor?'!

The Americans had a film show every night and the film that night was *The Corsican Brothers* in which he took the lead. A joyous shout greeted his first appearance in the film. Later on I saw him have his leg pulled by some officers. He was not in the audience that night as he had seen the film before, and surprisingly he saw the complete film for the first time when aboard the ship. I gather this was because he was called up as a reserve officer just as the film was being finished. During the next few days I often saw him on the bridge.

Our cabins were not so comfortable as our own were in the Vic. There was no heater, chair or sofa bed and the furniture was metal, not comfortable wood.

On 12 May I went up the 'tower' with Ken Smith. It was amazingly high with many lookout positions. The ship itself was bristling with armament and apart from the 16in guns its secondary armament was formidable. The AA defences were numerous although a lot of them seemed to be in very exposed places.

The ship spent much time exercising and its three aircraft were catapulted and were in the air for some hours. One of them broke a float on landing and had to fly off to Hatston. When picking up the aircraft the ship would steam at about 10 knots. After landing, the aircraft would taxi to a large net being towed through the water and catch a hook in it. More ropes then hoisted them on board with a crane.

Early in the afternoon we were 'attacked' by torpedo-carrying Beauforts and Hampdens. The Hampdens were very slow and unwieldy and came in from a long way out in a straight line making a good target of themselves. They could not take any avoiding action and had to fly on over the ship after 'dropping' their fish. The Beauforts were faster and looked as if they might survive due to this. The tactics are, of course, very different from the ones we used with the Albacores: We dived from a height, turned in, and were over the sea for a minimum time; we dropped the torpedo and were away with as much avoiding action as we could manage.

No afternoon tea was served, however coffee was obtainable all day long and as it was served with cream it was excellent. The general organisation was pretty good from what I saw.

On the 15th I was back in Hvalfjord and the good old Vic once more and found lots of letters waiting for me. But having arrived after coming all the way up from Scapa what did we do? We returned to Scapa! So it was rather a wasted journey in the *Washington*, but an interesting one nevertheless.

I did no flying from 5 May until 11 June. Then we did some intensive working up, based at Hatston.

Sub-Lieutenant J. Leggatt who was in my original St Vincent course was killed crashing into the island of Hoy in a fog. Sub-Lieutenant Wallis of 817 Squadron was killed when a taxiing Albacore struck him with its propeller. 'Mac' Laurie, an incredibly pleasant bloke who went to my father's old school Malvern was killed when the wings of a Swordfish he was flying came off. I had not heard of it happening to a Swordfish before.

I met a man who was just back from Malta. His aircraft was responsible for shooting one Jerry down and torpedoing one ship as well as doing numerous other attacks.

On 1 July I was back in the ship for the usual convoy work to Russia. To deal with any shadowers we now had five Hurricanes on board. Since their wings did not fold and so do not fit into the lifts they had to remain on deck. This meant that they had to be manhandled back and forth when other flying took place.

It was announced that an attempt was being made to lure the enemy ships out and into a submarine trap. Later there was a signal to say the operation was cancelled, so it seems the bait did not work!

The cruiser HMS *Cumberland* was with us on this trip. Before joining the Navy she was one of the few naval ships I had seen, as she was in Freetown harbour in 1939. The ship in which I was travelling home from the Argentine, the *Andalucia Star*, stopped there for about a week because of some scare.

When a shadower, a Focke Wolfe, duly arrived we sent up four Hurricanes, but they only managed to get in a long-range burst before it escaped into a cloud. After they landed we sent up two Fulmars piloted by Tony Garland, and the CO of 809 Squadron Lieutenant Savage, as a standing air patrol. They sighted the enemy but again fired at long range before it managed to get into a cloud. This was Tony's first encounter with the enemy.

On 2 July I did a three-hour A/S patrol. The sun shone day and night which was a bit strange, but we were within or near the Arctic Circle. Unfortunately we could not enter our flights in our logbooks as night flying! These three-hour patrols always seemed like three days. Generally speaking, during the first hour you are looking for periscopes under every wave. During the second the pilot is bored, the observer indifferent and the TAG asleep. For the third hour both the observer and the TAG are asleep and the pilot is propping up his eyelids with matchsticks. On this particular flight the observer had a bit more to do, as he had to photograph the Battle Fleet. It was a good day for photography I hoped the pictures would come out well.

On arriving back at the ship I made only my second deck landing in eight weeks. Both were bumpy! After landing on aerodromes one is inclined to make bad landings on decks and vice versa since the techniques were different. Some of the pilots' landings at Hatston had not been not exactly exemplary.

I got my head down half clothed at 2245 hours and was called at 0145 to relieve Sidney Price as Air Officer of the Watch. Sidney had recently joined the squadron; he stayed on in the navy after the war, becoming Captain of Culdrose and eventually a Rear Admiral. His nickname Prillam was developed when he was in the squadron. He was friendly with Ron Hallam and the two become known as Prillam and Prallam.

There was a bit of a flap on and the fighters had only just ceased standing to, when a moment later a signal from HMS *Nigeria* said, 'One aircraft to be presumed hostile in sight bearing . . .'

Three Hurricanes took off. A minute or two later there was a call from the lookout, 'One Hurricane in the sea bearing Green 60°.' The aircraft had developed a coolant leak and his engine failed. The pilot was picked up by the *Marne* and when we asked whether he was OK we were told, 'Yes, but shaken in the head'.

Meanwhile the first Hurricane attacked a FW. Despite being fired at with cannon he got in close, fired a long burst and had the pleasure of seeing bits fall off. Hurricane Number 2 came in down sun and was not seen or fired on. The Courier went into a cloud and this pilot had to contend with giving it a squirt at long range.

We had Vice-Admiral Sir Bruce Fraser (later Lord Fraser of North Cape) on board. The pilot of Hurricane number 2 told his story before an interested audience of Vice Admiral Fraser, Captain Bovell, and a few others including me. Strangely, Sir Bruce was at Bradfield; the old school does crop up quite a lot in my story!

A Hurricane burst a wheel on landing, but it was serviceable 20 minutes later. We started with six Hurricanes but now had only two serviceable.

At 0400 hours I went back to bed and slept until 0830.

We were now very near the returning Russian convoy, an unusual situation to be in. So far there had been no news of any attacks on the ships.

On 4 July a 'D'ye hear there,' announcement stated that we were 60 miles west of south Spitzbergen. The east-bound convoy was south of us and a cruiser force was south of that. This convoy was designated PQ17 and the world was to hear about it later and books would be written about it. We heard that heavy enemy ships were at sea and that enemy destroyers had sighted the convoy. As I was writing this in my diary the CIC sent a signal saying that U-boats and aircraft had probably attacked the convoy and the *Tirpitz* was no longer at its base.

Later we were steering 195° and at 1600 hours we changed to 270°. I surmised that the German fleet might be trying to get off into the Atlantic and thought that with most of our forces out of the way they might succeed. Fog came down and visibility was about 200 yards. I saw Tony Garland sitting hopefully in his plane with his beacon unserviceable. If he had taken off he would have had a pretty poor chance of finding the fleet again and might have had to land at Spitzbergen.

Next morning I arose at 0600 and stood by for an A/S patrol until 0900. 'Fighters stand to,' came at 0700 as a Focke Wolfe and a Ju-88 were sighted. One Hurricane and two Fulmars chased them but they went into cloud and disappeared. The other Hurricane went unserviceable on the deck, so out of six Hurricanes we had only one available.

I finally took off for an A/S patrol. The fleet looked wonderful, but just like toys in the calm blue sea. It was hard to believe that if those 20 odd ships were suddenly to disappear the future of Britain would be utterly altered.

A thick belt of fog lay ahead of the fleet and when David Johnson my observer signalled that fact we caused twenty ships and several thousand men to change course to land us on! There was a wind of only 25 knots over the deck and we were pulled up with a bit of a jolt by the arrester wires.

Later it was announced that enemy heavy units were after the convoy and that we had altered course last night to go to their aid. Then came the infamous and ill-fated order, 'Convoy is to scatter,' which to us implied that the heavy enemy units must have been close to the convoy. In fact the major cause of this was a false report from a Russian submarine that it had sighted the German fleet.

One merchant ship was sunk by our own forces after being torpedoed by an aircraft. I wrote, ' It is believed that we had achieved our object and deterred the enemy ships.' Unfortunately things did not turn out like that.

We set course for Scapa 1,000 miles away.

Another announcement was made, 'After the convoy scattered, two ships were hit by dive bombers and by torpedo aircraft. A Russian submarine has claimed two hits on the *Tirpitz* and on another warship as well. These two were reported to be close to the merchant ships.'

I wonder if the 'hits' on the *Tirpitz* were just as true as the sighting report made by that submarine.

In my diary I wrote, 'We seem to be pushing off in the direction of Scapa and leaving the enemy to make a clean haul. Actually it is not all bad as I have just been up to the Ops Room and learned we are due to meet an oil tanker and three destroyers shortly. Whoopee! Perhaps we will try to intercept the *Tirpitz* now. The second warship reported might be the *Hipper*. The Ops Room seems full of signals sent from ships, several of them incomplete, saying they were being dive-bombed. One signal said, ' I am on fire and sinking'. These merchant seamen take all the rap, can scarcely fight back and they get sunk, while we sit on our arses and practically clear out of the way. I only hope they refuel the destroyers from the tanker and then go south east again.'

On 6 July we refuelled the destroyers and went northeast again, but then turned back and steered a course for home. There were various reports in the Ops Room about the hunt for survivors of the convoy. Signals were received such as, 'Burnt out wreck position . . . no survivors, repeat no survivors'.

I observed, 'I think we ought to place the Battle Fleet nearer convoy next time. If it were adequately escorted I don't see how U-boats could put fish into the battleships and aircraft carriers. Those poor merchant seamen had no chance at all and we ought and could do more to protect them. Still, no doubt Admiral Tovey knows more than I do about these matters.'

There was no 'next time' for me. In view of the fiasco convoys to Russia were suspended for two months.

Out of 33 ships only 11 reached Murmansk.

In his wonderful book *Victorious the World Over*, Ray Barker, a shipmate (although I did not know it at the time), made some bitter observations with which I entirely agree. He said that the butchery of the merchant ships took four days, by which time we were back in Scapa Flow – having done exactly nothing to aid our merchant comrades. He concluded, 'I doubted whether we would ever again be cheered by merchant seaman.'

On the way home we received a signal – an unfinished one – reporting, '2PBs and 6 DRs . . .' i.e. Two Pocket Battleships and six destroyers . . .

The Admiralty was concerned about this and was urgently calling for more information. I wonder if this was a ruse by the Germans?

The Vic went to Liverpool to have her bottom scraped while we flew off to RNAS Hatston and spent some two weeks there practising air firing, ALTs and navexes. I had a Leading Airman McLean as my TAG for most of this time with David Johnson as my Observer as usual.

Of course rumour was rife and one of them was correct: we were going to escort a convoy to Malta.

13

MALTA CONVOY, AUGUST 1942.
OPERATION PEDESTAL
(THE SANTA MARIA CONVOY)

The Malta convoy of August 1942 was, perhaps, the most important one of the war. The battle of El Alamein had not yet started the breakout towards the west and the Germans still occupied Libya. Malta was in a desperate state for few ships had managed to get through to the island to bring the vital supplies of food, munitions and, in particular, fuel. Had Malta fallen the Germans could have used it as a base from which to attack our forces in Libya and later on, when the allies had landed in North Africa, they could have used it as an additional base from which to attack them if, indeed, we could have gone ahead with this operation at all. In the meantime Malta was a particularly important base from which we could attack German shipping bringing in supplies to the Axis forces.

Operation Pedestal had such a wide impact and had so many individual stories that dozens of books have been written about it. I do not intend to add to that number but merely to give a day-to-day account of what happened around me during those anxious but exciting days. My part in the operation was very minor: I carried out a few A/S patrols, my other duties I will describe later. Of the aircrews the fighter boys were the ones to whom honour must be given, but every man in the convoy made his own individual contribution to its success. And it must be called a success despite the grievous losses, for Malta received enough supplies to carry on.

In an operation of this sort we usually give very little thought to all the planning needed but, months before and somewhere in the bowels of the Admiralty or perhaps elsewhere, people must work like beavers to make all the millions of arrangements required. Every ship must be moved to its new assembly point leaving a vacuum that must be filled if possible. Fuel must be at the right place at the right time. The list seems endless and the miracle is that it all comes together at the right time.

After our working up at Hatston the squadron landed back on the Vic on 28 July.

We sailed into the Atlantic and not too far from Gibraltar we met the other ships. We had two battleships, three fleet carriers (*Victorious*, *Indomitable*, and *Eagle*) plus HMS *Furious* which was to carry RAF fighter aircraft for Malta, and the old carrier HMS *Argus* which was to carry spare aircraft, etc, for us. Then there were seven cruisers and twenty destroyers. All this to escort fourteen merchant ships.

All eyes were immediately drawn towards the middle of the convoy where the oil tanker *Ohio* was in position. She was an American ship manned by a British crew and although I did not know it at the time, the largest oil tanker in the world. When one looks at the size of giant tankers that now sail the seven seas the *Ohio* looks quite small. Anyway, our thoughts were with that tanker and her gallant crew and we all wondered whether such a vulnerable vessel would survive.

HMS *Victorious* before the Malta convoy, Operation Pedestal. HMS *Argus* is in the background.

Against us were the Italian Naval vessels consisting of three heavy cruisers with seven destroyers in one division. Three light cruisers with four destroyers in another and eighteen submarines plus E-boat squadrons. The Germans provided two submarines and four motor torpedo boats. However, of more significance was the fact that the Germans and Italians had considerable air forces available to them.

As for our fighters, the Vic had taken on six more Fulmars and six Sea Hurricanes and we had left behind some Albacores to make room for these. As before, the Hurricanes had to be kept on deck because their wings did not fold. In all, the carriers had some seventy fighter aircraft.

It was about this time that a contemporary of mine at Bradfield, Dick Grimsdale, joined the squadron. Unfortunately he did not stay long as he left us for an appointment in another squadron.

Admiral Syfret was in charge of Operation Pedestal. But the aircraft carriers came under Rear-Admiral Lyster who was Rear-Admiral Aircraft Carriers flying his flag in the Vic. He paid a casual visit to the wardroom and had a chat to the aircraft crews who happened to be there. He had also spoken to the ship's company when we were away at Hatston and had said that wherever he went he found trouble and relied on others to get him out of it!

On 6 August something rather unusual happened to me during an A/S patrol. After landing I found that one of my depth charges was missing. How it happened I couldn't think; I must say that I wondered why the aircraft was tending to fly right wing low all the time!

On the same day was interesting to watch an oil tanker refuelling three destroyers at once. Two formated on either side and one trailed behind.

We pushed two crashed Fulmars over the side to make more room in the hangar. I wondered how many former pots and pans went to the bottom in those aircraft; housewives had been encouraged to donate them so that the aluminium could be used for making aircraft.

On the 7th a pilot of 809 Squadron was killed. He did a steep turn after an aborted landing and hit the sea. Meanwhile Ken Smith was trying to keep formation on the CO and was 50 miles from the ship with his cylinder head temperature and oil pressure doing things they should not do. He left the formation, but then got lost and landed *after* the other aircraft. Using less power than the CO was using he found that the temperatures and pressures improved.

On the 8th the *Indomitable* left us for a while. She had been unable to refuel from the tanker, so had to go to Gibraltar to do so.

On the evening of 9 August and just after sunset I went up on to the flight deck. There was a lovely glow in the sky which turned to dark orange and then disappeared by stages. We were nearing our passage

1942. Hurricanes on the deck of HMS *Victorious* prior to Operation Pedestal.
HMS *Indomitable* and HMS *Eagle* are shown in line astern.

through the Straits of Gibraltar. A lighthouse twinkled in the distance and there was a soft warm breeze. None of the ships showed any lights and the silence was broken only by the swish of the waves. Who would think we were at war?

10th August. The RAF made a mess of things when a Hudson flew towards the fleet with its IFF switched off. R/T silence had to be broken to intercept them with Hurricanes. Next morning, 11 August, a Sunderland sent a message saying, 'I am being attacked by enemy fighters,' and fired at our Hurricanes! At 0900 hours an announcement said that a plane had flown in from 70 miles away, had seen the fighters from the *Indomitable* (our sister ship) and had flown away. It had Vichy French markings and was a flying boat flying from Toulon to Morocco. Admiral Syfret, the Commander in Chief, ordered it shot down as it would have reported our presence. In fact the Italians had known of our operation from the time we left Britain and had already set in motion their plans to intercept us. Also, the German agents at La Linea near Gibraltar could not have failed to detect our passage through the straits.

We were informed that the Allies had bombed some of the Italian airfields. We never heard any more of this and I often wondered whether this was a tale put out to keep our morale up; however, on reading *The Battle of Malta* by Joseph Attard I see that British Beaufighters and American Liberators attacked three Sardinian airfields and the Italians reported 22 aircraft put out of action.

The *Furious* flew off her Spitfires for Malta. Two made forced landings on the *Indomitable*. I saw one of these and the pilot did a good landing, but as he had no arrester hook he had to crash into the barrier.

Our cabin flats were closed and any possessions we needed were with us in the dormitories. There was an order given to cover our bodies with clothing to minimise injuries by fire.

We had a cruiser astern of us that acted as an anti-aircraft ship. She followed in our wake the whole time.

Being an Albacore pilot whose flying at this juncture consisted entirely of A/S patrols I was given other jobs. I did watches and last night I had part of the middle (normally 0000–0400 hours) watch. In daytime, during any actions stations that were sounded, I had to help spot aircraft for an Oerlikon which occupied a position over the starboard side of the ship and about 30 yards from the rear of the island superstructure and quite close to a multiple pom pom.

At this site, apart from the gunner, I had as companion Pat Urwin, a pilot. He was very keen on saying things like, 'At this moment the Germans are combing the hair on the back of their hands and getting ready to take off!' He later became Senior Pilot of 835 Squadron.

I saw the *Eagle* sink! I was walking along the flight deck and happened to look to starboard and was amazed to see four great fountains of water springing up from the port side of the ship. She had been hit by torpedoes. She momentarily rolled to starboard and then took up a permanent list to port, which gradually increased. I could not believe my eyes and wanted someone to talk to. I went into the nearby Pilots' and Observers' Waiting Room and said, 'There's a carrier sinking out there'. No one believed me at first and then someone looked out of the porthole and said, 'My God, there is!'

The *Eagle* continued to roll to port and men and aircraft were falling into the sea. It was dreadful to watch because one knew that at that moment people were dying. Some would have been killed in the explosion but others would be trapped and would be drowned.

Some of the *Eagle*'s planes were in the air at the time and they heard the sound of the explosions on the R/T.

Shortly after this two depth charges were dropped dead astern of us and it was said that some stuff came to the surface.

Fighter aircraft were up and seeking out the enemy, Martlets shot down one Ju-88 and one was damaged with an engine on fire.

Sunset came and we were told that groups of enemy aircraft were approaching from various directions. I closed up to my Oerlikon where I had been most of the afternoon.

There was an ominous silence. Then many alarms and excursions. We had a firework display as the fleet's guns opened up on the enemy aircraft. Our 4.5-inch guns (the ship's largest) came into action, the sudden loud noise making me jump. Then we spotted a Ju-88, which dived on to the fleet. Our gun was one of the first on to it and then all the guns in the fleet seemed to open up on it. I felt sorry for the crew in a way for there was no possible escape and the aircraft crashed into the sea.

While we were watching the Ju-88 I was suddenly drenched with water and discovered that a bomb had hit the water only 50 yards away. At the time I was only mildly interested in this fact with all the things happening elsewhere, but reflecting on it later I realised what a narrow squeak we had had.

Our fighters were up and one landed without his hook and went right along the deck and into a multiple pom pom. Fortunately no one was hurt. With light fading fast another with apparently only half a gallon of fuel left flew right over us, hit another Hurricane parked on the deck and caught fire. The pilot walked out. This was Hugh Popham from 18 Course St Vincent whom I have mentioned before. He was low in fuel and unfortunately the fleet was firing at anything that flew, so he landed on the only carrier he could find. The Vic was still swinging round into wind as he touched down. In his book *Sea Flight* Hugh reports how he went up to the compass platform and now discovered which carrier he was on as the skipper was *not* Captain Troubridge of the *Indomitable*!

Captain Bovell said, 'What do you mean by crashing on my deck against a wave-off?'

'Very sorry sir. No petrol.'

The Captain glared at him. 'Oh, I see. Very well.'

Later on I went into the Pilots' and Observers' Waiting Room and Hugh was lying on a couch reading. He had a cigarette held nonchalantly in one hand. It was rock steady and the smoke was going straight up. I was impressed!

I visited this room several times and among others I saw there was Sub-Lieutenant M. Hankey. He took off shortly afterwards, shot down an enemy aircraft and was last seen with an enemy aircraft on his tail.

It was only later that I heard that Dickie Cork, the Fleet Air Arm's top fighter pilot with seven kills, had been aboard the Vic, albeit briefly. He was the FAA's most experienced fighter pilot, having been a naval pilot in the Bader Wing of the RAF. He was killed some months later when his aircraft collided with another during either a take-off run or a landing. He was blamed for the accident and his parents died thinking that their son had caused it. Years later he was vindicated: it was not his fault.

We had four Fulmars and two Hurricanes missing. After waiting for some time I got my head down. Later on we were informed that one aircraft was missing, the others had all landed on the *Indomitable*. Later still we were told that no aircraft were missing.

12 August. I was up at 0500 hours. I was astonished that we had no dawn attack on us. We had lots of shadowers and our valiant fighter boys shot many down. Tony Garland was credited with half a plane – a flamer. In my diary I also note that 'Faj' Pennington (a New Zealander on my course at St Vincent) got one, but I just wonder how he came into the picture, as he was not aboard the Vic.

Several Ju-88s attacked us before lunch. Some were shot down before they reached us. One was hit over the convoy, stayed in the air quite a time issuing white smoke and then hit the sea. Another did a very pretty dive with smoke pouring out of it. On picking up sufficient airspeed it shot up again, stalled, and went full plop into the sea.

It must have been about this time that I got injured, but not by enemy action! The ammunition for the Oerlikon was kept in boxes that were lined with metal foil rather like strong silver paper. I plunged my hand into the box and cut it on the foil. I cursed the man who invented this system and I reckoned that I was not the only one to have this sort of accident.

We now come to an episode, very minor in itself, that I remember vividly. From my position over the side of the Vic on the starboard side I happened to peep over the deck and across to the port side and saw two aircraft, apparently Hurricanes, coming towards us from the port quarter and evidently about to beat us up (i.e. just fly low and fast across us). I suddenly noticed a white band around their fuselages and I just had time to yell 'Enemy . . .' to the gunner, and 'Fire!' when they were across us and away flying towards off at about 45° to our course. The bomb dropped by the aircraft on the right of its formation (the left to us) hit the deck and bounced almost over my head. I watched the bomb fly through the air and enter the water, thinking at that moment that if it went off I was a gonner. It was absolutely intact as it went over the side; reports that it had broken up on hitting the deck and caused some minor injuries were incorrect. The bits that flew about the flight deck were the fuse link that prevented it from exploding; apparently the Italians had not removed this safety device when they loaded it on to the aircraft. My gunner put in a few shots at the fast-disappearing aircraft, but had to stop for fear of hitting other ships. It was reported that no one fired at that aircraft but this is incorrect, we certainly did, and I think we were the only ones to do so.

In the meantime Captain Bovell, so it was reported, was also watching the aircraft approach and remarked, 'Oh well, our boys will have their fun – S . . . H . . . I . . . T . . . T . . .'

The aircraft that we all confused with Hurricanes were, in fact, Italian Reggiane 2001 fighters.

'Our' bomb made a very slight dent in the flight deck, which could be seen by the eagle eyed. For months afterwards I used to show it to new members of 832 Squadron!

As far as the other bomb was concerned I have a first-hand account from Ron Hallam, a pilot in 832 Squadron. He was spotting for an Oerlikon in a position forward of the island. He caught sight of the two aircraft approaching and when he saw the other bomb dropping he yelled, 'Duck!'. He stated that it did not explode but overshot the deck and went into the water beside him. This is contrary to other accounts. He said that a crewmember was hit in the back by something that turned out to be the fuse link. We thought that the man was Don Young (who later worked at Westland Aircraft), but I could not check this as he died a few years ago.

Since there are conflicting reports about the second bomb I must say that if the bomb had exploded I might have heard it even though the island shielded me at the time.

Reports in other books that the *Victorious* was slightly damaged were, of course, wild exaggerations.

Many years later I was at the Farnborough Air Show and someone told me that the pilot who dropped 'my' bomb was there. So he survived the war; unfortunately I was unable to catch him.

I had a quick wash and managed to get my head down for a short while in the afternoon, but was rudely awakened to do a watch. While doing it a raid started and the sky became filled with smoke from the anti-aircraft fire. Two bombs damaged one merchant ship. While up on the compass platform it was announced that 'Faj' Pennington had been shot down; however, this turned out to be untrue, he was alive and well.

A lookout suddenly reported a submarine surfacing to port. It had been blown to the surface by depth charges. HMS *Ithuriel* then fired at it at point blank range; there were several misses (!) but then there were hits on the conning tower. The crew surrendered and I remember seeing many of them lined up on the top of the sub before it sank shortly afterwards. Joyful pipes announced this to the unfortunate members of our crew who were below decks.

I was relieved from my watch and another raid started so I went to my Oerlikon position. Some Ju-57s appeared and we had a crack at them. I saw an aircraft flying at about 2,000 feet above us and told the gunner to fire a few shots at it, more to point it out to the gunnery officer than anything else. He called out, 'It's a Hurricane!'

We spotted six or seven aircraft diving on the convoy. No one had opened fire (they looked like Fulmars at the time) and we reported them to the ADP (Air Defence Position). Desultory fire was opened on them but not nearly close or near enough. The result was that bombs hit HMS *Indomitable* and smoke billowed forth fore and aft – a most unpleasant sight. A few of her aircraft were airborne at the time and they began landing aboard us. A Martlet ditched in the water beside us, clearly he was out of fuel. A destroyer picked up the pilot.

We were now the only serviceable carrier left and all the airborne aircraft had to land aboard us. We had no room for them so we landed them on, removed the radios if there was time and then pushed the aircraft overboard. The seas around that area must be rich with once serviceable aircraft all rotting away.

I did an A/S patrol for three and a half hours. Time passed very quickly possibly because I was very anxious to get a U-boat and was busy peering closely at each wave. I was kept waiting for half an hour before landing-on.

The *Indomitable* was a nasty sight. There was a gaping hole in her forward on the starboard side and the forward lift was bent up also.

Operation Pedestal. HMS *Indomitable* is hit by bombs and is on fire fore and aft.

There was a large hole in her after end. Her dead were committed to the sea after sunset. 40 men were killed and 55 injured.

We left the convoy an hour before dusk and after our departure the convoy was very heavily attacked. The Admiralty announced the sinking of the *Eagle* on the radio and later we heard a rather varnished version of what had taken place.

We were covering the return of HMS *Kenya*, which had been damaged by a mine dropped ahead of the fleet. The *Indomitable* and the *Rodney* left us during the night.

On 15 August we arrived at Gibraltar in the late afternoon. Eight Hurricanes were on deck dressed by the right and looking very smart. I just hoped that the locals were impressed.

All the other carriers that were with us on the convoy were in Gib, except alas for the *Eagle*.

16 August. No one knew when we were sailing except the Captain and perhaps some senior officers and the previous night there were various pipes concerning the morrow.

They must have been a ruse for we sailed at 0200 hours!

The *Rodney* had some trouble with her steering and nearly cut us in two! The immediate cause was the avoiding action she had been taking and on one particular occasion she had put 20° of rudder on, which was too much for the old ship. She had to be steered from the after steering position following that. We had her in company plus some destroyers. We mere mortals did not know where we were going, but we were steering west. However, we had survivors from the *Manchester*, the *Foresight* and the *Eagle* on board so we guessed it would be England.

The Captain spoke to the ship's company and held our attention for over half an hour while he told the story of the convoy. This was mainly for the benefit of those who were below decks most of the time. I thought it was a very interesting talk and would do well if broadcast by the BBC.

As regards that important convoy: only four ships got through and it appeared that the *Ohio* had not made it. However, after the fleet left the convoy the tanker was torpedoed, hit five times by bombs and then by a crashing blazing Stuka. When the only four other ships to survive arrived in Grand Harbour she was still 200 miles away with smashed steering gear, decks awash and on fire. It is a long story but eventually she was held up by two destroyers with a third one astern steering her towards Malta. The Italians deployed four cruisers towards her in order to sink her and therefore bring Malta to its knees. In the meantime Lieutenant-Commander Mars of the British submarine HMS *Unbroken* had disobeyed orders at the risk of his career and moved his boat to a place where he thought the Italians would be. He hit two Italian ships with torpedoes. The Italian commander, instead of continuing his way towards the *Ohio*, spent his time trying to sink the *Unbroken*! The *Ohio* continued towards Malta and arrived to cheering crowds on the day of the Feast of Santa Maria, hence the Maltese name for that convoy. Malta was saved!

The heroic symbol of the whole operation was the oil tanker *Ohio*. If the world lasts for another thousand years men of the sea will always talk of the saga of the *Ohio*. Without her getting through to Valletta the island of Malta would have fallen, for without fuel the aircraft and essential services would not have been able to operate.

On 17 August I did an A/S patrol and spotted some yellow objects in the water. I could not identify them but assumed they were bits of wreckage. On the evening of the next day six of us did a sweep, flying on diverging tracks. We found nothing although Gerry Conolley dropped his depth charges on something that turned out to be a whale and split it in two. There was a convoy near us and we did A/S patrols for it.

The Captain spoke to us and said that the ship would be refitting at Rosyth. 832 Squadron would be going to RNAS Crail.

Later we heard Commander Anthony Kimmins, who was an author and a reporter for the BBC, give a broadcast about the story of the convoy. He made us proud to be members of the Royal Navy. I hoped that lots of folks back home heard it.

The ship passed through the Hebrides on 21 August and at noon all fighter aircraft were ranged. These included three Martlets from the luckless *Indomitable* and eight Hurricanes as well as Fulmars. The Hurricanes took off first and did a precise bit of formation flying over the ship. The Albacores were ranged at 1300 hours and we had a half hour journey to Hatston in formation. In the meantime the ship headed for Scapa. We had only half an hour at Hatston for refuelling before taking off for Crail, flying in formation.

Everything was OK until we met the coast north of Aberdeen, when it became very bumpy; visibility became worse and the cloud base dropped. Soon we were down to 500 feet and stampeding the cattle. We dropped to 200 feet and were still in the base of the cloud. A wireless mast nearly removed my starboard wing and I then left the formation and flew by myself. After getting lost for a while I found Aberdeen and flew down the coast at a few hundred feet to Arbroath where we cut across to Crail.

I met Harry Hawken at Crail, it was good to see him again.

I returned to Crail after my leave and we started working up again. We did some more ALTs and some night ADDLS and then after two days half the squadron were sent to Machrihanish. We had a poor reception in the wardroom; perhaps they were not expecting us. The organisation was bad.

We got stuck into some really hard work: lots of ALTs; night ADDLS, dive bombing with smoke bombs and then with real bombs, dropping them on a rocky part of the coast further north.

Doug Harris arrived at Machrichanish from leave; I forget what he was doing there. He was one of 19 Course St Vincent and I had not seen him for a year.

My 21st birthday passed fairly quietly. I received no mail or telegrammes and was a bit depressed. However, all was explained on the 17th when a stack of mail and telegrammes arrived from Crail. Mary's read, 'Cheers you've made it stop congratulations and best of luck. Room 115,' 115 was her office number in the Admiralty. Another said, 'Congratulations from the remnants at Crail.' Then there were the family ones and others.

14

841 SQUADRON, RAF MANSTON

On the morning of 24 September everything changed for me and for five other officers. The observers had just received their briefing from the Senior O for a navex when it was cancelled. This was strange as the weather was good, or good for Machrihanish anyway so we realised something was in the wind.

The CO sent for six of us: Harold Willott, Bob Procter, Gerry Child, Arch Hugill, John Burbidge and me. He read us a signal that stated that three aircraft and crews were not to be embarked aboard the Vic but were to go to 841 Squadron at RAF Manston.

He said he did not know what sort of job we should be doing and asked whether any of us had any objection to going. We had none but asked that all efforts should be made to return us to 832 afterwards.

We did some hurried packing while our aircraft were prepared, and said goodbye to all and sundry. Harold Willott was the senior officer so became our little group's CO. With Bob Procter as my observer and Bob Kinghan as my Telegraphist Air Gunner we took off and set course for Stretton flying near the Isle of Man en route. Owing to a misunderstanding the aircraft never formed up until we were over the English coast where somehow we miraculously found each other and went on our way in loose formation.

As we neared Stretton the visibility deteriorated and a thunderstorm broke out bringing lightening which danced along the main plane. We were just beginning to get concerned about finding the airfield when two rockets sent up from Stretton were sighted to port.

Because of the bad weather we had to spend the night at Stretton in miserably cold Nissen huts.

We left Stretton as quickly as possible in the morning and arranged to land at Bicester to obtain a met report as there was a likelihood of fog putting in its appearance around the London area. One of our aircraft got lost, I forget which one, and had to land at Stratford, causing not a little amusement and wonder among the local RAF types who had never seen an Albacore let alone an aircraft with a bicycle attached to its wings. Having had a response to the pilot's question, 'Where am I?' this pilot and skilled navigator arrived in Bicester in time to find the other two aircraft taking off again.

A new route had been given to us, which took us south of London. From there we followed the railway line that led us through Ashford, took us over the balloons at Canterbury and shortly after this we landed at Manston, encountering some of the airfields notorious bumps on its grass airfield while doing so.

Up to this time 841 Squadron had consisted of four aircraft and eight officers. No air gunners were used so the men we had brought with us entered the scene and left it before they had even time to say, 'Hullo'. They were sent back to Machrihanish as quickly as possible and no doubt were able to give the rest of the squadron some insight as to what 841 did. I was to fly again with Kinghan many times after I had left Manston.

841 Squadron was attached to RAF Fighter Command and its job was to bomb 'E' boats, the RAF having no suitable aircraft for that sort of work. It might be thought strange to have slow biplanes attached to *Fighter* Command, but the point was that we were under the control of Fighter Direction Officers at Swingate, which comprised a set of tall RDF masts plus quarters at the base. Because we were attached to Fighter Command our aircraft were jocularly known as Albifighters.

VHF R/T was used for communications and my aircraft 4R was spirited away to be fitted with the new set. The other two aircraft are nearing their 240-hour inspection and they were to be exchanged for new aircraft.

The Commanding Officer of 841 was Lieutenant R.L. Williamson RN. I remember him as a tall man and eminently suited to be the CO. His squadron aircrew prior to our arrival consisted of Lieutenant S.M.P. Walsh, and the following, all Sub-Lieutenants: K. Lee White RN, 'Mac' Rutherford, J.J. Hitch, Norman, Patrick, and D. Waiting.

The name Mac Rutherford will be familiar to past and present FAA personnel. He founded the Fleet Air Arm Officers Association and is now a Vice President and is better known perhaps as Commander G. McC. Rutherford MBE, DSC, VRD, RNR.

My very first flight there was a night one to familiarise myself with the circuit and John Burbidge and Norman of 841 were in the back. Next day I flew with the new VHF set and the difference between that and the ones we had been using previously was remarkable; it was just like a very clear telephone.

Officially the Admiralty knew us as 832B Flight and the original squadron at Machrihanish was to be known as 832A Flight. I do not think

1943. Mechanics working on a black-painted Albacore of 841 Squadron that was used in night operations over the English Channel from RAF Manston. Officially this was an aircraft of 832b Squadron attached to 841 Squadron.

that the boys back at the squadron even knew about this, the nomenclature probably only cropped up in Admiralty signals and we very rarely talked about ourselves as B Flight. We were in 841 Squadron!

A ground party of about ten personnel arrived by Harrow from 832 Squadron to augment the ground staff of our squadron.

My aircraft was cleaned ready to be painted black and the two replacement Albacores arrived. During the night 841 sent out one aircraft to hunt for E boats. One was sighted and bombed, but no hits were obtained. The attack was, perhaps, slightly unusual in that the E boat crew were able to see the Albacore in the bright moonlight and could fire at it.

On 28 September night flying was carried out. For practice some vectors were given for us to fly and these took us over the channel towards France and then in a north westerly direction. We finished with a vector that took us right over the aerodrome. Bacon and eggs were served in the officers' mess on completion; this was normally a privilege reserved for aircrews after night operations; it must be remembered that with food rationing in force eggs and bacon were in short supply.

Next day Lieutenant Walsh, the Senior Pilot, flew us near the shore by Margate to demonstrate the technique used to bomb E boats. The target in this case was a 7-foot long dinghy towed at 15 knots by an MTB (Motor Torpedo Boat). The target was approached from behind at 2,000 feet and a gentle dive made at cruising rpm and boost and with no flaps used. At about 700 feet the nose was lifted and the stick of bombs released. The 'stick' in this case was a single smoke bomb representing the first bomb of the stick. After this bit of instruction the 832 crews took over and dropped 16 smoke bombs. Results were satisfactory but we thought some training at bombing with proper sticks would be helpful. This practice was followed by the three aircraft doing some formation flying in order to demonstrate to 841 that we were much better at it than they were! A mild beat-up of the aerodrome followed. We carried out some more vector and R/T practice during the night.

On 2 October the 832b Flight aircrew were taken down to Swingate to meet the controllers and the visit proved interesting and instructive. It was good to meet the owners of the voices that gave us the vectors and the beer they gave us on completion of the tour was appreciated too. We carried out some more practice bombing with varied success. The weather was hot with scarcely a cloud in the sky. To gather from the loud crumps we heard from the direction of France the Flying Fortresses were busy. An enemy aircraft flew high over the airfield at 1415 hours pursued by inaccurate gunfire. No bombs were dropped.

Two days later the CO announced that the 832B Flight was fully operational, which pleased us. We did some more practice bombing and this time the dinghy sank! However, this was not caused by the accuracy of our bombing but the fact that the boat was towed too fast and got filled with seawater.

Evening brought some loud bangs and flashes from the Dover direction as the channel guns went into action against an enemy convoy. The German guns replied and we heard that they had caused some casualties in Dover and Folkestone. Later on, the CO, with his observer Norman, took off despite adverse weather conditions in order to fix the position of the convoy for the benefit of our MTBs. Cloud was down to 800ft and when they found the convoy they were unable to dive bomb it. Instead they dropped their bombs by ASV (Air to Service Vessel). The results could not be observed.

Arch Hugill and Gerry Child took off and flew below cloud, the base then being at 500ft. They located the convoy and passed over it observing several lights from escorting vessels and some revolving searchlights.

They went to and fro over it until some large lumps of lethal metal began to move in their direction. Arch was a bit peeved at this and used the Albacore's manoeuvrability to the full to avoid the 'accurate light flak', to quote the official signal. Gerry's R/T plug was torn out during these aerobatics and Arch began to give his observer up for dead when he did not reply to his messages! However the trouble was soon rectified and they set course for home.

Their job was done; they had found the convoy for the MTB's benefit. They had orders not to drop bombs so they brought these back. On reaching Manston the cloud base was so low that they had to land at Bradwell Bay instead where they were glad to find that their aircraft was all in one piece.

So 832B flight received its baptism of fire.

In the meantime a bit of excitement at Manston was caused by two Wellingtons and a Halifax crash-landing after a raid on Aachen. One of the Wellingtons contained only the pilot, the rest of the crew having baled out over Germany after the failure of one engine. Being one of the nearest airfields to the continent Manston was often used for emergency landings by damaged aircraft.

On 10 October in the early morning and while still asleep, we had an air raid warning that took the Norwegian fighter pilots based at Manston by surprise. Apparently they were all busy washing when the warning went! At 0900 hours great gaggles of Flying Fortresses and Liberators, with protective formations of Lightnings, orbited the airfield at about 5,000ft before departing in a southerly direction. Sometime later a Fortress made a downwind landing on the airfield with smoke coming from two engines. Only one engine was working properly out of the remaining two. Later we heard on the news that these aircraft had taken part in the biggest raid ever, the target being factories at Lille.

There was a show in the RAF theatre in the evening. It was mainly local talent but Annette Mills the songwriter and actress also took part in it.

While this was going on Walsh and Patrick patrolled the Gravelines and Dunkirk area, during which time they were held by a searchlight and had a brief encounter with some heavy flak. On the way out they spotted six of our MTBs that appeared dangerously open to air attack; luckily for them no enemy aircraft were around. Later Arch and Gerry took off and patrolled the same area. They were more privileged and had no less than *three* searchlights turned towards them. These failed to illuminate them and the heavy flak that followed did no harm. 'Mac' Rutherford and Johnnie Hitch took off later.

At 1900 hours on the 12th a call came through to scramble one aircraft. The CO and Norman were the only ones in the crew room and were not due to stand by at all that night. Naturally they took off soon afterwards. Mac and Hitch followed them 20 minutes later and Bob and I shortly afterwards. I also had as a passenger an intrepid officer from the MTBs called Sub-Lieutenant. Bray. He wanted to see at first hand what we were up to; perhaps this would help him in his job with the boats. I only hoped that he realised that although we were out to kill a few Huns if possible, the latter were also out to kill some of us if they could. I must say that I certainly would not want to go out in one of his MTBs!

Apparently Swingate had spotted a blip out to sea. It was our job to try to find the source and if it was an enemy to bomb it. We stooged off Dieppe and all seemed quiet and peaceful. Of course if I had not been so naïve I might have done a bit of weaving, but I believed that if the enemy had any serious intent towards a lone aircraft flying on a steady course out at sea they would have shone a few searchlights in my direction. Had other aircraft been in the vicinity Swingate would have warned me.

Suddenly it looked as if there were some barrage balloons right in front of me. I could also hear some bangs. I realised that this was heavy flak exploding and immediately did a diving turn to the right.

Bob piped up, sounding rather nervous, and I don't blame him, 'Er, what's going on John?'

To reassure him I said, as calmly and steadily as possible, 'It's all right, Bob, that was a bit of flak we were avoiding.'

I must say that the Germans were remarkable. To have fused their shells so exactly that they burst at the right height and exactly ahead of my intended track shows how sophisticated their radiolocation (i.e. *radar* as it was called later) had become. Had they believed that an aircraft could fly as slowly as an Albacore I would not be writing this now.

Owing to poor R/T reception Swingate were unable to communicate with us and for a while the boys back in the crew room thought that we had bought it.

In the meantime the CO, with his observer Norman, had given a 'Tally ho,' when he had found an Armed Merchant Ship and three escorts off Boulogne. When nothing further was heard from him Swingate called him up to see whether he was all right. Nothing ever was heard and he never reappeared so we realised he must have been shot down by the escorts.

Back at Manston Walsh was frantically trying to get some search aircraft off to look for the CO. The RAF sent out a Beaufighter and some Hudsons, all to no avail. Walsh then took off with Mac Rutherford and Johnnie Hitch in the back, but they sighted nothing.

832 seemed to be fated to lose COs and during night operations at that. Williamson was married and had a family and the least we could hope

for was that he was a prisoner of war. His stratagems and ideas would have been a boon to any squadron. To us his loss was more than the loss of a good CO. In fact we never did find out what happened to him.

A new CO was appointed and Lieutenant Kiggel, RN, arrived.

On 17 October I had one of my most exciting – but frustrating – nights of the war. A signal from Group stated that 841 was to co-operate with four Hudsons of Coastal Command in the attack of a large ship due to leave Boulogne which was going to Dunkirk. It was decided to send only one Albacore, whose job it would be to ring the ship with flame floats for the benefit of the Hudsons who would then bomb it. As far as I could glean from the information provided, the Hudsons were manned by a Dutch crew and the idea was for them to sink the ship so as to boost morale back in Holland.

Bob and I set off about midnight armed with four 250 lb bombs plus our flame floats and were vectored towards the enemy ships. It was an extremely dark night and I could see nothing but blackness. As we reached a position to which Swingate had directed us I was able with difficulty to make out the wash of a large ship surrounded by four smaller ones.

Just as I spotted them they opened up with anti-aircraft fire, and at that very moment Swingate said, 'You should be over them now!'

Bob replied, 'You're telling us!!'

We took avoiding action and then returned hoping to come in on the front of the little convoy in order to start dropping the ring of flame floats. We dropped the first flame float right on top of the group of ships and followed this up with more floats. Under the glare of these the wakes were no longer visible. What was so frustrating was that I could easily have dropped my bombs with an excellent chance of obtaining a hit, but no, the Hudsons were supposed to do it.

Up till now there had been no sign of any Hudsons except for the occasional flare and flak to the west.

We were again vectored to the target and approached fairly close to the shore. The shore batteries suddenly opened up with some fairly accurate heavy flak. Having stirred up a hornet's nest we departed, hoping that we had done enough to illuminate the target for the Hudsons.

According to Swingate the dropping of the flame floats made the ship turn back in the direction of Calais, where it was damaged, probably by a mine, and beached.

The RAF alleged that one of the Hudsons had made a direct hit on the target and that this was the cause of the sinking. However, Swingate said that the Hudsons were nowhere near the scene at the time. I can only hope that the Dutch people were gratified to think that their men had done a good job!

In the eyes of 841 the ship was sunk by eight flame floats and one mine and not by any Hudsons making haphazard attacks on sandbanks. A star was painted on the side of my aircraft to indicate the success of the operation.

Anyway the great thing is that the ship was found next day with its back broken and decks awash. So that finished that, the war effort was boosted and that is all that really mattered.

There was no action for the rest of the month. Most of the time the moon had been at its brightest and the weather at its dirtiest so the inactivity was explained. We practised such things such as air firing and dummy dive bombing plus formations of five aircraft. I see from my log book that I also towed a drogue for the others to fire at. I had no complaints and did not have to shriek into the R/T, 'You stupid bastards, I'm towing this thing not pushing it!' Which is apparently what happened elsewhere when some shots went wild on a practice shoot.

I see that I flew an aircraft to Gosport to be painted black by the experts there and that I picked it up two days later.

On 6 November we were asked to do some flying at night to give the searchlight boys some practice at finding and tracking us. I was on the ground watching as the senior pilot flew. I was considerably surprised when he made no effort to escape from the lights; he just carried on flying straight and level. When he landed I tackled him about this and he said that it was impossible to get out of the searchlight beams.

I then took off and every time a searchlight found me I was able to dive, make a steep turn and lose the lights. On landing I was told what happened on the ground: the senior pilot said, 'Well, Fay talks a lot – now he'll see!' At that moment I made a beautiful steep turn and disappeared into the Stygian darkness!

Manston had an unusual air defence system that I had not known of anywhere else, although it might have been widespread for all I knew. The airfield perimeter had rocket-bearing cables mounted there. At the press of a button, presumably in the control tower, the rockets would streak skywards carrying the cables. If operated at the right moment they would catch any low-flying aircraft attacking the airfield. The timing must have been very critical and they were used only once when I was there – with no result.

On 8 November Operation Torch, the landings in North Africa, started, which revealed the reason for our removal from the squadron. Like the Malta convoy the Vic needed the space for more fighters. It was while I

841 SQUADRON, RAF MANSTON

was at Manston that we heard the good news about the battle of El Alamein. The war was beginning to turn our way at last.

On 23 November the career of 832B Flight was cut short by a signal telling us to go to Crail and be absorbed into an FAA carrier squadron.

Our departure from Manston was recorded in the RAF Daily Activity Report which stated:

'An FAA squadron departing from Manston made a successful dive bombing attack on the control tower, scoring a near miss with a roll of toilet paper.'

Bob Procter and Gerry Child did not fly with us on this trip. Arch and I had RAF passengers with us on the first leg of the flight to Stretton. I managed to fly via Oxshott and over the house where the Yates family lived.

Bob went with the ground crew in a Harrow; Gerry Child went by train with a prisoner and escort, the prisoner being one of our squadron.

At Stretton – that 'father of all fogbound places,' as I recorded in my diary, we were delayed for three days before being able to depart for Crail.

So ended the story of 832B Flight. It was a short-lived existence, but we did some useful work while we were at Manston and I wouldn't have missed it; it was a great experience. Above all I began to feel supremely confident about instrument flying and making night landings between lamps of low luminosity.

Back at Crail we found to our delight that we were rejoining our old squadron – 832. The day after we arrived we all went on one week's leave because the squadron had just returned from the Algiers landing in Operation Torch. Shortly after returning Harold Willott went to hospital with pleurisy. I was not to see him again until we met at a squadron reunion several decades later.

15

FROM THE CLYDE TO HAWAII

Having rejoined the squadron at Crail we exchanged details of our operations. We were sorry to hear that Sub-Lieutenant David Harvey had been lost overboard in the Mediterranean and was drowned. Otherwise the squadron was intact and full of rumours as to what we were going to do next. There was a strong feeling that we were going to America.

If any reader thinks that they have read some of the words of the following three chapters of my tale before they are probably right, for an article I wrote called 'Pacific Interlude' was borrowed by Mike Apps and he was able to use some of it in his book *Send Her Victorious*. I also used some of it in an article for *Jabberwock*, which is a magazine published by the Society of Friends of the Fleet Air Arm Museum.

On 7 December 1942 I flew to Machrihanish and a few days later I landed aboard the Vic. On the 15th I ferried two pilots to Machrihanish and as this took only 15 minutes the Vic must have been on her way to the Clyde at the time.

It was about this time that the escort carrier HMS *Avenger* was torpedoed by a German submarine as she was heading back from Africa, and blew up. The explosion that sank her left only 12 survivors out of a total crew of 550 men. One of the men lost was Hugh Anson-May, the man who met me at Luton and who knew my sister in the Argentine. Many years later I met his father in Uruguay and he was still very cut up about it.

We left the Clyde on the 20th. The ship had a new captain, Captain Mackintosh. He was a Scot who was actually the Mackintosh of Mackintosh, which meant that he was the leader of the clan. He was Captain of the *Eagle* when I saw her sink under him during the Malta convoy. I just hoped he didn't make a habit of that sort of thing. Captain Bovell became RANAS (Rear Admiral Naval Air Stations). Commander Surtees had left us too, he became captain of an escort carrier and some of his methods were to cause controversy. In his place we had

Commander Ross who had witnessed the surrender of the German High Seas Fleet in 1918 and its later scuttling in Scapa Flow. In the Dunkirk evacuation his ship made six trips and carried 11,000 troops to safety, for which he received the DSO. He was also a conjurer and would occasionally entertain us with his tricks. Both these new characters were as different from their predecessors as chalk from cheese.

As we sailed from the Clyde some Martlets landed-on from Machrihanish and then our new captain spoke to the ship's company over the broadcaster. 'We are going to Bermuda,' he said and added that a rough Atlantic crossing was expected. This was an understatement and by next day we had a wind of 40 knots and more against us. Seawater poured into the hangar and was inches deep at times and our aircraft received a good soaking. No flying was possible and life was a bit boring.

By the 25th we were right in the centre of the Atlantic and it was hard to believe it was Christmas day. We received all sorts of messages from the King downwards. The rumours of our future began to coalesce and we understood that 832 Squadron was going to convert to the American Avenger. We could only hazard guesses as to where we were going after that, but we had a strong feeling that it was the Pacific. We also assumed that the Vic would have a refit in the States.

Christmas dinner took place in the evening and as the wardroom was too small to hold all the officers at once we had to have a running meal. I shared a bottle of Liebfraumilch with Ken Smith and got my head down early as I was doing the dawn A/S patrol on the morrow.

I rose at 0630 and had a quick breakfast then went up to the flight deck and climbed aboard my aircraft. The weather was not promising as it was raining and the visibility was poor. However it cleared a little and off the bows we went.

The flight lasted three hours and as usual nothing was sighted. My landing was not exemplary, but they say that any landing you walk away from is a good one. My legs were aching after having to push on the rudder pedals so I was not too pleased when I was told I would have to fly again – this time it was an A/S search which lasted two hours, and four of us went out on diverging courses. I had Sub-Lieutenant Bill Thomson as my observer on this occasion. He was the squadron wit and would write humorous ditties; his most famous one I shall quote later. When I say that he was the squadron wit I think a good percentage of the Fleet Air Arm had exceptional senses of humour, I suppose that being associated with the sea as well as the air and the dangers thereof brought out the best in us. However, I thought that the best of all humorists in the squadron was 'Jeff' Jefford.

Despite the fact that I was dog tired after flying most of the day it was always a source of satisfaction to know that once again I had landed safely on a carrier deck. Deck landing was always an adventure except, perhaps, in the calmest of conditions and after a successful landing there is a tremendous sense of something accomplished. The best part of any landing is the feel of an arrester wire having been caught by one's hook and bringing the aircraft to a halt. I had now done forty-four landings without a crash, which was quite a good record considering the weather we had been having.

Captain Mackintosh gave a talk to the pilots and observers in the wardroom. He had been trained as an observer himself and among other matters he spoke of the peril of mixing alcohol with flying. To illustrate his warning he said, 'I once had a flight with a pilot who had been drinking. When I came out of hospital . . .!'

We could not imagine Captain Bovell giving us a talk like that and making a joke. We respected him a lot but not being a flying type like Captain Mackintosh he was not on the same wavelength.

On the 27th we tried to refuel one of our three escorting destroyers, HMS *Redoubt*. For a long time she kept too far away for any pipe lines to be passed to her. Eventually she came in closer on our starboard side and formatted on us. Makeshift-looking attempts were made to pass the equipment, although I supposed they were the normal drill. Then she came in too close and did some damage. In order for her to steer clear her wheel would have to be put to starboard, which would have caused her stern to go to port. As she was right up close she could not do this! She eventually managed to get clear and the refuelling attempt was abandoned. The damage she did to us was enough to render unserviceable the mechanism for raising and lowering the radio masts. When not operating aircraft the masts are normally kept vertical. When aircraft are taking off and landing the masts are angled outboard to a horizontal position.

The two aircraft on A/S patrol had to land-on with the masts vertical, which is quite a dangerous situation.

Our new captain had decreed that Air Officers of the Watch should take a turn as OOW (Officer of the Watch) under the supervision of the duty OOW, so when I was up on the compass platform on duty there I was virtually steering the ship by giving orders down a voice pipe to the Quartermaster. I found it most interesting work.

After six of our aircraft had landed successfully the following signal was made:

TO 832 Squadron. FROM Victorious.
MANOEUVRE WELL EXECUTED. 1735.

The *Victorious* is refuelled at sea.

We appreciated that but thought this was a typical naval way of doing things and wondered what RAF aircrews would think if, after doing a successful mission, they received a signal saying that their manoeuvres had been 'well executed'!

Most of us were kept awake during the night of the 28th by the rough weather. The swell was considerable and those of us in the Admiral's Day Cabin who were not roused by the fact that they were alternately almost airborne and then squashed into their bunks were certainly woken up by the crash of a large percentage of our cups and saucers which were thrown on to the floor. I wondered how the crew who were asleep amidships were faring; better than we were I reckoned, as they were not at the extreme ends of the seesaw. However, our hearts went out to the crews of the destroyers they must have been suffering hell. The only good thing about the weather was the fact that any U-boats would be keeping well below the surface. When I paid a visit to the quarterdeck later on I found that the ship was steering more or less across the swell so it was rolling badly but not pitching too much.

I remarked in my diary on the 29th that I seemed to be destined for one crash per year! I was chosen to stand by for the first A/S patrol in the event of the weather settling down a bit. Sure enough 'Flying Stations' was piped and I had to leave the warm wardroom and climb into my aircraft. I had Jimmy Duckett as my observer; the only time he ever flew with me. The ship was pitching so much while waiting to take off that at one stage the aircraft started to slide towards the side of the ship and the flight deck party had to gather round it and hold on. The take off was not too bad and the air above was smoother than the sea below.

After an hour and a half in the air the visibility decreased owing to fog and after signalling to the ship we were told to stand by to land-on. I presume I was told to jettison depth charges, probably owing to the bad weather, because that is what I did. They were supposed to be on 'safe' but one of the four exploded, no doubt causing a few hearts to beat faster in the crews of those below the waterline.

After a short delay the ship turned into wind and I made my approach. The ship was rolling all over the place and so was I in my efforts to keep in a straight line just as I touched down the ship made what I referred to in my diary as a 'God Almighty roll to starboard'. This made me land heavily on my port undercarriage, which was forced up into the mainplane. Commander Figuls Price, generally known as Commander Price, our new Commander Flying did not seem mad at me and people said it was bad luck. Well, it was my first prang on deck and my personal record of 44 landings without a crash was broken. Sometimes I blame myself for not going round again; but would things have been any better? I don't know.

I went up on deck fairly early on the 30th in order to watch the approach to Bermuda. An A/S patrol had taken off earlier and soon it came into land. Despite the calm sea there was a swell from the starboard quarter and this caused the ship to roll somewhat. John Randall, who was a permanent member of 771 Squadron when I was a temporary member, was the pilot and his total experience of deck landing was four landings some days ago. The rolling was too much for him and he did the same as I did only worse. He smashed his port wheel, slid across to the side of the ship and broke up the port inner mainplane, narrowly missing a man standing at the side.

The ship circled the north of Bermuda and anchored about one mile off shore. Throughout the day it was amusing to watch American planes: if they were land planes they would beat us up; if they were floatplanes they would land alongside and then taxi slowly around us taking a good look.

'Hands to bathe', was piped at 1130 hours. The temperature in the water was 70°F. so I put on my swimming trunks and went in. A man was standing by in case any of us got into difficulties and a marine with a rifle stood by in case of sharks. The water felt coldish but refreshing.

At 1315 hours the ship's company put on their Christmas play. It was extremely well done and most enjoyable. At the end of it the captain spoke to us and gave us the bad, or good news depending on one's point of view.

He said that the Albacores were being changed for Avengers, that we were going to Norfolk, Virginia and that we were joining the American fleet after the ship had been altered to take American bombs and torpedoes. Having heard of the terrific battles that had taken place in the Pacific since Pearl Harbor this last bit of information filled every man present with a mixture of excitement and awe. The strange sound that came forth from our collective throats was something I shall never forget.

It looked to us as if we would not see England again for some time.

We were woken up by sixteen bells being sounded to notify us of the New Year, and a sleepy voice said, 'A Happy New Year to all on this ship'. Since the Royal Navy insists that we live *in* a ship and not *on* a ship, I wondered what the Captain thought of that, but perhaps I was being pedantic.

It was auspicious that we would fly off to America on 1 January. A new year and a new start we thought. We 'rose and shone' at 0545 and ranged the aircraft at 0700, taking off at 0800. We seemed to fly for ages before we sighted land but the total flight took only an hour and a half

After cautious and wide circuits of the airfield the squadron landed at Norfolk Naval Air Station. Apart from the considerable confusion caused to the airfield circuit on the sudden introduction of slow aircraft, our arrival caused a minor sensation, for some of the Americans had not seen bi-planes before. To them it was as if some Time Travellers from the First World War had suddenly materialised. It was a pity, perhaps, that the bizarre appearance of our aircraft had not been accentuated on this occasion by bicycles strapped to the wing struts, for in home waters this was a practice often carried out when flying from ship to shore.

This was my last ever flight in an Albacore. It was a shame really as I much preferred it to the Swordfish, and it was the Swordfish that I was to fly again towards the end of the year.

At Norfolk, Virginia, we were astounded at our welcome. Where was this much hyped hospitality and organisation? We stood waiting for our luggage to be collected for nearly two hours and had endless forms of red tape to sign. Then we had some very rude women hall porters to deal with. Our own Royal Naval Air Stations at their worst were never like this and foreign visitors, especially in groups, would be particularly well looked after. To counterbalance the pinpricks we received during our stay in Norfolk, however, there was some wonderful hospitality and kindness shown to us at other times and places; but, here we were in Navy Norfolk where, it was said, the locals were not only anti-British but anti-American as well!

The Avengers we were going to fly were all in a hangar and we spent the afternoon being shown around them. Unlike our thoughts on our welcome we *were* impressed.

Later the Royal Navy changed the name of the Avenger to Tarpon. Later still it was changed back to Avenger when it became policy to call American aircraft by their American name. To avoid confusion I shall keep to the better-known name of Avenger. But, for the time being, I shall also refer to our fighters as Martlets as they were known better by that name than by their later one – Wildcats.

The Avenger first flew in January 1942 and by June about 60 were being rolled out each month. By the end of 1942 over 600 had been built, and during 1943 the average production rose to 150 per month. From 1942–1945 nearly 10,000 aircraft had been constructed – a record for the greatest number of naval strike aircraft ever produced. Only a proportion was completed by Grumman, for in late 1942 the Eastern Aircraft Division of General Motors started to take over production.

On 2 January I carried out my first flight in an Avenger. My take-off felt a bit odd owing to my pushing the stick forward too much; the Avenger takes off better if the stick is held in a more or less neutral position. When I reached 200 feet I put my hand out to raise the undercarriage, unfortunately I had omitted to tighten the throttle nut and the engine lost rpm immediately. This is a classic error and one I was not likely to repeat. I climbed to sufficient height where it did not matter if the engine throttled back.

The aircraft climbed at a fast rate compared to other aircraft I had flown, but the controls were very stiff to operate and most movements required alterations of the trimmers. The Americans call that sort of plane a 'tab ship'. An apt description! I spent an hour getting used to the aircraft. My landing was a bit bumpy, but that was to be expected.

That evening I went into Norfolk town. It took about half an hour to get across the airfield by bus and then about 40 minutes in a streetcar to reach the centre of town. It was pleasant to see some bright lights again, but after doing a bit of shopping I was glad to get back to my quarters and get my head down.

We were getting concerned about the fact that we had neither received any mail nor were we allowed to send any. We thought the folks back home would be worried, especially as there had been some sort of naval battle in northern waters where the Vic had operated for the past months.

Two or three days after our arrival I was duty officer. I had few duties to do that I had not had experience of before, but on this occasion I was approached by PO Laidlaw who said that he had had trouble with a rating who had refused an order given him by a leading hand. He said that he had now got him settled and had turned a blind eye to it. I do not know why he should have told me this seeing that the matter appeared to be settled; however it was not, for when I was going round one of the huts in which the ratings were living Laidlow suddenly stopped in front of the rating and pointed him out to me. I did not know what Laidlaw expected me to do, matters of indiscipline were things we rarely had to deal with. On this occasion I tried to look intelligent (in my diary I asked myself, 'Is this possible?!') and asked for his name. Nothing further was heard of the matter.

I approached the Ready Room in a hangar where I was going to sleep, and was challenged by two American sentries on my way in. After showing them my card I said, 'Good night', but they never replied.

We had been preceded at Norfolk by a squadron called the TA Squadron. It was not a front line squadron. Their function was to look at the Avenger from the British point of view and one modification called for was the observer's window, which had to be modified to enable the observer to take sights.

There was a Canadian in our dormitory and he appeared to have a good opinion of England. Among things I heard him say was, 'In England an American is an honorary member of practically every mess he enters and pays very little. Over here with the British it is always "Cash please!"' Another time he was asked by some Americans why we said so little and kept so much to ourselves and he replied that they, the Americans, were the hosts and were expected to speak to us first.

They say that when you are in a foreign country you look out for the bad points and not the good ones. But we really were getting a little fed up with the manners of some people, particularly the women. I was in the Ships Service Store with Sid Price and Gerry Child and we were drinking milk shake and munching some doughnuts when a female looked at me and pointed to a notice about not eating at the counter and said, 'Can't you read!' Now, in Britain they would have said, 'Excuse me, Sir, but there's a rule about . . . .' or something of that sort.

We knew we were going to be attached to the US Navy of course, so when an American, recognising a British uniform, said to one of our officers, 'What's it like being in the second best navy?' His riposte was, 'Oh, we're not going to actually be *in* your navy, we are only attached to you.'

On 10 January there was snow outside the door when I opened it in the morning. This caused any early flying to be cancelled. I was not down for flying in the afternoon, so instead I was given a job to do. I had to get a plane back from the assembly and repair depot. I took a Petty

Officer and three ratings and a tractor and set off. After wandering into all sorts of buildings, most of which were meant to be secret, I was at length directed to the correct one. After signing for the plane I got in the cockpit and worked the brakes while the tractor pulled it along until we reached a hangar. All this took an hour. I may add here that the American idea of having brakes operated by a hinged flap on the rudder pedals was infinitely superior to the method employed on the Albacore. In that aircraft engine power was needed and a small handle on the control column operated the brakes; right or left pedal operation would cause only that brake to work. So to move an Albacore with no engine power meant that there were no brakes!

Concerning my walking into restricted places: the famous American bombsite that is supposed to be guarded day and night by armed guards was, in that place, under the protection of one unarmed rating!

The mail position was eventually solved and on the 16th we received some mail at last. I had a telegramme from Mary, which read, 'Every good wish for Christmas and New Year good luck and fishing.' The fishing in this case referred to any possible torpedo attacks made by us.

Familiarisation flights continued and among other things we were able to use automatic pilots for the first time. Another innovation we had not seen before was a radar altimeter. Until those times it was not possible to tell one's altitude except by an altimeter worked by the ambient air pressure. It was at Norfolk that we heard for the first time the word 'radar'. Prior to that various names had been used such as ASV, RDF and Radio Location. I get a bit annoyed when I read books in which authors in books have their characters using the word *radar* for events occurring before the war.

Some days later some more pilots and observers from the TA Squadron were appointed to 832. Among these were Frank Low, RN, destined to become our Senior Pilot and, later on, our CO; and Lieutenant Bill Bailey, RN, who was to be the Senior Observer. Then there were Bruce Petrie, John Stringleman, Hugh Saunders and Jack Loftus, all of whom were New Zealanders. Among the Britons was Doug Briggs, who was the best man at my wedding some years later, and John Swinn, John Swift, and Derek Hill to name a few. We learned that we were to become a twenty-one aircraft squadron and believed that we belonged to the largest Fleet Air Arm front line squadron at the time. This, however, was erroneous, for 836 Squadron operating Swordfish had that honour. But the members were spread throughout the MAC ships and it is likely that some squadron members never met each other.

We all received lectures on the American deck landing system. To a man we believed the method to be hopelessly complex. It was difficult to execute and required constant practice, particularly in the last stage of the approach when a tricky piece of handling had to be carried out. On their merits, the signals from the batsman, who stood on the deck and controlled the approach, were really quite sensible. Unfortunately, however, the important signals were the complete opposite of the British ones. For example, both arms raised from the side and outstretched 45° above the horizontal meant, in the British case: 'Go higher!' but in the American case: 'You are too high'. In other words the British signals were an instruction of what to do whereas the American signals were 'mirror' signals advising the pilot of the position of the aircraft in relation to the correct approach path.

The American landing procedure consisted of a flat approach towards an imaginary point anything up to fifty feet above the stern of the ship. At a position over the stern the batsman would give a 'cut' signal and the pilot would close his throttle. So far so good, but the aircraft was not a few feet above the deck at the time but anything up to fifty feet, and in a nose-high condition. To avoid an extremely heavy arrival on the deck the stick had to be eased forward quickly, which naturally made the aircraft drop more rapidly, and then eased back to cushion the landing. All this would take place in a few seconds of time and required considerable skill, acquired and maintained by practice, to make a good touchdown.

The British method consisted of a nose-high descending approach at about 10 knots above stalling speed; in other words, the same procedure as would be adopted when making a precautionary approach or a landing into a small area. The aircraft would be held in this position until just prior to touching the deck. The throttle would then be closed and the touchdown made.

Flying training continued with the emphasis now on ADDLS. After considerable practice, some of which we carried out at Monogram airfield, I was permitted to carry out landings on a carrier, the USS *Charger* while she cruised up and down in Chesapeake Bay. Mentally, everything seemed rather shattering when I made my landings, especially as the Americans preferred one to land with a boisterous bang rather than the light caress that was the intention if not always the substance of the British system. I found that cutting the throttle when still high above the deck, and the subsequent hard drop, completely alien to my previous experience. My morale was not improved by the fact some Avengers at this time had seat belts but no shoulder harness, and the Avenger I was flying was one of those. I feared for my head during the rapid deceleration that took place after catching an arrester wire.

During the time on the *Charger* I learned, without hearing many details, about one group of four Martlets that had had a very bad day.

139

One aircraft spun into the deck and the pilot was killed; another aircraft went over the side still attached to the arrester wire, the pilot being uninjured; a third aircraft did not arrive and the pilot's body was washed ashore several days later.

While at Norfolk my life was saved by the expression on someone's face. I was walking in front of an Avenger, the engine of which was being run up by a fitter. I was, naturally, a fair way in front of it and as I moved it passed out of my view. The engine appeared to be running at almost full throttle and chocks held the aircraft back. It was roaring away like an angry bull straining at a chain. In front of me was Reg Highland who was watching the aircraft. Suddenly a most alarmed look appeared on his face. Then he turned and ran. I followed, glancing to the left as I went and saw the Avenger was moving; the aircraft had jumped the chocks. My angry bull was no longer tethered, its chain had broken and the enraged beast was charging forward, gaining momentum with every second. It ran about fifty yards and then ran full tilt into a hangar wall. Some ratings ran up to the cockpit and brought out the fitter who was unconscious with blood all over his face. A few moments later someone was brought out of the rear cockpit in a far worse condition. This was Leading Airman P.J. (Jock) McEvoy, a TAG. Both men were put in the back of a small truck with Surgeon Lieutenant Mumford, who happened to be nearby, and taken to the sick bay.

McEvoy died of his injuries. He was from Eire and in his small way he made up for some of the discredit of that country for not allowing us bases there, which was ironic for had Britain been invaded the Germans would have swept through Eire with scarcely a pause. The lack of bases in Eire must have cost the lives of thousands of people.

We had been in Navy Norfolk for about three weeks when we were inoculated against various diseases. The one I received for Yellow Fever really got to me. I felt ill and had to lie down with a feeling of dizziness and sickness. I looked in the mirror and saw that my face was white. My pulse was feeble and beating only once every few seconds. I recovered fairly quickly, which was fortunate as I was told I was going on leave. The place to head for was, of course, New York. I had a hasty dinner and five of us went to the station in a taxi and then took a bus for the ferry to Cape Charles in Delaware. While on board I had a chat to an American CPO and his wife, the latter told me that the soldiers in England were having such a wonderful time that they were going to go back after the war. This was good to hear, although I must confess I was a bit taken aback to hear her remarks what with the food rationing, bombing, blackouts, etc.

We had an interminable wait for a train at Cape Charles. It was impossible to get a Pullman and the seats we sat on were not designed for sleeping in comfort. In New York David Johnson and I went to the Barbizon Plaza Hotel which apparently had special facilities for officers. We had a welcome bath and shave and then breakfast. Guy Richardson had arrived the day before and the three of us walked round the city for while. We had some tea in the White Ensign Club, which was in the Barbizon Plaza. We spotted some new members of 832 there.

After dinner David and I went to Radio City, the world's largest cinema. We arrived in the middle of a leg show on stage by the Rockettes. They were really spectacular and were absolutely together in every movement. Then came the film *Random Harvest* with Greer Garson and Ronald Colman, which was a truly first class film, we enjoyed every second of it. After the news and a cartoon film there was some music by an orchestra, which played pieces from *Die Fledermaus*. Next came some very clever 'acting' by performing dogs, a bit of singing and then, as the entertainment was continuous, those fantastic Rockettes again.

Back in the bar of the Barbizon Plaza an American and his wife invited us over to their table. Her name was Mary and she had a friend called Ellie whose husband was in my birthplace, São Paulo. Quite a coincidence! This was where my opinions of Americans started to change and became diametrically opposite the ones I had first formed at Navy Norfolk. Here was this group whose opinion of England and the English seemed to be as good as mine. The conversation ranged from England to the marines in Guadalcanal and back again. They were all kindness itself and of course, ' if I was ever their way in Virginia . . . .etc., be sure to look us up.' We took up the invitation of Mrs Anne Benedict and Ellie to visit them next evening.

At the hotel they have system of shoving your breakfast through a flap in the door. So I had breakfast in bed! Afterwards David and I went to the Empire State Building. Despite the adverse weather conditions we had a good view and a guide pointed out all the interesting points. 1,200 feet seemed higher than it would from an aircraft.

Next day we went to the Science Museum at the Rockefeller Centre and were intensely interested in the war section. In the evening we took a taxi to Anne Benedict's place. There was a thick layer of snow on the streets and when we turned into side streets it was heavy going. We got stuck once and took ten minutes to get away. On leaving the taxi our shoes filled with snow! We had a delightful evening with the two ladies and their friends. The party tended to split up when two US Navy men and their ladies arrived, but anyway we had to leave to catch a train back to Norfolk.

In the train we met Andy Anderson and Ray Richardson, a New Zealander who had recently joined the squadron, not to be confused with Guy Richardson.

There then passed an hour of extreme disquiet. One thing I cannot abide is British people in uniform making a nuisance of themselves in foreign countries: they let themselves down, they let the Navy down and they let their country down. In our carriage there were three drunken British sailors. They started singing songs out of tune and very loudly. They were obviously disturbing the rest of the carriage and making a very bad impression. I stood it as long as I could and then suggested to Arch Hugill as the senior man that he talk to the sailors and try to quieten them down. Now, we were taught that if a sailor looks as if he going to attack an officer he should run away! This is to avoid the man being charged with striking an officer, which is a very serious offence. I had a mental picture of Arch rushing down the aisle hotly pursued by an angry rating! Fortunately after talking to the men for a few minutes they quietened down and went to sleep. Then one of them was sick! I felt more and more ashamed of my fellow countrymen.

I considered that the man who designed the seats in those trains must have been a sadist! In no position can one be comfortable. Added to that a great wave of hot air rushes up from near the wall and brings a sweat to that side of the body. The other side might be freezing!

Back to the Air Station via ferry and bus, then a welcome wash and a meal. I grabbed a place in the Ready Room and slept for three hours. The three days in New York were not nearly enough; I decided that sometime I must go there again and do the place properly.

After my return, the *Victorious* put to sea for some local trials during which two Martlets were lost. One piloted by Sub-Lieutenant Farthing dropped into the water on takeoff due to a faulty engine; he was picked up by a US destroyer unhurt. The second accident was caused by the pilot coming in too fast on his approach. When the main wheels hit the deck the tail went down and the aircraft became airborne again sailed over the first crash barrier and went into the second. This was strong enough to prevent the aircraft hitting the aircraft parked forward. It is worth mentioning that an accident of this sort would not happen in the modern aircraft carrier, for crash barriers are not necessary with angled decks. If the last stage of the approach is faulty the pilot needs only to increase engine thrust and overshoot. Our Avengers landed on better than most people had predicted; however, satisfaction was short-lived and had we had a lot of trouble at this time a later tragedy might have been prevented, for it was possible that the *Victorious* would have had modifications carried out at Norfolk instead of at Pearl.

While at Norfolk, Virginia, it was observed that American sailors had some hardwearing trousers made of denim and called blue jeans. Commander Ross thought that it would be a good idea if our crews had the same. Accordingly these were issued and the Admiralty agreed that these were a suitable and practical part of a sailors' uniform. Thus the crews of the *Victorious* were the first in the Navy, and indeed, the first in Britain, to have this item of clothing.

The ship left Norfolk for Panama on 5 February, but owing to thick fog did not leave the area until the next evening. As my own cabin was below the water line I was once again sleeping in a dormitory well above the surface, this time in the Captain's day cabin on a rather hard camp bed.

After an uncomfortable beginning to the voyage due to gales the weather began to get hot and we donned tropical kit. The ship did not appear to have been designed with the prospect in mind of ever operating in this sort of climate, for it was stifling below deck and even the cold water in the taps was hot. Cuba was in sight all day on 9 February.

Bill Thomson produced his most famous song 'Take Me Back to Navy Norfolk' sung to the tune of 'Take Me Back to Dear Old Blighty'. In it he described all the things that we found irritating about the place. His last few lines puts our general feelings succinctly:

> Oh, isn't it blooming awful
> Living in Navy Norfolk
> The arsehole of the USA!

We had a certain amount of trouble with deck landings. Two tyres and one wheel were broken on one day and on another there was a barrier crash and a broken propeller owing to an arrester hook failure. These were comparatively minor incidents for, on the day after, a Martlet pilot was killed. His plane caught fire in the air and. being too low to bale out he was killed when his plane hit the water.

Before reaching Panama the ship's company stood by for a practice attack by American bombers, but they never appeared. Our gunners did, however, have some practice in shooting at drogues; two of these were shot down, one by the 4.5in guns and the other by the light armament.

We arrived at Cristobal on 11 February at mid-day, passing the USS *Stalker* on the way in. We intercepted a signal from the USS *Massachusetts*, which said, 'What's the Limey flattop?' I did not learn what answer was given, but for the purpose of security our ship was generally referred to as the USS *Robin*. Years later an American author approached me about a book he wanted to write to be called *The USS* Robin, *RN*. Unfortunately it never saw the light of day.

At Cristobal two days were spent in removing guns and other protuberances from the sides of the ship to enable her to pass through

Photo from Fleet Air Arm Museum

1943. En route to the Pacific HMS *Victorious* squeezes into a lock in the Panama Canal with inches to spare on either side.

the Panama Canal. In the meantime the officers took the opportunity of letting their hair down and held a party on the quarterdeck. When the band departed its pianist carried on for a while and when he left, Frank Low took over. Frank was a really gifted pianist and was in great demand on occasions like this.

We left dock on 13 February in the early afternoon and headed for the first of the three locks that lead up to the lakes of Panama. We passed through green jungle and some items of interest were pointed out, in particular the place where Ferdinand de Lesseps made an attempt to build a canal. I kept saying to myself that twelve years ago when, as a small boy aged 9, I passed through the canal in the opposite direction en route from New Zealand to England, I little dreamed that one day I would come through the same canal as an officer in the Royal Navy.

Eventually we reached the locks. We could see that it was going to be a tight squeeze, but the men driving the little trams that towed the ship did not seem to realise this. The ship was allowed to go too far to port and hit the lock entrance. The port submarine lookout's position was knocked off, but fortunately this was the only damage done and the ship continued on with two feet to spare on either side.

It took nearly four hours to get through the three locks and at last we were free to swing at anchor instead of being restricted to mere inches of latitude.

The hook was pulled up early next day and a start was made through the middle lock. It was all rather comic as prayers were held on the flight deck at the same time. Everyone was too hot to sing and as the ship scraped the walls of the lock there were cries of, 'Get her over!' which interfered with the decorum of the service.

We were four days at Balboa while the various pieces of equipment that had been removed at Cristobal were put back on again. The opportunity was taken for all to have shore leave and everyone had a thoroughly good time. It was almost with relief that we entered the Pacific in company with three American destroyers. The feeling was that the sooner we got the job over the sooner we would return to Britain, although it seemed exciting to read about travel in foreign parts, the thoughts of the majority of the crew at the time were always on their homes and how soon they would see them again. There could not have

Photo from the collection of John W. Herbert

1943. American PT boats escort HMS *Victorious* as she enters the Pacific.

been a man among us who did not believe that he would see a lot of action or wonder whether he would ever see his family again.

When we had progressed a mile or two into the ocean a dummy attack was made on the ship by American torpedo boats. The attackers made smoke screens and then emerged from cover to make their assault simultaneously. Even by twisting and turning at high speed we could not avoid them, but naturally the story would be different if it had been a real attack and we had been able to use our armament. I expect the Americans were impressed with the manoeuvrability of the *Victorious* compared with that of the existing US carriers in the Pacific.

There was an anxious moment. One boat made an attack fine on the port bow. It finished up ahead but slightly to port of the ship, tried to turn away to avoid hitting us and when this was insufficient its engines were put full astern. It missed the ship by about thirty feet and the men on board were preparing to jump overboard. As our bows passed it we carried out an emergency turn to port to swing our stern clear.

Our next excitement was dummy dive-bombing attacks by Airacobras, and this was impressively done. The ship's gun crews had some firing practice at drogues and the light armament shot one down.

The captain told us that we were going to Pearl Harbor and that the squadrons would disembark there for working up.

As the years pass, history is often distorted and I read recently that the *Victorious* embarked only American squadrons aboard. This is not true; the squadrons aboard were British. It is correct that the *Victorious* had an American fighter squadron on board in addition to our own for one operation, but the implication that we merely lent the ship and not our Fleet Air Arm to the US Navy is a severe distortion of fact.

There was a slight flap next day when a message from one of our aircraft was misread. A British merchant ship was wrongly thought to be a cruiser and we ranged six Avengers with torpedoes before the error was discovered. Shortly after this episode I took off for a radar calibration flight with my usual crew, Bob Procter and Leading Airman Bob Kinghan. We climbed to 10,000 feet and flew out for 55 miles in touch by radio with another aircraft on the same duty. Bob Procter then told me that a lot of oil was coming into the rear cockpit so we reported to the other aircraft that we were returning.

As we had hoped, the ship had picked up the message, but she could not call us owing to radio silence. She had already been steaming into wind for ten minutes when we reached her. As there was only two knots of wind at the time she had been churning away at 30 knots to produce sufficient wind over the deck for a safe landing.

I made an approach to the deck but found that due to oil on the windscreen I could see neither the batsman nor the deck. I opened the throttle and went round again, making a circular motion with my hand to indicate the trouble. On my second approach I came in from the port quarter and did not turn into wind until the last possible moment, so I was able to see the batsman for most of the approach. The aircraft hit the deck with a solid bump, but a comforting one in view of the circumstances.

With the modicum of experience that the squadron had now acquired it was realised that the ship, in its present condition, was not really suitable for landing Avengers safely. These were, after all, the largest and heaviest aircraft ever landed on a British deck and with a maximum setting on the arrester wire hydraulic system the wires would still pull out for a considerable way. This meant that if an aircraft caught any wire forward of the fourth, it would go into the crash barriers. Our flight deck personnel were becoming skilled at lowering the barriers as soon as an aircraft had caught an arrester wire and in this way had saved many aircraft from damage. Also, 'Tommy' (Lieutenant Thompson USN), the popular batsman who had been appointed to the ship, had been bringing the aircraft in on a lower approach in an attempt to prevent them landing too far up the deck. To a certain extent we were living in a fool's paradise thinking that with the combined skills of the batsman, pilots and barrier operators everything would be all right until we reached Pearl, where suitable modifications could be carried out to the ship.

On 22 February two sub-flights took off to carry out practice torpedo attacks on the ship. I was in the second sub-flight and the formation flew ahead of the ship for forty-five minutes before turning and flying on a reciprocal heading. When we saw the ship we were at 11,000 feet and our escorting fighters protected us from 'attacks' by other Martlets. We went into line astern and started the dive. My ASI was soon indicating 290 knots and I was delighted to find that the aircraft would turn quite well at that speed despite being a 'tab ship'. We started our turn in towards the ship rather far away which gave us a comparatively long run over the water. Hitherto our attacks in the slower Albacores would, ideally, consist of a dive, a very short level flight over the water during which the torpedo was dropped and then a turn away. For the faster Avenger the technique had to be altered slightly.

On this occasion we managed to outwit the ship but only because the ship's radar had been giving trouble and we were seen visually too late for any effective avoiding action to be taken. When low on the water and at the correct distance, speed and altitude, I pressed the button that takes a photograph, and turned away. From the photograph the height, distance, angle to the ship, aircraft attitude and whether a 'hit' was scored could be ascertained. On this occasion none of the photographs could be developed owing to a sudden influx of water into the ship's photographic section, which ruined the films. However, although the attack was carried out by only six aircraft we knew that it had been well coordinated and with the ship in the best possible position for good hits to be obtained.

Photo from David Johnson

Pacific 1943. An Avenger about to take off from HMS *Victorious*.

Photo from the collection of John W. Herbert

1943. An Avenger on fire after crashing and cutting a fuel line on the side of the ship.

An Avenger of 832 Squadron on its final approach to the deck.

1943. Pacific Ocean. An Avenger on deck aboard
HMS *Victorious*. Martlet in background.

The fighters had one 'prang' when they landed. Then the Avengers started to come in. The second aircraft went over the port side and hung suspended on the arrester wire, unfortunately knocking a man down on the deck just before dropping over, and killing him. The position of this aircraft caused much difficulty and the rest of us had to remain in the air for an extra hour and a half before the deck was cleared. I made a good American-style touch down and, due to the high wind speed over the deck, had practically stopped before catching the first wire, much to everyone's surprise, including my own.

A few days later I had the First Dog Watch as Air Officer of the Watch I took over the watch just as some Avengers were landing-on. I was looking at some items in the hooded table to see whether there was anything of interest when I suddenly heard Commander Price the Commander Flying, and Commander Mitchell USN, the American Adviser, shout, 'Put on the brakes!' I was not very interested as I thought it was something to do with an aircraft taxi-ing up the deck; however, I walked over to Commander Flying's position to have a look. As I did so I heard Commander Price shout, 'Good God!' I looked out on to the deck and saw one of the worst sights in my life. The Avenger that had just landed was going up in a sheet of flame. I could just see John Eyre the pilot starting to get out of the cockpit. I went to the voice pipe and told the Bosun's Mate to pipe, 'Fire on Deck! Fire on deck!' I could not think of the correct wording at the time and just wanted to let everyone know that something had happened. It was only after about five minutes that Commander Price called the hands to Fire Station.

The story, as I learned later, was that the aircraft had caught the first wire, but had rolled gently towards the port side of the ship. The port wheel had gone over the edge and had cut a pipe supplying petrol to the flight deck. The fuel had then ignited. The observer, Bill Browne, had got out of the rear cockpit but then tripped over a wire and fallen into the flames. He ran along the deck trying to put the flames out and had then been taken into the Pilots' and Observers' Waiting Room.

The pilot, John Eyre, had got out all right but was badly burnt. In the meantime the TAG, L/A Lovell also burnt, had, unknown to anyone on deck, run down a companionway and gone straight to the nearby sickbay. His disappearance caused me considerable worry as the Commander Flying sent me to find him and as he was not to be seen anywhere it was assumed that he was still in the blazing aircraft.

The fire raged. It was drawn into ventilators and smoke started to appear in various parts of the ship. The boat deck started to burn and the Admiral's barge and a cutter were destroyed. Then some stored timber caught alight. It was a full hour before the fires were under control. I was not a little worried about the depth charges in the aircraft exploding, but they just melted and were ditched. I was also momentarily alarmed when the remaining aircraft on anti-submarine petrol started dropping depth charges. I thought, 'Now we have a sub to deal with as well!' But the pilots were merely jettisoning their loads in order to lighten the aircraft and extend their endurance.

The observer and pilot died next day and the air gunner the day after. It was a severe jolt for us as we had not realised how much damage shock could do and we had been told that they all had a chance.

About fifty years later I was talking to a New Zealander about this and he told me that Commander Price (the Commander Flying) had been blamed at the Court of Inquiry for insisting that pressure be kept up in the fuel pipes that ran along the side of the ship. In fairness I have no official confirmation of this.

John Eyre had been Senior Pilot. Following John's death Frank Low took up that position, which he held until he became CO shortly afterwards.

In his next broadcast the captain told us, among other items of interest, that the ship had steamed 100,000 miles since her launching. The same afternoon a Martlet crashed on landing and caught fire. The petrol tank was ripped open and petrol spewed out. Water from hoses spread it still further and flames drifted down the deck until Commander 'F' shouted for the fire party to use foam only. The fire was then quickly put out.

I did not fly again on the voyage until the squadrons took off for Hawaii, landing at Ford Island, which was to be our home for the next two months. The prime purpose of the ship's visit to the Pacific was to fill a gap. The Americans were short of carriers after the recent actions and we had offered to 'lend' them ours, despite being hard pressed ourselves. The *Saratoga* and the *Enterprise* were the only two in the Pacific at the time and the *Enterprise* was due for a refit.

The *Victorious* entered harbour later and came alongside quite near to our hangar. I did not see her arrival but was told she made an impressive sight with the ship's company dressed in white and lining the flight deck. On shore the American band played British tunes, our Royal Marines played American ones in return.

16

PACIFIC INTERLUDE

Most people think of Hawaii as a paradise. To the ship's company that had lived through long cold months of duty in Arctic waters broken only recently by the Malta convoy and the landings in North Africa it must have seemed doubly so. Palm trees, beaches, green hills and lots of colour made an unbelievable contrast to the cold, grey and white of the inhospitable seas north of the British Isles.

Unlike our experiences at Norfolk, Virginia, in Hawaii we were treated like kings, I had always read that the nearer the front line one goes the more friendly people become, both in one's own service and in that of other nations as well. This was certainly true in our case.

Sometime during our time with the Americans we were issued with a list of hand signals detailed below and which I inserted into my diary. Looking at it now I cannot remember whether it was issued as being of historical interest or whether we were ever supposed to learn them. Possibly the former as some of the instructions seem archaic.

The following is a partial list of hand signals now used in US Naval Aviation:

SIGNAL	MEANING
Shake elevators	Form vee
Series of small zooms	Form vee or close up
Series of pronounced zooms	Join up
Wave back with palm of hand	Take open distance (open out)
Pat side of fuselage	Close up
Swish tail	Form column
Leader shades eyes with hand and looks from side to side	Form scouting line
Succession of pronounced zooms followed by circling	Rendezvous scouting line

Shake wings and elevators by rotary motion of stick	Break-up
Shake ailerons	Execution signal
Cranking motion of hand	Retract or extend wheels
Flap hand up and down	Lower flaps
Head moved backwards	Slow down
Head moved forward	Speed up
Head nodded to right or left	I am turning to right or left
Rock wings from side to side	Attack
Blow a kiss	Leaving the formation
Leader pats self on head, points to number two	Leader shifting lead to number two plane
Leader with forearm erect, hand open, chops	Directs course to be steered
Closed fist or open palm tapping characters	Dot, dash system of Morse
Taps earphones followed by holding nose	Radio out of commission
Taps earphones followed by patting head	I have taken over communications
Taps earphones and nods head	Radio is now in commission
Taps earphones and points to plane being called	You are being called by radio'

I liked the 'Blow a kiss' signal, but just could not imagine some hoary old squadron commander doing it!

There was an intensive working-up period awaiting us. During this time we lived ashore in the BOQ (Batchelor Officers' Quarters) and in one of the cabins there was a small round hole in the wall; beside it were the words, 'I was only cleaning my gun'.

While we were carrying out our training the ship was once again to become a shambles. She was moved to another berth and men swarmed all over her carrying out repairs, putting in more guns, and above all modifying the arrester system so that the Avengers could land on safely. As well as increasing the braking effect of the wires more of them were fitted aft of the original number one wire. There was room for this because a flush deck had replaced the 'round down' that drooped area of the flight deck at the stern, when the ship was in Norfolk.

In contrast to the hard work that lay ahead of the aircrews the other squadron personnel were to have an easier time as all the maintenance was to be carried out by American personnel on Ford Island. No one begrudged our ground crews this, they had had a tough job when

During the war aircrews were amused by the cartoons of Chris Wren in *The Aeroplane*. He drew his 'Oddentifications' of various aircraft, to which he added verses. The one for the Swordfish, printed towards the end of the war, stating that, 'Stringbag the sailor has had his day', drew a response from an operational Swordfish squadron pointing out, in verse, that Swordfish were still carrying out operations.

ODDENTIFICATION—XXXVII.

If you had been at Matapan
You'd know this biplane in the van
For half the sea fights in the War
Have seen the Fairey Albacore.

ODDENTIFICATION—LXXXIII

Straight off the drawing board, angles and all,
Comes the Avenger on Jap preys to fall.
Formed like the Martlet, but fuller of meat,
Destined for vengeance where'er the Fleets meet.

ODDENTIFICATION—L.

" The time has come," the Walrus said,
" To talk of many things—
Of pusher-screws and ' Shagbats '
And strutted, swept-back wings—
I'm an aeronautical wonder
And if that is not enough,
Then I've wheels that I can land on
When the sea's a bit too rough ! "

ODDENTIFICATION—XLV

Lots of struts in all directions,
Curved and cut-out centre sections—
Stringbag the Sailor's had his day,
But in his own distinguished way
He's left his mark on history's page,
The champion of the biplane age!

maintaining aircraft on board ship in the Arctic and even when the squadrons were ashore at Naval Air Stations their task in maintaining the aircraft – and they often had to work in the open air – was unenviable. To show their gratitude to the Americans our men presented a Softball trophy to the crews of Carrier Aircraft Servicing Unit 1 (CASU 1) before leaving Hawaii.

I paid a visit to Honolulu. For the first time in public and because I was wearing khaki I was wearing wings on my chest, which I always considered the correct place for them instead of on the sleeve. The inhabitants of the island were certainly a mixed bunch: there were Hawaiians, Americans, Chinese, Filipinos and now British. I thought Honolulu's streets were too narrow for all the traffic. The Americans claimed that the road between Honolulu and Pearl Harbor was the busiest in the world at that time. When I travelled that road on the way back to Ford Island I shared a taxi with six American sailors, one of whom was trying to be sick behind me. Fortunately he did not succeed.

Our first flight from Ford Island was a tour of the area for familiarisation purposes. For an hour we flew round Oahu, the island on which Honolulu and Pearl was situated. The whole island was, geologically speaking, a deeply eroded volcanic dome with a mountain Mauna Kaala (4,000 feet) dominating it. Much of the land was covered with a mantle of green. With fields, cows, farms and valleys it was quite reminiscent of England. Two well-known landmarks we flew past were Diamond Head and Waikiki Beach, which I visited that same afternoon in company with Sidney Price and Ron Hallam.

We went by ferry from Ford Island and caught a taxi on the mainland and went to our hotel, the Moana, on Waikiki Beach. The afternoon and evening passed pleasantly in company with a relay of Americans who talked to us. Among them was one who had spent some time in Canada and one of the remarks he passed concerned the American habit of using expressions derived from their games and sports. These pastimes were unfamiliar to the British who therefore did not laugh in the right place. And this caused the Americans to think the British had no sense of humour.

The three of us slept in one three-bedded room. We found the room had many cockroaches in it and in the bathroom was an insect of enormous proportions. I telephoned the desk downstairs and asked if they had another room. 'No, we haven't, but I'll send up a boy with a spray'. The insects must have been listening because they disappeared about a minute before the boy arrived. Eventually we found a few creatures for him and also persuaded him to leave the spray with us. We went to sleep with the lights on to avoid having bugs dropping on us in the middle of the night.

Photo from the collection of John W. Herbert

Martlets and Avengers getting ready for take off. At this time the aircraft still used British markings. These were changed later in case trigger-happy gunners mistook the aircraft for Japanese.

Two days later the squadron carried out a simulated torpedo attack on an American ship going by the identification of *PC.588*. We 'attacked' the wrong ship at first, but eventually found the right one and my camera showed I had carried out a good drop, and next day I was permitted to take up a 'runner', a real torpedo with a dummy head.

We had had our British roundels on the aircraft changed to the American stars. Our markings could have been mistaken for Japanese and to obviate our premature demise by trigger-happy American gunners we had had to change. This was, of course, a sensible decision, but I was disappointed because I would have liked to emphasise the British presence and point out to the locals in particular that the British were in this war as well as the Americans; indeed, some of our shipmates had overheard some locals saying that the ship was British but that the squadrons were American! Months later, while doing an A/S patrol in poor visibility and approaching San Diego, my frustration was complete when I came across a British merchant ship. How heartening it would have been for the British crew to know that it was a British aircraft that was circling them! Instead I could imagine them saying. 'Oh, just another of those innumerable American aircraft!' The fact that all the aircraft in Hawaii had the same identification markings caused some confusion when we took off to drop the runner, and both Bruce Petrie, in another Avenger, and I initially followed some American Avengers after becoming airborne. When I eventually dropped my torpedo I was gratified to see it run. We carried out so many simulated drops that it was a rare thrill to drop a real 'fish'. American torpedoes were shorter and fatter than our own and could be dropped higher and faster. There was a story that although they ran very well their main trouble was that they would not explode! Apparently a squadron had dropped some in a harbour at some Japanese ships and not one had gone off.

Sometimes in the evenings I would listen to the radio. The programme took a lot of getting used to. I would be engrossed in a news item when suddenly the reader would say: 'Now here is a very important announcement'. I would sit bolt upright expecting some vital war news, but there would follow an advertisement for aspirin. How different from the BBC!

One day after a trip to Waikiki I was returning to Ford Island in the ferry when I saw that the British aircraft transport ship the *Athenia* was in harbour. Later I had two members of the crew as passengers on a

Torpedo instruction. American torpedoes were shorter and fatter than the British ones.

Martlets and Avengers ranged on deck. The USS *Saratoga* is in the background.
Note the American markings.

flight and I was able to learn what the ship had gone through. She had
sailed from Britain for Java with forty Hurricanes. As soon as the planes
had been landed they had been bombed and completely destroyed.

We started doing some night flying. It appeared to be the intention to
concentrate on night attacks more than the Americans did. Fleet Air Arm
aircraft (Swordfish and Albacores) operating from Malta had had some
wonderful results with night torpedo attacks and we hoped to emulate
them in the Pacific, although unlike the Swordfish and Albacore the
Avenger was neither silent nor very manoeuvrable, it was, however,
considerably faster.

In between night flying I was allowed to drop another runner by day.
We had had some trouble with the torpedoes just prior to this. We had
been dropping them at 300 feet above the sea and at 175 knots airspeed;
but there had been several failures; on this day we tried dropping them
at 150 feet and 147 knots. This time all the five torpedoes dropped ran
well. My own had a transfer error owing to dropping in a side wind, this
meant that as the 'fish' was moving sideways when the nose hit the
water, the tail was slewed round and the torpedo track was initially at
an angle to the one intended until the gyros took over and corrected it.
I think my torpedo missed ahead of the target, but it looked good to see
the track go practically under the ship.

During our time in Hawaii the Commander-in-Chief Pacific Fleet
Admiral Chester Nimitz came aboard. A remarkable man, he was picked
and promoted by President Roosevelt ahead of other admirals to take

1943. Pearl Harbor. Admiral Nimitz and Captain Macintosh walking the deck of HMS *Victorious*.

over from Admiral Kimmel after the action at Pearl Harbor. Admiral Nimitz had more men under his command than any other military leader.

He was born in Fredericksburg in 1885 and a museum dedicated to his memory is situated in that town. It is well worth a visit and several decades after the war I went there. As there was no mention of the Royal Navy in the museum I sent along a photograph of the Admiral and Captain Mackintosh walking the deck of HMS *Victorious*.

We had been issued with revolvers, but did not use our own when we went along to the range for practice shooting. John Burbidge, Bob Procter and I all did better than we expected, shooting both right and left handed. Had we come down in the jungle and used our own revolvers against the Japs I fear that I would have lost face, followed in rapid succession by my life, for I had eased off the tension in the trigger spring in order to be able to shoot faster. I did not realise that this also had the effect of reducing the force with which the hammer strikes the percussion cap and very few rounds would have fired. I know this because I tried firing this revolver some months later!

David Johnson was given a Japanese pamphlet that had been dropped to some American marines. It allegedly gave one an amnesty if you followed the instructions as follows:

1. Come towards our lines waving a white flag.
2. Strap your gun over your left shoulder muzzle down and pointing behind you.
3. Show this ticket to the sentry.
4. Any number of you may surrender using this one ticket.

Then followed some Japanese characters followed by the words, 'Sing your way to peace, pray for peace.'

Accompanying was a description by a Marine of exactly how 'kind' the Japs had been to the Americans and their allies.

David also received an evaluation of the flight characteristics of the Japanese Zero fighter. Suffice it to say the Zero was superior to any Allied fighter for the first two years of the Pacific war.

I had some trouble with my aircraft on the next flight. I turned into wind on the runway, opened the throttle and on becoming airborne put my hand down to raise the undercarriage. The wheels came up, which was normal; what was not normal was the sudden blow like a wet smack that I received in my left eye. Not knowing what the substance was, my first thought was 'oil' and I told Bob to stand by for an emergency landing and to inform the control tower. In the meantime I investigated the substance further and checked my instruments. I found that the liquid was hydraulic fluid and it was coming out of a pipe on the port side of the aircraft. I turned downwind at a suitable height and started to pump the wheels down by hand. First the starboard wheel came down, then the port, and I ceased pumping with a sigh of relief as the undercarriage indicator needle touched bottom. On the approach to land I remembered that the flaps were also on the hydraulic system, but exhausted from pumping I said to myself, 'To hell with this, no more pumping, I'll land without flaps'. Observing this attitude caused me to float half way down the runway before touching down, cheered on by the tower controller who told me to keep going as I was nearly down. Owing to the lack of flaps I touched down several times before I finally landed! After landing I was turning to port when I smelled burning and at the same time Bob told me to get off the runway and stop at once. We found that the tail wheel had not come down and that the rear of the fuselage was scraping along on the ground. On stopping, two fire engines and an ambulance came alongside; fortunately none of them was needed. I wiped fluid from my eyes and face and tried to mop up slightly. On examining the aircraft I found that little damage had been done and after telephoning the control tower to thank the controller for his help I went to the dispensary to bathe my eyes.

Next day nine of our aircraft went to Maui to carry out a dummy attack on Pearl, together with many American squadrons. Bob and I were to night fly that evening so did not go, and were able to watch the attack. Martlets and P40s 'fought' it out overhead while Avengers and Dauntless bombers made dive and glide bombing attacks. What I thought was the last attack was made by the Dauntless aircraft which came down one after the other on the ships in harbour; they did it well and would have made difficult targets for flak. I was wondering which of the Avengers were ours, for with similar markings they were impossible to distinguish from the American ones, when suddenly the most spectacular attack of the day took place – and it was our boys doing it! They came in low from the opposite direction to anyone else and bombed and fished the harbour and then beat up the aerodrome and our quarters. Very spectacular and very satisfying to watch!

Our night flying programme was not going too well. Either the flares did not work properly, or the radar did not pick up the target, or the aircraft were not able to get into the correct formation.

One night we tried some simulated deck landings at Barber's Point, but owing to the proximity of the hangars on the particular approach that we were using, the exercise was not very satisfactory. On the way back to Ford Island the army shone searchlights on me four times and finally I picked my transmitter and said: 'Ida Control from 4V. Are these searchlights *really* necessary? Over.' Back came the reply: '4V from Ida.

An Avenger of 832 Squadron about to become airborne.

Sorry, I have no control over the searchlights. Out.' The CO, Lieutenant-Commander Lucas, was able to be more forthright than I was; his remark to the tower was, 'Why were those searchlights shone on me during my approach? They are extremely dangerous and unnecessary.' Later the army telephoned and apologised.

The next night practice torpedo attack was unusual for me in that I found the formation fairly quickly. Having got into position I was then told to lead the strike owing to another aircraft becoming unserviceable. As I had never led a strike by day, let alone by night, this might have proved exciting for all concerned, but as we never found the target I was not put to the test.

I was told, how true this was I don't know, that some of the ship's crew were near mutiny, having compared their miserable quarters with those of the Americans. This was probably an exaggeration and all they were doing was having a jolly good moan. I remarked in my diary that I could not say I blamed them! I suppose the worst inconvenience they had to suffer in the Pacific – both on this trip and the later voyage to the Pacific – was the unbearable heat aboard the ship, especially as the steel flight deck would accumulate heat during the day and radiate it downwards during the night.

I had a letter from my father who surmised, correctly, that I was in America to pick up new aircraft. He hoped I was not in the Pacific!

One of the most boring jobs we had to do was flying the aircraft while the air gunner had practice in firing at a drogue, and one morning I rose at 0545 hours in order to fly to Barber's Point and to work from there during the day as Ford Island was going to be used for a fighter exercise. Someone had boobed, however, and we had to return to Ford Island at 1000 hours to carry on from there. I tossed a coin with Ron Hallam as to who was to lead one particular sortie. I lost and got prepared to lead John Stringleman in 4D and Ken Smith and his observer, Reg Highland, in 4M. The latter aircraft was to tow the drogue. Everything seemed to go wrong. First I had to wait for ammunition for the turret; then white smoke started to come from my engine cowl. After investigation I was told it was all right to fly. While this was happening the crews of the other two aircraft got fed up and taxied past to take off. Five minutes later I was ready and taxied down the side of the extremely wide Ford Island runway. I reached the end and waited for a green light from the tower. Then on the radio I heard, 'Ida control from 4 Dog, 4 Mike has gone down in flames.' When there was no reply this was repeated. Then the tower came back and said that the position of 4M was located.

I went back to the crew room and informed Bill Bailey the chief observer what had happened and then went to speak to John Stringleman who had just landed. He was as white as a sheet, and no wonder. He said that an American Corsair had hit 4M in mid-air and the two aircraft had exploded. He had felt the heat from the explosion in his own aircraft. Ken and Reg and the pilot of the Corsair were certain casualties, and had probably known nothing about it. John said that he had seen the Corsair turn towards them and had assumed that it was going to beat them up, but it had straightened up and dived straight at them.

Next day, in brilliant sunshine, a funeral service was held in Oahu cemetery among the soft green of the Hawaiian hills for our two officers and the American, a Captain of the US Marines. It began with a slow march by all the mourners, the escort and the firing party to the graveside. The padre read the service and the Royal Marines fired their volleys. The British party then stepped back and the Americans held their service. It was all very impressive and very sad.

I had to sort out Ken Smith's things. Like me he kept a diary, unfortunately it was full of service stuff that was secret so I had to destroy it. He had a gift for writing that I did not possess. He wrote a short story depicting an attack by the squadron on an enemy fleet. He also wrote poems.

As regards diary writing it was, of course, forbidden. Nevertheless down through the ages men have kept diaries in wartime; without them history would have been less interesting. In my case I kept one mainly because, with my parents living in the Argentine, I was unable to tell them of my doings; if I were killed at least they could read about my experiences. To safeguard them I always took a diary back to Chipstead with me when I went on leave and then started a new notebook on my return.

The Vic put to sea on 12 April for some trials and Bob and I had to do a radio exercise for its benefit. We stooged around at 14,000 feet and I used oxygen for the first time. This might seem strange to present-day pilots but then we seldom ventured much above 10,000 feet for long.

I wrote in my diary, 'The film In Which We Serve was shown one evening in the officers' quarters. I had seen it before in London, but I went to see it again. Never before had the difference in the American and British outlook been so clearly demonstrated to me. The Americans laughed at all the wrong places and their laughter often drowned a good joke, and others they missed. Sorry if I appear rude to the Yanks, I expect they said the same thing about us.' Having written that in 1943, I must say that nowadays some of the American TV humour appeals to me more than some of the British. Our programmes have deteriorated in the last few decades.

The Vic put to sea for exercises and the squadron took the opportunity of carrying out a practice torpedo attack on her. Our fighter planes took to the air as well, one squadron acting as our escort and the second defending the target. Before we reached the ship the opposing fighters 'attacked' us. There had not been such a melee of aircraft around us for many a long day and matters got so out of hand the CO of our escorting fighters, Lieutenant Shaw, called out on the R/T, 'Black Base from 7 Leader. For God's sake call off your chickens unless you want another death around here'. I did not hear this remark at the time because my accumulator went flat and both intercom and radio were not working. We had to carry out the attack as best we could without those aids. On the way home I went down low on the water and flew at full boost and maximum RPM to check the airspeed obtainable. We reached 200 knots, a paltry speed by today's standards, but quite impressive to me at the time. I did not appreciate how much fuel this high speed would require and just before reaching land my engine coughed gently, I glanced at the fuel gauge and saw that it read zero. I swiftly changed tanks and all was well. The short period of high speed flying had caused the engine to use 143 gallons of fuel in 1¼ hours' flying – about twice the normal consumption, and three times the consumption for flight in maximum endurance conditions.

Trying to keep cool in the aircraft in this climate was very difficult. Most of the time I was sitting in a pool of sweat and I could feel it dripping down my chest and under my clothes.

On another operation practice we had a rendezvous with some Dauntless dive bombers for a combined attack on the 'Vic'. We formed up over Lanai and then headed towards the target climbing to 14,000 feet as we went. We were 'attacked' by fighters and were probably all shot down in theory if not, fortunately, in practice. Over the target we started our dive, initially maintaining our 'V' formation in sub flights. I thought: 'Line astern at last. Thank God, my neck's stiff through looking to the right at the leader. Faster! Trim that stick over to starboard. Frank is turning now, pull her over, *heave*. The controls are extremely heavy at this speed. Ah! He's straightening out. That's better, a nice straight dive now. Watch for fighters. Have I gone deaf? I can't hear a thing. You idiot, you've forgotten to blow out your ears. Pop, crackle. That's better, but that hurt. No fighters around now, Petrol? Enough to last for some time. Switches all made. 3,000 feet. Frank must be going for the starboard side; yes he's turning in. Open bomb doors. Turn in with him. 900 feet. Damn, the ship was turning all the time and it's the port side Frank was going for. Hell! Now I'm on the bow. Only one thing for it – turn 90° bank, pull back, back. Blast that destroyer! Throttle back and lose height. Now we are round again and the ship has turned into position for us. Lovely! Watch that height. 150 feet that's fine. Distance OK now. Press the tit.

Now get away. Watch for aircraft and destroyers'. I spoke aloud: 'I hope we would not have to do that on a real attack, Bob.' 'Yes, I hope not too. I could have dropped a brick on that destroyer!'

On yet another attack the fighters were able to follow us down and we had to do some tight turns to avoid them. One fighter dived through the formation from behind and then carried out a steep turn right in front of the CO's plane. I saw the aircraft give a sudden jerk (Bill Bailey in the rear of the aircraft was looking out of the blister at the time and received quite a whack). I gripped the controls and waited. Then it came. It was not like hitting ordinary slipstream, it was more like the proverbial brick wall, and the sudden jolt and bang seemed to nearly shake the engine out of the fuselage. Bob piped up from the rear: 'Bloody fool, I could have shot him down all the time he was making his approach.' 'Yes, I could have got him with my front gun too.' I replied. Our attack on the ship was remarkable as all the Avengers arrived on the water simultaneously while all the fighters were milling around. The CO said it was the most dangerous attack he had ever seen. Commander Mitchell, USN, declared it was the *best* attack he had ever seen!

A few days later the ship excelled herself by shooting down a Queen Bee, or pilotless target aircraft. Apparently the Queen Bee was a careworn old thing that had been diving on US ships for years, had been fired at thousands of times and never been badly damaged. This time it started a dive from 10,000 feet, was hit plumb on the nose by one of our shells and had come down in flames. The Americans were not a little upset at the loss of their toy!

Night flying continued. We were making gradual progress. My big moan on one flight was that I was flying on the inside of a large formation; when the formation turned, my aircraft was flying too slowly to maintain flying speed and tended to stall, an experience which modern pilots in their fast aircraft never undergo. At last, however, the time came when we seemed to have everything right: we all formed up correctly; the radar worked; we found the target and carried out a brilliant simulated attack. I even had time to carry out a second run on the target, for practice, and came in nicely with the help of radar. We all landed with our morale sky high.

As the time for our departure from Hawaii grew nearer we were given a short survival course in Honolulu. We were taught what fish and fruits to eat. We learned that all shellfish were edible. The marvels of the coconut trees were explained to us in such detail that we felt that given one tree we could almost make a radio out of it. The keener ones debated how to distil alcohol from coconut milk! We were informed that sharks were more frightened of us than we were of them (except one kind of shark) and that one way of scaring them was to put one's head under water and stare at them! We hoped that all sharks had been briefed with this bit of information!

One of the most interesting restaurants in Oahu was TRADER VIC'S situated between Honolulu and Waikiki, and John Burbidge, Bob Procter, Boris Morris and I repaired there one day. It was a bar-cum-restaurant constructed to look like an old South Seas trading station. The entire building was made from coconut trees and leaves and decorated inside and out with native tools and implements from the South Seas. It was an impressive place with loads of atmosphere. Possibly it would not make such an impact nowadays for TRADER VIC'S restaurants have spread even to London. We had an excellent meal and each of us received a souvenir certificate entitling us to 'full trading privileges'.

After the meal Bob and I drove into the mountains to solve the mystery of The Upsidedown Falls. We had heard the name, but no other details. Before arriving there we visited a high point where people had jumped over to commit suicide. We were told that sometimes the wind was so strong that their fall had been broken and they had walked away unhurt. When we reached The Upsidedown Falls we found that water came over the edge of a high rock – and then got thrown up into the air by a strong wind, hence the name.

One of the attractions of Waikiki is, of course, the surfboarding. As a beginner I used the small body board and had quite a lot of fun. No way was I going to be good enough to use the bigger board and I certainly would not have had time to gain experience and stand up. Unfortunately I cut my foot on a piece of coral and knew nothing about it until I went ashore and found blood pouring from it. Luckily there was an efficient US Navy corpsman standing by and he saw to my needs. Strangely, some 50 years later I was on Waikiki beach and I dived in and hit my ankle on a piece of rock. But in this day and age there was no efficient First Aid man to attend to me and I lay on the beach whilst my wife, Dorothy had to go and fetch help. It was only later that my memory from those far off days returned and I recalled that someone had remarked that in that particular part of the beach there were rocks. Why were there no warning signs?

Two other memories of Waikiki stand out. In 1943 there were only two hotels there – The Moana and the Royal Hawaiian. Nowadays the hotels stretch all along the beach. The other memory is of getting off a bus there and finding someone filming me. I ignored him and tried to look natural. I wondered vaguely whether he was an amateur or professional, but thought I would never find out. To my astonishment, years late, I was watching a TV film (*The War At Sea* if I recall correctly) when suddenly

'Jeff' Jefford and Sidney Price.

The author and Andy Anderson.

Bill Hughes.

1943. Hawaii. At Trader Vics. John Fay, John Burbidge, Boris Morris and Bob Procter.

1943. Some members of 832 Squadron.

this scrawny-looking Sub-Lieutenant (A) RNVR appeared on the screen, getting off a bus!

Our CO disappeared quite suddenly. Unknown to us he was an alcoholic. Apparently he was rude to the Captain who promptly sent him back to Britain. Frank Low took over as CO. He was one of the best COs I ever had: he was approachable and knew his job backwards. He was RN and so had been flying for considerably longer than any of us.

When passing her one day I was able to get a look at the Vic. There was quite a difference! She had been painted a blue-grey colour and there were no less than 14 Oerlikons on the starboard side alone, and there were some 40mm cannon, which were an innovation to us. The passageway outboard of the island and at flight deck level had been pushed out and fitted with six or seven Oerlikons. The goofers' platform also had two but there was still some room for 'goofing'.

On 3 May I was in the air a total of 6 hours 10 minutes, a record for me, and possibly the squadron. Apart from a positioning flight to Ewa I did an ALT and then a night shadowing exercise, this time with Derek Pearson and LA Smith. An observer once described Derek as 'the cleverest man I know'; small wonder then that Derek did well in the Civil Service after the war.

Frank Low and Johnny Randall. CO and Senior Pilot.

The first Avenger landings on board the ship since the modifications were carried out revealed the fact that the arrester wires were now too resistant and that the damping must be eased off to avoid possible damage to the aircraft. Since first writing about these times I have been informed by Ron Hallam that there was another cause of accidents: the arrester wires had too large a diameter, consequently the arrester hook would grip the cable instead of sliding along it as would occur in the case of the aircraft landing with a slight yaw. Thinner cable solved that problem. Ship and squadron exercises continued apace after this was done, with the emphasis on day and night torpedo attacks. We also carried out night shadowing exercises; radar was invaluable here as, generally, the only thing visible in the blackness was the ship's wake, and if this was found without radar it was by sheer luck. Our night torpedo attacks were becoming consistently good; Frank Low, dropping the flares very skilfully.

On 7 May our aircraft were loaded on to the *Victorious* from the dockside and our baggage taken on board in the evening. We left harbour early next morning on a cloudless day. Slowly we passed between Ford Island and the main Pearl Harbor docks. Ahead of us was the USS *North Carolina* also moving out. We acknowledged her salute. There were few people about, but a band on shore played us out. We passed from the harbour and moved into the wide Pacific. But where to now, we wondered?

At 1030 hours the captain told us we were on our way to Noumea in New Caledonia. Later in the day we passed the USS *Enterprise* and the USS *Washington*, although they were too far away for us to see them. The *Enterprise* was returning home for a long overdue refit. The *Washington* and I were old friends as I had once sailed in her from Scapa to Iceland as mentioned previously.

On 10 May after a long A/S patrol, during which I left much of the flying to the Automatic Pilot, I thought my landing was a bit ropey, but I was surprised at the number of people who said it was good. Even my TAG said, 'Nice landing, Sir'. I was also complimented after the next flight and thought I would soon be getting a swollen head!

On 11 May we crossed the equator. The Navigating Officer spoke over the broadcaster: 'We are now crossing the equator. This is the third time the ship has done so'. Our eyebrows shot up. Then came the explanation: 'We crossed it for the first time today when on course, then again when turning back into wind to land on aircraft'.

Next morning I was awakened early to carry out the first anti-submarine patrol. I had a very unusual accident, not a flying one this time. I came out of the 'island' in semi-darkness and walked aft towards the Pilots' and Observers' Waiting Room. All of a sudden I felt myself being lifted into the air. My first thought was 'God, the ship must have hit a mighty big wave to be pitching such a lot!' The thought must have lasted about half a second, then I was elevated five feet up into the air and thrown forward on to the deck. A clanking sound behind me revealed the trouble: one of the crash barriers had been raised just as I stepped on it. I had come out of the 'island' so quickly that the Petty Officer operating it had not got time to stop it coming up during a test. Luckily I was not hurt. Upon reflection I think I was lucky. If the barrier had come up a fraction of a second before or after I would have been thrown backwards or had my spine injured. Worse, if I had been stepping across the barrier it would have come up between my legs.

Just before lunch I was watching some Martlets land-on. One aircraft had its arrester hook torn out and it careered along the port side of the flight deck and then went over the side. The aircraft dinghy came out and after a few seconds the pilot appeared. He was not hurt.

I wrote in my diary: 'Today is Friday the 14th May, tomorrow is Sunday the 16th' for the ship was crossing the International Date Line. On the return voyage I was to fly on the day *after* August 2nd and it was still August 2nd!

On one of the anti-submarine searches that took my aircraft one hundred and fifty miles ahead of the ship I spotted two objects floating on the water and giving off smoke. To see anything at all in the ocean was unusual so I approached warily. The enigma was solved when I suddenly realised that they were smoke floats dropped by another aircraft to find the wind velocity.

About 15% of the squadron aircrew consisted of New Zealanders, and this figure probably held true throughout the Fleet Air Arm at the time. If the other officers were not originally familiar with New Zealand words, as I was from boyhood, they quickly became acquainted with the terms *kiwi, Maori, Haka*, etc. So when Lieutenant-Commander Webb gave a short talk on the broadcaster on the subject of the French Island of New Caledonia and mentioned kiwis, we thought we knew what was coming. He said: 'Among the fauna to be found on New Caledonia is the kiwi'. Pause. 'A bird normally found on the lid of boot polish tins!'

After a week's voyage we arrived at Noumea in New Caledonia. The ship's company lined the flight deck for entering harbour and the Royal Marine Band marched up and down the deck. We probably looked smart and efficient but it was all wasted, as the nearest ship was the aircraft carrier USS *Saratoga*, which was over half a mile away. Initially we were rather surprised at how small the 'Sara' (as she was affectionately called) appeared, but this was deceptive as close to she was enormous.

American forage caps were cooler and more comfortable than the normal ones and many officers wore them. Here they are being 'modelled' by the author, who is striking a pose, and by John Herbert a fighter pilot of 896 Squadron. The white ensign on the tail of the Martlet was the only indication that it belonged to a British Squadron. John Herbert's photograph is from his collection.

Noumea was not a large town and was quickly explored. We met and talked with many people including one American who had Irish parents. He said he had been taught from birth to hate the English, but he didn't. One surprise was to find Ron Spackman in Noumea. He was a New Zealander who had been with me since the first day of training – and had been taken ill with dysentery in Hawaii. He was now en route for home for sick leave. I thought him one of the luckiest men alive, for on the morrow he would be back in the land I had always wanted to revisit.

Bob Procter had made friends with an American Warrant Officer, an engineer. Barker was his name and he was a member of the crew of the *Saratoga* and he invited us round the ship. There were several points of interest that we would have done well to emulate in the Royal Navy. The neatness of the flight deck was one case in point: all the objects such as barriers and wire raisers lay flush with the deck as near as possible; another was the lifts, although ours had the advantage of being faster they were not nearly large enough. Their hangar was wider than ours and it was a lot higher and they were able to save space by hoisting some aircraft up to the roof. They did this with fighter aircraft but not with Avengers. I was surprised to learn the principle of the ship's engines: they are steam turbines, yes, but the turbines turn dynamos, which in turn supply current to the electric motors connected to the propeller shafts. This is the same sort of principle as our diesel-electric trains.

1943. The USS *Saratoga.*

After dinner in the Warrant Officers' mess we went into the hangar, which was used as a theatre. Artie Shaw was a CPO in the US Navy and first of all we had to endure one and a half hours of music by his band. I'm afraid I did not like his sort of music, especially as in this case the bad acoustics in the hangar made the sounds into a cacophony. Afterwards we were shown a film *Stand By For Action*. It was quite a good film but the sound reproduction was poor.

Our stay in Noumea was short-lived. Two days after our arrival there was a mild flap and the battle fleet (or to use the new and less inspiring idiom the *Task Force*) put to sea. The fleet consisted of the aircraft carriers HMS *Victorious* and USS *Saratoga*, the battleships USS *North Carolina*, USS *Indiana* and eleven destroyers.

The *Saratoga* landed-on sixty aircraft in forty-five minutes, watched intently by all of us. This done, the force headed for the Coral Sea where we might possibly meet the Japanese fleet, apparently it had sailed northwards from Truk but could turn south and into our area.

We sent off nine aircraft on anti-submarine patrols later and they landed after lunch. This was the first time our aircraft had carried out any landings in full view of the *Saratoga* and we were anxious as to how they would go. I watched from the goofers' platform and was in mental agony when the deck was clear and the ship into the wind before the aircraft were in position, but every aircraft landed well and we had them all aboard in seven minutes which compared well with the Americans. Later that day I was watching some of our Martlets landing-on. There was a misunderstanding when one of them wanted an emergency landing and the others did not realise it, but all was well until ... it happened! A Martlet landed. As it touched down its guns went off due to an electrical fault. I was down like lightning behind a metal shield, not that this action would have helped me much for any bullets coming my way would have hit me before I had had time to move. It was thought at first that the shots had passed over the flight deck and gone into the sea without doing any damage, but it quickly transpired that, in fact, three people were hit, one of them being the Navigating Officer. The bullets apparently ricocheted round Commander Flying's platform before hitting him. He was not badly hurt.

The Japanese fleet did not turn south, and our task force headed back for Noumea. I carried out one more anti-submarine patrol before arriving, using the automatic pilot for quite a long time on this occasion. The observer was able to use the system to a limited degree from the rear cockpit and instead of saying 'Stand by to turn on to 210°', Bob was delighted to be able to say, 'Stand by *to be turned* on to 210°'! On this particular flight my electrical system went unserviceable and we re-

From the collection of John W. Herbert

A damaged Martlet is removed from the ship by lighter.

turned to the ship early. After landing, my arrester hook, which is electrically operated, would not retract and a rating had to run behind the aircraft holding it clear of the arrester wires as I taxied up the deck. I went too quickly for him and Commander Flying shouted over his amplifier 'Slow down'. I could not hear what he was saying, but hearing the note of urgency in his voice and thinking that another plane was coming in to land behind me I accelerated forward. The man holding the hook fell flat on his face!

We spent a few days in Noumea visiting other ships and generally enjoying ourselves and had one exercise at sea for three days, then the squadron disembarked to Tontouta, an American airfield about 40 miles from Noumea. I was one of the party that travelled there by open lorry. I wisely took my flying goggles with me, for the dust was thick and blinding; before long I was getting cash offers for them! The first part of the journey lay through green country round steep bends and winding roads. Then it led into the mountains and became, according to the notices, a *'route tortueuse'*, as indeed it was. There was a bend every hundred yards and more often than not a steep drop to one side. The country was no place to try a forced landing and I resolved that if I had an engine failure over that area I would bale out. Houses were few and far between, but in the middle of nowhere there was, of all places, a laundry! At last the road reached flat country and before long we arrived at a row of tents. These were our quarters! That part of the squadron that had arrived the previous day were already busy carpentering and making all kinds of fittings for their temporary homes. After lunch I was allotted a tent, which I shared with Jock Landles and four others. We had blankets and mosquito nets, but despite these we were bitten and worried by insects all night.

So far as ablutions were concerned we had rows of some 22 toilets arranged in the open air. I was not averse to performing in public for at Bradfield the loos had no doors, but some of us were a bit sensitive about it at first. John Burbidge has reminded me that the only difference between the officers' toilets and the ratings' ones was that the officers' ones had lids!

The climate at that time of year was like a hot English summer. Next morning I went along to the local river with Jock Landles, Andy Anderson, Doc Mumford, Derek Pearson and Derek Hill. The river was a bit shallow, making swimming difficult. However, next morning after breakfast of porridge, cake and beans we obtained pack lunches and went on a walking tour. We climbed a hill about 1,000 feet high, went along a ridge, followed a dry river bed for miles – or so it seemed – and after a spot of lunch continued on our way until we found a real river where we were able to swim in water that was very clear and about 30 feet deep. Arch Hugill came along shortly afterwards and told us a truck

An American destroyer is refuelled from HMS *Victorious*.

was about half a mile down river. Jock, Arch and I swam there while the others walked. We came back to base in the truck.

After a few days many of us were sporting beards, without permission. Consequently when some senior officers from the ship came along we made ourselves scarce. Unfortunately I had to go down to the airfield with Derek Hill and John Randall to find some practice bombs. We were waiting for a lift back to our tents when suddenly I spotted a staff car. 'Look out!' I said. 'There's Commander Webb.' The three of us turned our half-bearded faces away from the car and pretended not to see it. As it drew abreast, however, discipline became too strong for us and we saluted with our bearded faces still pointing in the opposite direction! Fortunately the car did not stop, but in another part of the airfield the captain had come along and spotted the beards belonging to Johnny Swift and Arch and told them they were a disgrace to the British Navy!

In between living the lives of Boy Scouts we did do some flying! Among other exercises we tried some skip bombing on an old wreck. We dived from 2,000 feet, levelled out at 50 feet and then released the bombs. Most of us overshot the target at first, but we improved with practice.

Our Avengers were often parked with the wings folded. I was down among the aircraft one day and an Australian private came along. He

Photo: David Johnson

An Avenger taxiing up the deck with wings folded. The pilot could fold and spread the wings mechanically from the cockpit. This was not possible in the Martlet.

gazed at the aircraft for a while and then expressed the view that we must dive at a tremendous speed when the wings were folded like that! We privately hoped that we would never find out.

We were sorry to hear that Lieutenant-Commander Metcalf, the flight deck officer in the Vic, was killed when he was beating up the ship in a Martlet. He got out of control and crashed into the sea. To us he seemed an oldish man (he was probably only about 30!) and was well liked.

Despite being a batsman short following Metcalf's death we had Bill Hughes back in the squadron, much to his delight. He had left the squadron at Norfolk to become a batsman, a job he loathed.

After some days at Tontouta we flew back to the ship, flying along the coast of New Caledonia for about an hour before turning to carry out a practice torpedo attack. We could see how very mountainous the country was, the only flat area being in the Tontouta area. We thought it would be a good thing to get back on board the ship for a while in order to catch up with correspondence, repair the damage the mosquitoes had done and get some clothing, but our stay on board the ship was shorter than expected. After taking off on exercises next morning, the rain came down heavily and due to the poor visibility we had to land at Tontouta, together with several aircraft from the *Saratoga*. Having had no breakfast we had to make do with lunch only. We were then given a message from the ship telling us not to return until next day, and there we were with shoes, socks and flying jackets only! Foolishly I went to an open-air cinema that evening and when it came on to rain I got soaking wet. Next day I had to take off, do an exercise with the *Victorious* and then land-on in my wet things. I was certainly glad to get into something dry.

The consequence of this episode was a week in the sick bay with fever. When I was better I went across to the *Saratoga* with my belongings, for the squadron was to operate from her and two of her fighter squadrons were to be transferred to the *Victorious*. This was the first time a British Squadron had operated from an American carrier and proved quite a news item when given to the press after our return home. I was in a cabin with two Americans: one a Doctor Martin, and the other a gunner. The officers were situated in the forward part of the ship and the ratings aft, so in contrast to living in the Vic we had not got the vibration of the ship's screws to worry us. To balance this, however, the Sara rolled even in a calm sea and I wondered what would happen when the weather got rough.

For the first time I was able to view the Vic from another ship at sea, she looked strong and beautiful and rock steady; when turning, she was like a destroyer, in contrast to the Sara which wallowed round like an unstable floating box.

1943. 832 Squadron aboard the USS *Saratoga*. HMS *Victorious* is in the background.

We were told that the fleet was to be the covering force for an American landing in New Georgia in the Solomons. This meant that we would be in the Coral Sea ready and at hand in case the Japanese fleet put to sea to interfere with the landings; it did not mean that we would take part in the actual offensive.

What I considered at the time to be a crazy practice was the American custom of going to General Quarters (Action Stations) at sunrise. Since the sun rose at 0530 I seemed to spend most of my spare time trying to make up for lost sleep. Another idea we did not like was the fact that there was no separate wardroom anteroom as there was in the Vic. We relaxed and ate in the same room, consequently I might be reading a book or playing cards when along would come a steward to say that he wanted to set up the table. I would move to another table and along would come another steward . . .

Bruce Petrie and his observer Doug Briggs had the squadron's first accident on the Sara when a wave-off was given as the aircraft was touching down. Bruce opened the throttle to go round again but in the meantime his hook had caught an arrester wire and into the sea the aircraft went. At one time we heard that the crew had not been picked up and that the depth charges had gone off, but the depth charges were ones dropped by a destroyer in error and the crew were, in fact, all right.

Next day I had one of the early anti-submarine patrols and I flew off and landed on the Sara for the first time. Compared with the Vic the deck looked enormous. Bob said my landing seemed a heavy one; Jock Landles, who was watching, said that it was the best of the lot, which showed how opinions could differ!

Two days later John Stringleman and his observer went into the sea when their engine failed about ten miles from the ship. The USS *Fanning* picked them up and later that day they were hauled across by breeches buoy, but only after 25 lbs of ice cream had been sent across by way of payment, as was the custom. Little did I know that I should shortly be partaking of that same ice cream!

It all happened early next morning when I was due to do the first anti-submarine patrol. As on another occasion, everything went wrong from the start. First, the seat of my aircraft jammed in the fully down position so that all I could see was the sides and front of the cockpit. It took ten minutes pulling and shoving by an American rating to get it up. While he was doing this he accidentally knocked on my identification light, which displeased the Flight Deck Party as it was fairly dark and the ship was still blacked out. Then I found that my fluorescent light would not work, however, as it was nearly dawn I let that go. The next occurrence might have paralysed me with laughter had I not been in a hurry to taxi to the take-off position. I found that two members of the Flight Deck Party were signalling me into position at the same time. This would have been nothing to worry about except that they were signalling in opposite directions! Whenever I obeyed one man and went in the required direction the other man would wave his arms frantically. When I obeyed *him* the first man would go into apparent paroxysms of rage, I could almost hear him thinking, 'These bloody Limeys'. Fortunately this ludicrous situation did not last and before long I was in the take-off position. There then occurred the incident I mentioned at the very beginning of this book.

A few days later I was watching the take-off of a Dauntless dive bomber belonging to one of the American squadrons. Smoke started coming from the engine, but it became airborne quite easily and the pilot went round for an emergency landing. He did not put his flaps down and received a wave-off from the batsman. He came round again, but after the turn into the 'groove' seemed to be flying slower and slower. All of a sudden the aircraft stalled and crashed into the sea. Someone said that they saw the pilot's head go forward and hit the aiming sight; another said that the pilot never wore shoulder straps as his life had once been saved through not wearing them. Anyway, the air gunner got out but the pilot did not.

For a period, the battleship element of the task force was operating about fifty miles ahead of the aircraft carriers and one day I had to take off and fly to the battleships and carry out an ant-submarine patrol for them. The old Sara had only just turned into wind and so was rolling heavily as I took off. With one exception it was the most frightening take-off I have ever experienced. On part of the take-off run I had not only to use full rudder, but a touch of brake as well in order to keep straight. After becoming airborne we had some trouble with the radio and flew to a position astern of the ship in order to drop a message on the deck and let them know our intentions. Unfortunately, the wind was blowing across from the starboard, which I knew would cause the air over the deck to be very disturbed owing to the unusually large size of the funnel. I did not know it then, but an American pilot had once been caused to crash when dropping a message under similar conditions. I put my flaps down and flew faster and higher than I would normally for a message drop. Even so, no sooner was I abreast of the island when the aircraft was out of control, or nearly so. I opened the throttle fully and eased back the stick and also tried to prevent the wings rocking violently. In a few seconds we were clear of the disturbance but had not dropped the message. We were not going to repeat the performance so Bob started flashing Morse by Aldis lamp. Flashing from the air to American carriers was not normal practice, however, and we were ignored. Shortly after this the radio suddenly became serviceable so we were able to continue the flight.

Some welcome mail arrived aboard the *Saratoga* from home. It had come out from Noumea by destroyer to the *Victorious* and was then flown across from her to the Sara by Avenger. I did not see the landing, if I had my heart would have been in my mouth, not only for the pilot, but for the mail as well, for on touchdown, the arrester hook was torn out and the aircraft continued up the deck, went through all three crash barriers and into five Dauntless dive bombers parked up forward. Fortunately no one was hurt and nothing caught fire. If we had lost our mail I think the pilot would have been keelhauled!

By this time we felt that the ship had started to wear a groove in the Coral Sea, for it had been cruising about in one spot for three weeks and we were becoming more than a little bored.

When Captain Ross (our Commander at the time) read these words he wrote to me the following:

> I have read every word with interest and your narrative weaves in and out of mine in a remarkable way and (naturally) brings out the FAA side. At the point where you speak of wearing a groove in the Coral Sea I actually mention the fact that we wore a hole in the chart literally, as the Navigator showed me. I'm sure it was tactically very unwise as these were the very waters where the *Lexington* was sunk a year before. As for it being an 'interlude' I think I hit on very fundamental reason for the strange lull in the South Pacific. It was while reading of how the Japanese C-in-C Yamamoto was shot down on his way to inspect the fleet in the Solomons that the date struck me. It was 13th April 1943. And we were still working up out of Pearl Harbor. Had he lived on as their sort of combined Nimitz and Lord Nelson, things might have taken a different course.

The Americans in the wardroom were mystified by the fact that on our blackboard some figures had started to appear followed by the words, '. . . more days'. The figures were diminishing by one as each day passed. The board now read '39 more days'. The explanation lay in the fact that one of the squadron wits had informed all and sundry that after 60 days at sea a certain practice between consenting adults (now legalised in Britain) was lawful in the British Navy! Someone had started a countdown!

At last the enemy appeared! One of the American Dauntless pilots spotted a solitary Japanese aircraft called 'a 'Betty' about 50 miles from the fleet. He dived on it, firing his front guns, but apparently did not hit it.

It was about this time that an event took place about which we did not hear until we had returned to our own ship. In poor visibility the *Victorious* and the *Saratoga* were on a collision course, with the former steering straight for the side of the other. This was due to the Sara not zigging or zagging as she should have done. The only man on either ship to see the situation was our Captain Mackintosh, who was on the deck above the compass platform. He shouted down to the officer of the watch: 'Hard a port, full astern port engine!' and somehow a tragedy was averted. If the ships' positions had been transposed nothing could have prevented a collision for the turning circle of the *Saratoga* was considerably inferior to that of the *Victorious*.

The action in New Georgia was proceeding satisfactorily. The interests of the British, however, were centred more on a place thousands of miles away – Sicily, where the Allies had landed. The headlines of the respective ships' newspapers reflected the contrasting view: The Americans put the Sicily item last, almost as an afterthought; the British paper had banner headlines about the landings in Sicily, but events in New Georgia still came second in importance.

Our morale suddenly rose when we heard that we were on our way back to Noumea, but our hopes were dashed when a few hours later some sort of flap arose and plans for our return were cancelled. The *Victorious* began to get somewhat short of food and some dehydrated potatoes were flown across to her. We ourselves, temporarily living in a well-stocked ship, had eggs for breakfast every day; in the *Victorious* at sea we had about one per week. Our living quarters in the *Saratoga* were not, however, as pleasant as they were in the *Victorious*; the fact that the paint, which was a fire risk, had been stripped off the walls of the wardroom and other living space did nothing to keep one's spirits up. A day or two later we really did set course for Noumea and anchored again in the harbour.

Squadron personnel were transferred back to the *Victorious* where, after being in a dry ship for 28 days, severe inroads were made into the bar stocks and an impromptu party was held.

I reproduce here three items of correspondence that passed between Captain Mullinnix, Captain of the *Saratoga*, Admiral Ramsey and Captain Mackintosh:

In reply, address   USS SARATOGA
Commanding Office USS Saratoga and refer to

CV3/A4-3
(700)(10-hr)July 24, 1943.

From: The Commanding Officer.
To: The Commanding Officer, HMS VICTORIOUS.
Via: The Commander Task Force FOURTEEN.

Subject: Operations of 832 Squadron, Fleet Air Arm,
Period 27 June to 24 July inclusive, 1943.

1. During the past four weeks Squadron 832 has operated from this ship as a unit of the SARATOGA Air Group. Availability of the 'Tarpons' of that squadron increased the potential striking power of the Air Group very materially. Routine daily operations were conducted with gratifying precision and efficiency, in both fair and foul weather.

2. Close association with the officers and men of 832 Squadron in this ship has been most pleasant. The SARATOGA is happy to have been host to them. The bearing of the Royal Navy personnel has reflected the leadership and engaging personality of the squadron commander, Acting Lieutenant-Commander (A) R.N.Low. The Commanding Officer takes pleasure in congratulating you, and the officers and men of 832 Squadron, especially Lieutenant-Commander Low, upon the operating proficiency and high morale prevailing in that unit.

H.M. MULLINNIX.
UNITED STATES PACIFIC FLEET
    TASK FORCE FOURTEEN   (tin)

Serial 131

Recd. July 26 1943
FIRST ENDORSEMENT to
    CO SARATOGA ltr. CV3/.
A4-3/(700)(10hr) of
July 24, 1943.

From: Commander Task Force FOURTEEN.
To: Commanding Officer, HMS VICTORIOUS.

Subject: Operations of 832 Squadron, Fleet Air Arm,
Period 27 June to 24 July, inclusive, 1943

The personnel referred to by Captain Mullinnix also were under my intimate observation during the period of their duty in the SARATOGA. It is a pleasure to me to fully endorse his remarks. The officers and men of the VICTORIOUS adapted themselves so smoothly and efficiently to the operations and routine of the SARATOGA that the only distinguishing feature to me was their uniforms.

I was particularly pleased to hold several interesting conversations with Lieutenant Commander Low who obviously is a squadron leader and an officer of the highest type.

D.C.Ramsey

No. 190/5207

Second Endorsement

From: The Commanding Officer, H.M.S.Victorious
To: THE COMMANDING OFFICER, 832 NAVAL AIR SQUADRON

I am very gratified to receive such a good report, and congratulate you
and your Squadron.

(L.D. Mackintosh)

Note that we were still calling our aircraft 'Tarpons' at that time.

Back aboard the Vic – and how good it seemed being surrounded by
Britishness once more – we made severe inroads into the bar. After all
we had been in a dry ship for a month. We had a singsong round the
piano and Jeff Jefford and John Randall made up some witty songs! John
had one about 'Who pranged 4 George?' to the tune of 'Who killed Cock
Robin'. 4 George being the aircraft in which he had his crash. A lot of
the banter was anti-American and I just hoped that if any of the
Americans heard us they would not take offence; it was just our way of
having fun. I expect they had plenty to be witty about when they
returned from any British establishment

We had a visit from the American Admiral who was going to higher
things in Washington. Both he and Captain Mackintosh made good
amusing speeches. Next day the Captain requested our company in the
evening. We thought we were going to have a gen session but it turned
out to be a small party. The Captain asked me about my accident. He
said he had seen it and that it looked horrible. I can't remember my reply
but no doubt I said that it *felt* horrible too!

17

THE VOYAGE HOME

On 31 July the *Victorious* set sail for Pearl with 53 American Officers aboard as passengers. Our task was done and we were on the first leg of our journey back to Britain. Avengers from the *Saratoga*'s squadrons came along to beat us up as we departed. Their show was rather marred by the fact that two of the aircraft collided! Fortunately it was only a case of the propeller of one aircraft taking bits off the tail of another, and bits of metal fluttered down round the ship. Then the fighters came in and gave an impressive, if nail-biting display.

In addition to our American passengers we had two Japanese prisoners of war on board. It might be thought ironic that after the immense effort that went into transferring a British carrier to the Pacific the only enemy with whom contact was made were prisoners of war. It must be remembered, however, that in strategy mere presence and availability can achieve much. The *Victorious* had been part of the US Fleet during the vital interval that occurred just before new US carriers were entering the Pacific to replace ones that had either been sunk or were badly overdue for a refit. It is doubtful whether the landings in New Georgia could have taken place without the covering force of which the *Victorious* was a vital part, alternatively operations elsewhere might have been curtailed or postponed as other units of the fleet were stretched to fill the gap.

Prior to leaving for the Pacific the *Victorious* had crossed swords with the enemy in other oceans. On her second trip to the Far East she saw much action. In between these and on this deployment she steamed from Britain to the Coral Sea and back without sighting the enemy. For her it was truly a Pacific Interlude.

From Honolulu we went to San Diego. Since the possibility of being torpedoed by a submarine was now minimal we were allowed to sleep in our cabins.

On a beach at San Diego. John Burbidge, Guy Richardson and an American boy.

From the collection of John W. Herbert

1943. A US Navy Blimp flies over HMS *Victorious* as she approaches San Diego.

As the ship approached San Diego we were wearing white cap covers over our normal dark blue ones and as we stood there for entering harbour we all looked extremely smart after wearing khaki for so long. We were beaten up by blimps doing a full 40 knots, which gave us a laugh. During the entry into the rather long harbour we were overtaken by a string of US destroyers and only one gave us a salute by calling the hands to attention. To starboard of us was the Naval Air Station and was alongside here that we eventually docked.

The NAS itself was on an island and the quickest way into San Diego was to go over by ferry. John Burbidge, Guy Richardson, Roger Kerrison and I went ashore. We were approached by a negro and wondered why.

He said, 'Are you gentlemen seeking transportation?'

We went straight to the Coronado Hotel as A types are wont to do. To our surprise we were told that they could not serve service men with alcohol until 5.0 p.m. The barman said he was allowed to serve beer, but he had not got any! A civilian told us that the law applied to all the western states. John remarked that if happened in England there would be a revolution! We found a little place down the road.

'Have you any beer?'

'Yes we do, but only in quart bottles.'

As if *that* mattered!

I had never seen so many pretty girls to the square mile in my life and wondered whether it was because we had been at sea so long! However, on analysis I realised that expert make-up was part of the picture. Even so I retained for life this image of so much beauty and when many decades later I remarked to an American lady about it, she diplomatically said, 'It's because the men are so handsome!'

Next day John Burbidge, Guy Richardson and I went swimming from the beach. A boy of about 12 called Eddie Kimble joined us. He was a bright young spark whose main idea of being with us was to get our wings! His father was in the new USS *Lexington* and he said that his father told him two months ago that a British carrier would be coming there at this time.

So much for security!

We were told (fortunately *after* our swim) that we should be careful where we stepped as there were stingrays about.

We sailed next day at 1400 hours with the Royal Marine band playing us away.

On an A/S patrol I also had to give the ship some practice in giving D/F bearings. I flew with Sub-Lieutenant George Watson (Bob being on watch), and LA Kinghan. The bearings were hopeless and we managed to get lost because of this. I remarked in my diary, 'God help us if we ever needed a real D/F bearing!' In the end we had to use the beacon to get back to the ship. George told the operator that the bearings were no good and that his Morse was poor anyway! He then got a bottle from Lieutenant-Commander A.S. Webb because any messages sent to the ship were officially addressed to the Captain and George was being rude to him! This is a similar situation to that which occurred when we were in the Home Fleet: one of our pilots, Sub-Lieutenant Reid sent a message that the ship was making black smoke. He received a ticking off from the Captain. Ever afterwards he was referred to as, 'Black smoke Reid!'

An amusing incident occurred when I flew later with Bob Procter. After tracking a ship by its wake we found the ship and I read its name – **Fort Yukon**. I told Bob and he thought I said 421 and wondered why I was trying to read the flags, and wrongly at that! I did a solo ALT and took a photograph with the torpedo camera from 500 yards. We then flew back to the ship and dropped a message on the deck. Shortly after this I had a leak from the hydraulic pressure gauge and landed early before things got worse.

While in the Canal we were told that no fewer than 18 carriers had passed through since our last visit in February.

We went through the locks in the Panama Canal and eventually arrived at Cristobal where we were permitted to go ashore. We stayed only one night but had a riotous time for just a few hours before leaving next day for Norfolk, Virginia. Once again, as we were in a proper war zone we had to sleep in dormitories rather than our cabins.

On 31 August despite heavy rain and thunder and lightning we sent off two aircraft on an A/S patrol. With a decrease in visibility it was decided to bring them back. However, only one aircraft arrived and it was assumed that the other aircraft had got lost and had set course for America some 300 miles away.

We arrived at Norfolk next day and found that this aircraft, with Smith and Bill Thomson on board had, indeed, arrived in America safely. The Naval Air Station was not expecting us and, indeed, had no room for our aircraft or the crews. We were told that we would go to Willow Grove near Philadelphia instead.

The *Indomitable* was in port. She caught a fish off Sicily and was to be in Norfolk for some time being repaired. I paid a visit in the evening and was surprised how luxurious she was compared with the *Victorious*. There was more space everywhere and she seemed much more comfortable. And the Vic was supposed to be her sister ship!

We rose early next day and went by ship's boat to the NAS. This was unusual as this was the first time I had travelled by that means of transport from ship to a NAS. Once again we caught the ferry to Cape

Charles where we boarded the train for Philadelphia. On our arrival there we were struck by the beauty of the railway station and thought that it would serve as a good template for some of our stations in Britain. We had some time to wait so as usual we finished up in a bar. Some free drinks arrived rather mysteriously and by careful observation we discovered that a lady sitting behind us was the kind donor. Kennedy and I went over to thank her. She said she loved listening to our accent and had missed her train because of it. She was a very pleasant and motherly sort of person.

We eventually climbed into the bus that was going to take us to Willow Grove Naval Air Station, which is about 25 miles north of Philadelphia. We sang squadron songs from our departure point to one end of Philadelphia. Then the driver discovered he was going the wrong way so we sang all the way back again. We hoped the inhabitants of the city could not hear the words of the songs!

We arrived at 0100 hours next morning and tumbled thankfully into bed at the BOQ (Batchelor Officers' Quarters).

On 4 September we were split into two groups for leave. John Barnes and I went off to New York, booking into the Barbizon Plaza once again. We ran into Brian Shaw who had remained in the ship but was on leave from there so we had dinner together. John and I saw the play, *The Skin of our Teeth*, which we did not like much, but it must have been successful for it came to London later on.

Next day after breakfast in bed as before (the breakfast is shoved through a slot in the door) we went to The Museum of Natural Science at the Rockefeller Centre, just as I had done in January. I could not resist seeing my beloved Rockettes again so off I went to Radio City. Years later when I heard that my niece was going to visit Radio City I wrote to her and told her to give my love to Susie. She wrote back, ' Susie didn't remember you!'

Next day John and I thought we ought to 'do' New York as tourists so we went downtown in the morning and gazed through the haze at the Statue of Liberty, went to Staten Island on a ferry, had two minutes there and came back on the same ferry inspecting the Manhattan skyline and did all the other things tourists do.

John went off to have lunch with a friend so I went to the top of the Empire State building once again and had lunch there. In the evening we saw the play *Arsenic and Old Lace*. It was very enjoyable, as British audiences found out when it came to London.

There was a bad railway accident near Philadelphia and about 100 people were killed. This made us change our travel plans and we took a train to Camden and a ferry from there to Philadelphia, boarded a subway to the centre of the city and then got on a tram. After about five minutes travel the air raid warning went and all traffic had to stop. We assumed this was a practice warning as we could not conceive of the Germans coming this far to do any bombing. After twenty minutes the all clear went. If all traffic had to stop in England during a warning there would never be any work done. After travelling along the road for a while the tram suddenly turned right and shot down onto what looked like railway lines. It went down a hill and through some woods and through places that no tram would ever do in Britain. It was quite a new experience for us.

We bussed to Willow Grove and arrived three hours after our ETA.

On 8 September I took an Avenger over to Brewster Field for compass swinging and on the way back I had a 'fight' with a Corsair. It was a most impressive aircraft and could outmanoeuvre me all the time. Its turning circle was prodigious. No wonder it did so well in the Pacific.

The Italians surrendered and changed sides! What a turn-up for the book! To celebrate I went to an Italian restaurant in Philadelphia. I ordered clams and they tasted awful. I then had spaghetti. My method of eating this dish was to cut it up so that bits didn't dangle off the fork. I had an amusing time watching other people wrapping it around their forks and trying all sorts of tricks to get it into their mouths.

I fear the Italians got their own back on me! The clams were obviously responsible. I was as sick as a dog and had to be taken by ambulance to the sick bay where I had embarrassing things done to me. I recovered quickly and three days later I got straight out of the sick bay into the back of an Avenger and was flown by Jock Landles to Norfolk.

We went to the Aviation Officers' Mess in the evening. We were not wearing whites but khaki, which was our rig. The duty commanding officer wearing a revolver came in and went up to Frank Low and told him we must 'Clear out!' Frank stood up and said, 'We're not wanted here!' All the British downed glasses and walked out. I wonder what would have happened if a British officer had done the same thing to Americans in Britain – but then our officers don't normally go around wearing revolvers.

Digressing somewhat, many years later Westland sold two Whirlwinds to the Batista Cuban government just a few months before Castro took over. I went out to test the aircraft and to check out the pilots. I was talking to one of the officers in the dormitory that I had to share with them and he told me that some Cuban officers were in an American officers' mess and they were told to clear out in a similar fashion to that which I described above. After telling me this the officer spat on the marble-like floor and rubbed it in with his foot so I wondered if this sort of behaviour had had any bearing on that situation!

All aircraft were taxied to the ship next morning over the same route we took last February. My tail wheel had a great chunk out of it so the whole aircraft was oscillating up and down as I went along.

There were a few small Russian ships near us and we invited some of their officers to dinner. They could speak only a little English and we spoke no Russian, but we got along famously. We finished up by taking them along to the Commissioned Officers' Club. Very soon the party developed into a sort of singing contest: they would sing a song and we would retaliate by singing some of our cleaner ones. It never got too rowdy and it was a great occasion to have Russian, British and Americans all sitting down at the same table.

One remark made by a Russian is worth recording,

'The war in Russia –very bad. The war in England – very bad. The war in America – Coco Cola.'

Russians and British were fraternising strongly by the end of the evening. One of our number got very drunk and kept telling everyone, 'Drink to Stalin, the man who saved your effing life.' Most Americans did, whether willingly or unwillingly I don't know.

After some days in Norfolk, we sailed on 16 September north for Argentia in Newfoundland. A balance sheet typed out in the squadron office revealed that from 1 January to 19 September, 832 Squadron had carried out 4,511 flying hours, made 842 deck landings, and the aircraft propellers had rotated 32,497,200,000 times! We had flown the equivalent of 21 times round the earth. On the debit side we had lost four aircraft, had 6 personnel killed, and had had 14 deck landing accidents.

Owing to the weather no flying took place until 1000 hours when we launched two Avengers. It got foggy again and it was decided to land-on the aircraft. There was a window of opportunity and the aircraft started to make their approach, but Wings said, 'No, there's a squall ahead, wave them off,' which was a strange action. What did it matter so long as the squall was ahead and we were not in the thick of it? The aircraft were waved off twice and the squall got nearer. Johnny Swift, quite rightly, I thought, ignored the batsman and tried to make a landing just as the ship was turning out of wind. He caught the Christ Almighty wire and slightly damaged the aircraft in the barrier. An American Major was in the back; we hoped he learnt his lesson that flying was dangerous! After stooging around for a bit Hugh Saunders brought his aircraft in and made a good landing.

There was no flying on the 19th owing to the bad weather. We left our destroyers behind and went ahead on our own, arriving in Argentia off Newfoundland at about 1900 hours. It was a miserable-looking place! It was rather like Iceland but not quite so bad. In July 1941, Roosevelt and

Churchill met for the first time in Argentia to issue a joint declaration on the purposes of the war against fascism.

We sailed at noon next day. I missed seeing the world's biggest battleship, the USS *Iowa*, which passed us; I must have been below decks at the time. We were initially going to take a northern route to Britain, but the Captain said that there was a bunch of U-boats ahead of us and we were going to take a more southerly track instead.

I was in my cabin which was just below the waterline during the afternoon of the 21st when, 'Submarine alarm, close all watertight openings!' was sounded. You couldn't see me for dust as I leapt out of my cabin and up to the next flat. I didn't even stop to get my Mae West life jacket. The possibility of a torpedo being already on its way to the ship lent me wings. It turned out to be a false alarm.

On 22 September fog came down while four aircraft were airborne. One pair found the ship and the other two circled on radar. The latter were eventually able to land-on after the ship had put on searchlights, fired rockets and star shells and even broken R/T silence. I wrote about this episode in an article and afterwards Peter Perrett of 896 Squadron contacted me and said that he was one of the fighter pilots who got caught in the fog. Peter became Commander Flying at Yeovilton some time after the war and he and his wife Joan entertained me royally when I went to Auckland for a New Zealand Fleet Air Arm reunion. In the afternoon I went up on deck to hear, but not in time to see, an aircraft crash over the side on landing. The pilot, Sub-Lieutenant Cullen was picked up unhurt, but no doubt very cold.

The U-boat situation was developing rapidly at that time. After a period of four months during which no shipping was lost in this ocean the Battle of the Atlantic was on once more and U-boats were increasing in numbers daily. There was a large convoy to the north of us and it was west bound. I heard that the American escort carrier USS *Bogue* was somewhere near us. This ship was somewhat larger than other escort carriers and she had had a modicum of success against U-boats. On this particular trip she saw no action

The Captain gave us a talk, mostly about the history of the ship. Since commissioning the ship had sailed the equivalent of seven times round the world. And after leaving Britain she had sailed the equivalent of two and a half times round the world.

18

ANTICLIMAX. AN UNEXPECTED OPERATION

We drew nearer to Britain and so did some well-earned leave – we thought! We flew off the ship and landed at Machrihanish in the Mull of Kintyre while the fighter boys went to Northern Ireland. At Machrihanish we ran into our old CO Lieutenant-Commander Lucas and also our old commander, Commander Surtees, now a Captain, who was going to the *Argus* soon. After refuelling we went on to Hatston in the Orkneys from where we blithely believed we would start our leave. But no! We were told not to drink that evening, and rumour ran riot. The next thing we knew was that torpedoes were being put on our aircraft. After having travelled back from the ends of the earth we thought it was an anti-climax to be sent on some operation before we had even been on leave. To make matters worse some of our observers and air gunners had not left the ship and were being substituted by crews from 846 Squadron. This is no reflection on 846, but clearly we would have liked to have our own crews with us for whatever lay ahead.

I noticed an officer checking radios who looked familiar, and I thought I must have met him during my time in the Navy. I said, 'Where have I seen you before?' He replied, 'Bradfield!' The penny dropped; in fact we had been in the shooting eight together. He was J. de M.C. Thompson.

Next day, 27 September, we rose at dawn, and after breakfast repaired to the operations room where the Captain briefed us. He told us the *Lützow* was out and that we were to fly to Norway to find and strike.

We flew first to Sumburgh in the Shetlands where we took on a full load of fuel and met the crews of six Beaufighters who were going to escort us. After hanging around for what seemed like hours we took off at about noon. I remember the take-off being a long one and the aircraft appeared reluctant to climb. We formed up and went right down on the water to keep under German radar cover. I am afraid that our opinion of the RAF was not enhanced by the fact that of the six Beaufighters that were supposed to escort us only two accompanied us until Norway came in sight. Then they disappeared.

The weather was good. Had the *Lützow* been at sea in that area there is no doubt it would have had strong fighter cover and our squadron would have been decimated. Apart from having no fighter cover I found that my front gun was working only intermittently! Later I was informed that in my sub flight only one turret gun was working. So altogether we were pretty poorly placed for any operation. Fortunately, when Norway came into our sight our anxious eyes could see no sign of the enemy and it was with some relief that we turned for home.

I am able to augment my remarks by quoting from *Touch and Go* (a book about the TAGs of one particular course) edited by R.G. Fletcher in which he quotes from John Minards of 846 Squadron as follows

> ... we took off for the type of attack for which we had been training for months. From then on things started to go wrong: as we circled the field waiting for the Beaufighters to take off, the third one, in doing so, ground looped and hit a petrol bowser. This accident caused a delay on the ground and, as time was of the essence, it was decided that we should press on with just the two Beaufighters for escort, but after a short while they left us and returned to base. In the meantime, the order was given to test fire the turret guns which led to the embarrassing discovery that of the twelve guns only three were serviceable, owing to a number of reasons which it was too late to remedy in the air. In my own case, I was able to effect a temporary arrangement whereby I was able to pull back the breech-block to cock the guns for firing.

Back at Hatston we received the following signal:

To Hatston, 832 Squadron.
(R) HOSS, 18 Group. Victorious, Admiralty.
From C. in C. Home Fleet.

I am sorry your good and strenuous work bore no fruit, but it was a fine effort.

A few days later while on leave I was walking down Regent Street when I ran into Wings (Commander Price) from the Vic. We got chatting and he said that a mysterious signal had been received by the ship addressed to 832 Squadron. I was astonished that security was so good that even our own ship had not heard of the operation. I quickly enlightened him.

The *Victorious* went into dock in Liverpool for a refit, which took six months. After leaving her in September 1943 I saw her only twice more: once when I spent a night aboard her in Liverpool, and once many years later in Portsmouth where she was being modernised and having an angled deck fitted. But this was not really the same ship: she had been rebuilt from the keel upwards. One of the most poignant pictures I have ever seen was a photo of her after the ship breakers had reduced her to one deck above the waterline. My old ship had disappeared into thin air and no longer existed. Had she been sunk she would still be an entity, albeit a rusting one. But now her very structure had been ripped out and distributed to the four corners of the earth in many different forms. The affection of her crew, however, remains undiminished and every year old wartime shipmates get together for a reunion.

I had over two weeks' leave and visited a lot of my old haunts and many old friends and relations. It was a thoroughly good leave.

With the leave over on 18 October I took a train to Thurso in company with Willie Wilson, David Johnson and Bruce Petrie. At Thurso we had a good breakfast at The Royal, we even had poached eggs, which were a luxury in wartime.

We crossed to Stromness and from there to Hatston. There was no appointment waiting for me yet but Jock Landles was appointed to Inskip and Arch Hugill to Arbroath.

Next day John Barnes, David Johnson and I went on leave again, 'Pending appointment!' So our long journey was all for nothing. We had a meal on the ferry and the sea was quite choppy. One soldier on board managed to be sick, but he was vomiting over the windward side!

We had breakfast at Perth and then the journey seemed to go on forever. The train had to detour near Rugby and we were two or three hours behind schedule getting into Euston. Being so late it was impossible to get across London and I put up at the Hotel Russell for the night. I telephoned my aunt and she told me that I had had a telegram appointing me to Crail dating from that day. So my journey south was not really necessary. What a waste of time! After going all the way up to Scotland and back I was damned if I was going straight back again so I decided that after all that travelling I would arrive at Crail in two days' time. We had an air raid during my stay in the hotel, but the raid was light and no bombs were dropped round that district.

At Chipstead I leant that Frank Low was to make a broadcast about the *Victorious*. This took place shortly after the 9 o'clock news. As usual Frank was relaxed, informative and interesting.

During the night several enemy aircraft flew fast and low over Chipstead.

Next day a lot of Frank's talk was in the newspapers. The Captain too had been speaking in London about our trip and there was a photograph of the Vic passing through the Panama Canal.

19

THE SERVICE TRIALS UNIT. 778
SQUADRON, CRAIL

I spent the night at Oxshott and next day left Chipstead after tea, had dinner in London and caught the night train to Edinburgh arriving there at about 0500 hours and had to wait for an hour to catch a train to Crail. After breakfast I went to the Captain's Office and found that instead of doing instructing as I thought I was appointed to the Service Trial Unit, which I thought was one of the best jobs going. I was extremely pleased

Jerry Connolly and Peter O'Shea, both former pilots of 832 were at Crail, as was Mike Hartree, another contemporary of mine at Bradfield. The number of times I mention Bradfield one would think we ran the FAA!

The main task of this squadron was to make landings on new aircraft carriers; however, as the name of the squadron implies there were other tasks as well and to this end we had to be familiar with many naval aircraft. So I had the thrill of flying many different types such as the Barracuda, the Fulmar, the Martlet II, The Hurricane, the Seafire, the Harvard (which was very similar to the Yale) the Hellcat, as well as the Swordfish and the Avenger. I also had some dual instruction in a Walrus.

The CO of the STU was Lieutenant-Commander Lane, RN. He had the nickname of 'Tubby', why this was so I never found out for his figure belied that appellation.

Other members were: the Senior Pilot, Lieutenant Desmond Whatley, RN, a tall man who was described in a FAA Magazine as the man with the come-to-bed eyes. Then there was 'Winkle', E.M. Brown, who carried out the first landing by a jet aircraft on a carrier. He became one of the most famous pilots in the navy. He rose to the rank of Captain and had what must be the highest number of deck landings of any pilot, British or American. He carried out 2407, and by the end of his career had flown 487 different types of aircraft! An incredible record indeed! He is also the author of several books.

We also had P.G. Lawrence, he was generally known as PG, so I shall call him that here. And there was also Keeting, Schonfeldt, Morgan, Morrel, Stroud, 'Steve' Stevenson, Johnnie Underwood and David Adamson. David was a good friend; his ambition at the time was to become a dentist after the war. In the event he emigrated to Canada with his wife and became a doctor. Before leaving the UK he went to Porton Down and took part in some of the experiments to find a cure for the common cold.

Tony Hazeldine was somewhat older than the rest of us. He lived in Crail with his wife and they were most hospitable people. He took up farming near Taunton after the war and I visited him there.

I had been at Crail for only a few weeks when David Johnson joined the STU. He used to be my observer before I had the short appointment to Manston; he later married Tony Hazeldine's stepdaughter. Another new pilot, Sandy Powell, and a man called Luke also arrived. Another newcomer at Crail during my appointment there was Lieutenant Day who used to be a FAA engineering officer aboard the Vic with me.

Reg Elliot arrived back at Crail from leave. We were in 19 Course St Vincent together and he was now an instructor. The TAGs in the squadron as recorded in my logbook were Bob Kinghan, (now a Petty Officer I was glad to see), and PO O'nion, but for the most part I flew with L.A. Selby.

I had my first flight in a Barracuda (often called a 'Barra') two days later and, after my Avenger experience, I wondered how this extraordinary looking aircraft was going to perform. The first British designed monoplane torpedo bomber of the Fleet Air Arm, the Fairey Barracuda, began entering service in late 1943. It had first flown in 1940 but there was such a high priority for RAF aircraft that it was slow to finish its evaluation trials. No fewer than 2,572 Barracudas of all marks were delivered to the FAA, which is a surprising figure considering the troubles that had to be overcome. Among them was the tendency at one stage for the wings to come off in a dive, which gave the pilots no confidence in the aircraft. However, the most obvious fault was its lack of power. One good feature of the aircraft was its Fairey-Youngman trailing-edge flaps, which I remember as being very efficient dive brakes.

I got airborne using plus 18 lbs boost and this was a pretty high figure. Boost is the pressure in the induction system measured in pounds per square inch above or below atmospheric pressure – equivalent to Manifold Pressure in the US. I was pleasantly surprised at the aircraft's handling qualities; although it was seriously underpowered, it was extremely manoeuvrable compared with the Avenger. The stick forces were incredibly light, it was certainly not a 'tab ship' as the Americans referred to aircraft like the Avenger where trim tabs had to be used to assist in moving the control surfaces.

I carried out only 18 hours in the Barracuda and I see from my log book that although one flight was for a bomb sight test and another for a radio check the rest of my flying in the Barra, apart from the familiarisation flight, was for transport duties. The most important of these was transporting myself down to Eastleigh when I left the squadron! Fortunately a Barracuda was required there just at the right time.

Some of the Barracuda pilots had never seen an Avenger before and I once watched a Barracuda pilot observing an Avenger taking off. He was open mouthed at the rate of climb as the aircraft left the deck. As someone who loved Avengers this was very satisfying to me!

I did a fair number of hours in the Swordfish, an aircraft that I had not flown for two years. My flights were mostly for radio trials, which meant flying south down the coast in order to get a reasonable distance from the base. After flying more modern aircraft it was quite a come-down to be in an open cockpit in freezing weather watching the poppet valves going in and out and not having a very good view for landing. Give me my old Albacore!

We had a few ENSA shows while I was there and they had certainly improved over the last year. It was during these that I ran into Ransford Slater and his wife. This was the last time I saw him for the next news I had of him was that he was dead. Apparently he had flown over his house to wave to his wife and had hit some power cables.

It was while visiting Abbotsinch to pick up an Avenger that I saw a copy of the *Illustrated London News*. There were pictures of 832 Squadron in it and other ones of the ship. Abbotsinch had an extremely soft and wet surface and PG, who took me there in an Avenger, made a bumpy landing. My take-off was equally rough.

I had to fly down to Speke on 6 November on to pick up some tail wheels for Martlets, and Dick Barnett went with me. We took the opportunity of visiting the Vic in Liverpool where we put up for the night. It was good to see again my old ship where I spent nearly two years on and off; it felt like being home again. We actually had eggs for breakfast – my first for a fortnight – quite a luxury! The ship was, of course, in chaos as she was having a fairly major refit that lasted until March 1944. Tunnels were being constructed to the lower decks to avoid having to go up through two or three watertight compartments; half the hangar deck had been removed, presumably in order to get at the ship's engines; all the mutiple pom poms had been taken away, whether temporarily or permanently I did not know. In addition to all that the island was being reconstructed inside and on top of the island a platform was being extended, presumably to fit new gun positions.

A few of the ship's officers were still on board, but there were several new ones including the first-lieutenant. The replacement for Captain Mackintosh was Captain Denny.

I said goodbye to my old ship for the last time. She went on to do valiant deeds off Norway and in the Pacific, and she was the only warship to sail completely around the world during the war.

Next morning I tried to get what we had come for – the Martlet tail wheels – but found they had all been sent to Perth the previous day!

Back at Crail I did some ADDLS in an Avenger using the British system. It was not easy at first especially as our signals were the opposite of the American ones. There was a letter from Bob Procter giving me news of some of the lads. Bob himself was now a staff officer. John Burbidge was at RAF Syerston and Bill Thomson was on a Fighter Direction Officer's course at Yeovilton.

I found the Fairey Fulmar very easy to fly, but made the remark that it did not seem to be as fast as our Avengers! I had great fun flying the Hurricane and Seafire and brushed up on aerobatics – something that I had not done since flying the Yale in Canada. I can't say I was all that good and felt that a spot of dual would help me with one or two queries I had. When I came to fly the Martlet my greatest difficulty was in winding the manually operated undercarriage up and down! I was never strong and we seldom had much exercise, indeed my six-pack, i.e. stomach muscles, had wasted away since I had joined the service. Otherwise flying the Martlet was rather like flying a smaller and lighter version of the Avenger.

I got talking to Mr and Mrs Schonfeldt at a party and he told me an interesting story about the *Ark Royal* and how someone was given a DSC (Distinguished Service Cross) for something that *he* had done! Apparently he and his pilot found the *Bismarck* a few minutes after the Catalina. At the same time another Swordfish appeared on the scene and sent off a sighting report of 'One Cruiser' instead of 'One Battleship'. Schonfeldt had sent off a sighting report, a correct one, at the same time. The Catalina crew then saw his Swordfish and thought it was a fighter catapulted off the *Bismarck* and pushed off. The other Swordfish returned to the *Ark* while Schonfeldt and his pilot shadowed the *Bismarck* alone until getting short of fuel. By some mistake the crew of the other Stringbag were given gongs while he and his pilot got nothing.

Some days later I had an exciting flight in a Barracuda. At 10,000 feet I had a dogfight with Dave Adamson who was flying a Seafire. I learnt one thing, and I hope I am correct in my assumption, and that was that when doing an avoiding turn it is better to *ascend* at the same time rather than descend.

On 17 November Bob Procter and Sid Price turned up at lunchtime while on their way to Speke. A reunion of 832 types took place. Apart from us three there were David Johnson, Gerry Connolley and Peter O'Shea. It was good to get together again. Bob told me that they did a night ALT the previous night and Hugh Saunders' carburettor had iced up during a glide and he had to ditch. The crew got out and managed to walk ashore; but they were frozen.

Landing an Avenger after a round trip to Arbroath and Easthaven I received a ticking off via the Lieutenant-Commander Flying ('Little F' as he is known) for taxiing too fast. My punishment was to be made duty officer, but as I did not hear about this till after the time I was due for the sentence I had no extra duties.

I had some more ADDLS; the batsman being PG. Unfortunately he wanted to be a personality batsman (like Lieutenant Everett mentioned before during my training days). I could not understand his signals. He kept waving his arms up and down and I thought he meant, 'Go faster!' when he really meant, 'Go lower!' One thing that can be said for the American system of batting, which are 'mirror' signals and not orders, is that you cannot be a personality batsman with that system! Next day I did some more ADDLs with the CO doing the batting and things went quite well.

My sister Maryele, now living in Uruguay, was expecting a baby around this time and I was getting worried that I had heard nothing. However, I had a telegram that said, 'Shirley arrived'. That succinct message told me that it was a girl, and I assumed all was well or the message might have added something.

On 28 November I heard that someone in a Barracuda had taken off the previous night with his dive brakes on. He went into the drink and was killed. And a second death occurred when a fitter walked into the prop of a Barra.

On 9 November Winkle Brown came back from some trials in HMS *Ravager*. As he was to leave the squadron soon a farewell party was held for him. The CO spoke about Winkle's exceptional ability as a pilot, which was a portent of Winkle's career as the best-known pilot in the navy.

My first flight in a Walrus was as a passenger. I had to take a Martlet to Machrihanish, navigating there was simple (not that Machrihanish was difficult to find in good weather), for David Adamson had to go there as well in a Firefly, and I just followed him. Tony Hazeltine arrived shortly afterwards in a Walrus to take us back; however, we found when we reached Ayr that the aircraft had not been refuelled and we put down there to correct matters and have some lunch. On the way in we flew over HMS *Unicorn*, a new carrier, and a battleship, which I did not identify. After take-off we could not get past Glasgow owing to thick weather, so we put down at Renfrew.

We three took a train to Glasgow and Tony went on to Edinburgh while David and I looked for accommodation. The only place we could find that had any to offer necessitated David and me sleeping in a double bed! Fortunately David's grandmother, who lived in Glasgow, offered to put him up so I had the room to myself after all. The owners of the hotel looked at him a bit sideways when he arrived next morning. Obviously they had dark thoughts about him! On going out to get dinner I ran into another branch man, a New Zealander, who was on leave from HMS *Chaser*. Research in Google reveals the fact that she was of the Attacker class, and my new acquaintance was most likely to have been in 835 Squadron flying Swordfish. Later on *Chaser* did good work in Arctic convoys: her aircraft sank three U-boats.

We all returned to Renfrew next day and the Walrus took us back to Crail.

Next day I had to do a smoke-float test (looking back I wonder what on earth this was for!) and then take someone to Arbroath. While there I met CPO Rosser, I knew him as a PO in 832 Squadron and I was glad to hear of his promotion. Afterwards I brought a Third Officer WRNS back to Crail, I knew her only by the nickname of 'Pooh'; her name turned out to be Roscoe. The Wrens at Crail were a smart lot, I remember being impressed by their marching.

We had a gas mask drill. Unfortunately I had left mine behind at Chipstead so I hid in the heads while the test was going on! I wonder how I got away with having no gas mask when I went outside the Air Station?

I again flew some people to Arbroath. It takes 15 minutes to get there, and since Crail is on a peninsular it must have saved them hours of travel by land.

It was about this time that the 1939-43 Star began to be distributed and that I eventually received mine. I wore it proudly as my only medal for about a year before several more campaign medals joined it. The 1939–43 Star was later changed to the 1939-45 Star; we were a bit sorry about this as we thought ourselves somewhat superior to those young blokes who had joined later than we had!

There was a theatre group in the Air Station called The Jackdaws and they put on a very impressive play called, *Well Caught*. I wondered whether the director was an actor in Civvy Street, the services in wartime have a variety of talents that were put to good use.

I had a delightful surprise when I flew to Machrihanish in an Avenger taking David Adamson as a passenger. I discovered that 832 Squadron was there! Gerry Child was there also; he was now in 846 Squadron. It was grand to see all the boys again, I felt as if I was back in the squadron for a while. On account of this we stopped for lunch . . . I flew back later after I had managed to start the engine, which was giving a lot of trouble.

Two days later I went to Machrihanish again but this time in the back of an Avenger piloted by Whatley, while Sandy Powell went in a Hurricane, PG in a Barracuda and Stroud in a Stringbag. What a varied collection! Next day, with me as a passenger Whatley went out to land-on the *Nairana*, but found that a Barra had pranged on the deck so we went back to Machrihanish. He completed the trials next day with the aircraft at a very low weight.

On 16 December with me in the back Whatley did the first landing on HMS *Vindex*, a sister ship of the *Nairana*. We went up to the bridge and the first person we saw was Commander Price, my old Commander Flying from the Vic! Whatley did four good landings on the ship and then as it was getting late we spent the night aboard; I shared a cabin with a Lieutenant from the Admiralty Press Division. I had seen him before somewhere and it transpired that I had met him at Hatston. I had a long talk with him and he took notes about my views of American aircraft.

After all the trials had been completed the ship embarked 825 Squadron and like HMS *Nairana* was used on Atlantic convoys with success, its aircraft assisting in the sinking of at least two U-boats.

We took off next morning for Machrihanish, a Fortress that had flown all the way from Newfoundland landing just after us. We had to stay the night there as the weather closed in, but fortunately the monotony was relieved by a good ENSA show in the evening.

Mary had a friend who was married to a New Zealander called Montgomery, a Lieutenant. He was told to look me up; but got the name wrong. Anyway he contacted me at last. Apparently he was looking for some young sprog pilot still on course, instead he found a pilot with the 1939–43 medal up, but young anyway, even if I felt old at 23.

David Adamson and I had Christmas leave so we rose early on 21 December and went down to Edinburgh and then to Kings Cross where David's wife was there to meet him. Since the train was one and a half hours late she had had a long wait.

While on leave I ran into Bill Jennings of 19 Course in a shop and he told me that Ron Spackman, who had left 832 with dysentery when we were in the Pacific, was back in England having been in his native New Zealand for the recovery. Montgomery, the New Zealander I met at Crail, was at a party I went to in Oxshott. It was his fiancée, Paula's twenty-first birthday. It's a very small world for I was once at Oxshott when I ran into a boy I was at school with in New Zealand, called Gregory. He was not FAA, but a fishhead in HMS *Achilles*. Another man I met briefly who was at school with me in Wellington, New Zealand, was Hugh Morrison. He was with me at Croydon School in Days Bay. Just to make things confusing this is now called Wellesley College and this was the name of the school I first went to in the city of Wellington.

I was riding back from Oxshott to Chipstead on my motorbike when I had a slight accident, although it could have been far worse. Some town roads at that time were made of wooden blocks over which tar had been placed, but with wartime economies the tar had not been replaced when it wore off, consequently the wood was exposed and when they were wet it was extremely slippery. I tried to make a turn but the bike went straight on and fell on its side. The float chamber was broken and petrol dripped out. I could not get a new one there, so I bought some sticking plaster and made a patch and was able to ride along by alternatively turning the petrol on and off. Back at Chipstead I made a better patch and then rode into Croydon where, thankfully, I was able to get a new float chamber. My only injury was a bruised hip.

Back at Crail I heard that 'Avenger' was now the official name for 'Tarpon', thus coming into line with the Americans, but the reader will recall that I have been using 'Avenger' all along. And the name of the 'Martlet' was changed to 'Wildcat'. I will now refer to the Martlet by its new name.

I had to fly to Arbroath in a Swordfish at short notice to take some spares for a Mosquito. After landing I found that somehow a portion of my elevator had received a bash – how this happened I did not know. This held me up until next day; however I ran into Jimmy Wilson, ex 832 and an observer, who was on a photographic course. In the evening I went to a concert by the Gordon Highlanders. A man with no voice at all sang a song and after receiving some half-hearted applause, he said, 'Thank you very much ladies and gentlemen and for an encore I would like to sing . . .'! After his song the show became very good. A man read out some notices in the voice of a parson and was really funny. In the same voice he told the old joke that I repeat for anyone who has just come into adulthood: 'I have to announce the formation of a Young Mothers' Union. The meetings will be on Thursdays. Any lady wishing to become a young mother should see me in the vestry afterwards.'

At Crail the cabin heating had broken down so I slept warmly at Arbroath as *their* heating was working! On my return to Crail I had some dual instruction in a Walrus with Whatley. I found it terrifying! Not only because could one not see the propeller going round because it was aft of the cockpit, but the fact that it had a wheel instead of a control column.

I had my first flights in a Hurricane in December. Now, after one more trip in one I had my first flight in a Seafire on 9 January 1944. This aircraft of course was merely a Spitfire with an arresting hook, plus any strengthening that was required to the airframe. My first flight in this noble and famous aircraft was on 9 January 1944. As previously warned I found the stick very sensitive in the fore and aft direction. I suppose its main faults were the fact that the engine could become overheated when taxi-ing out to the take off position and, because of the long nose, the view was restricted. When taking off it was difficult to see ahead until the nose went down. The view was not too good on the approach to land either. I never deck-landed it but the weak undercarriage used to cause trouble when landing on a deck as opposed to an aerodrome. After flying the aircraft around to get the feel of it I tried flying with flaps and wheels down, and carried out some stalls. Then I took it up to 10,000 feet and tried some loops and rolls. I made four landings on the airfield and found no difficulty.

The same day Lieutenant Burr DSC and bar was killed in a Barracuda. Apparently he dived straight into the sea. I felt sure that it was not a pilot error but that something was amiss with the aircraft.

A minor trouble that was insignificant compared with the above was the breakdown of the cinema in the evening: first the sound kept giving trouble then the projector packed up. With the cabin heating still not working we were feeling pretty wretched. David Johnson and I were even more miserable next day when we had to take a Swordfish up to 4,000 feet and fly almost to Newcastle doing a radio test. David did a lot of talking to a ground station and at various intervals he would ask me to write a number on a map giving our approximate position. Wearing all the clothes I possessed and with frozen fingers this was not easy. In my diary I stated that I would never praise a Swordfish again! However, my sufferings were nothing compared with the boys in the Arctic and Atlantic flying off escort carriers and I had the greatest admiration for them, and indeed for the amazing aircraft that the Swordfish was.

I was the Squadron Active and Passive Defence Officer. I cannot remember a thing about it except that, fortunately for the safety of the squadron and anyone near us, I had little to do. I mentioned in my diary that on a misty day when there was no flying we had an exercise sprung on us. We all survived!

I went to Arbroath to do some tests with the arrester wires but found when I got there that my hook was the wrong sort. Back I went to Crail to have a different hook fitted. At Arbroath I had to make several runs along the ground at the wires, almost becoming airborne in the process. David Adamson in a Wildcat had a go. On his first run his hook jumped the first wire and then the second wire took off his tail wheel. That's the first time I've seen that happen.

An electrician Commander, just off a cruiser, wanted to have a look at an Avenger and a Wildcat. I folded and spread the wings for him and he seemed quite pleased with my toy. Which reminds me that shortly after coming back from America, and when the ground crews had never seen an Avenger, I was taxiing fast towards a group of aircraft at a strange aerodrome. This naturally alarmed a group of men standing near some aircraft for they could see that I could not possibly get through a gap. They started waving frantically at me and then their faces changed to looks of surprise when I folded the wings as I taxied along.

I took David back in my Avenger to a chilly Crail. The cabin heating was still not on and letter writing was difficult. David Johnson, with whom I shared a cabin, had borrowed an electric heater. The trouble was that with only one electric socket in the room we could have only one apparatus on, so it was either the radio on or the heater. David was now busy connecting up the two items to the one plug so we could have both on together. In those day multi sockets in rooms were almost unheard of. I can't remember whether there were such things as adaptors, but they were probably in short supply anyway.

I went to the pay office to make out an allotment of £15 per month as a sort of forced saving. I had not been able to save anything during our American trip as the cost of living there was higher. £15 would not go far in 2006 but in those days a Mars Bar cost only 2d (two old pence). The modest Mars Bar is a useful indication of inflation and I reckon that my £15 would be worth about £180 today.

I did several ADDLS on 15 January fully loaded. This was prior to my carrying out some tests on the *Pretoria Castle*. Lieutenant Whatley was on leave and I was the Avenger King for the moment.

In the evening Mrs Hazeldine threw a party for some of us and for her daughter Poppet's benefit as she was returning to school the following day. Poppet, or Daphne to give her real name, was the girl that David Johnson married, so perhaps this was the first time they had met. We depleted the Hazeldine's beer supply somewhat and then played Vingt-et-Un. I lost a lot of money the first time I was banker so I was pleasantly surprised when I ended a shilling or so up at the end. We walked back to the Air Station after midnight and I narrowly missed stepping on a dead cat on the way.

If you draw a straight line from Ayr to Machrihanish you will find that it narrowly misses the Isle of Arran, and you will comprehend why a little carelessness could have caused the write-off of a valuable Avenger – apart from the loss to the FAA of another pilot. It happened like this: I had to take an Avenger to Machrihanish, but twice I had to turn back because of low cloud and poor visibility. In the end I got through to Ayr and proceeded in a westerly direction for Campbeltown. After flying for a while I had a blurred view of some land and I thought it was the area round Campbeltown, which is fairly flat. Fortunately I did not look down at my instruments at that crucial point or have my attention diverted for any reason. I belted along and to my horror found that all around me were hills going up into the clouds and enclosing a small harbour. I did the quickest steep turn that has ever been carried out in an Avenger and exited that place at a rate of knots. I believe this was Lamlash harbour in the Isle of Arran and I was north of my intended track. I wonder what the inhabitants thought when an aircraft came roaring in and narrowly missed their hills.

I was disappointed to find that 832 Squadron was on leave so none of my old friends were at Machrihanish.

Next morning I was supposed to rendezvous with HMS *Pretoria Castle* at 1100 hours. The ship was built in Belfast as a passenger liner and converted into an escort carrier and used principally for trials from April 1943. After the war when she was converted back to a passenger liner she was renamed the *Warwick Castle*. She was scrapped in 1962.

I had a lot of trouble starting my engine but eventually set off. I found two escort carriers close together and thought one of them must be the *Pretoria Castle*. I circled these two for half an hour. One of the carriers must have got tired of this and flashed to me, 'Go away . . .' I did not wait to read the rest! I found three other escort carriers, but none of them seemed to want me so I flew back to Machrihanish. A signal was then sent to say that we could not find the *Pretoria Castle* and requesting a new rendezvous. This crossed with one from the ship to say that an amended one was at the same place but at 1430 hours.

In the afternoon I found the ship straight away and landed aboard. Flying was cancelled for the rest of the day and I spent some time trying to find my way around the ship, getting lost several times in the process.

Next morning I did eight landings. The object was to check out the arrester gear at 16,000 lbs all up weight and at a speed of 55 knots. Some of the landings were carried out at a wind speed over the deck at only 18 knots consequently the deceleration was fairly high after catching an arrester wire.

I flew again next day and spent some time waiting to land-on as the deck was not ready. I note rather too laconically in my diary that during this time some shots were fired in front of me from the shore.

Unfortunately I do not seem to have investigated this as I made not more mention of it. My last two landings were made directly into the sun, which gave the flight deck a golden glow and completely hid the batsman. I caught a glimpse of him only when I reached about 100 feet from the ship.

I had dinner with the Captain in the evening. This is the only time in my life I have met a VC! As mentioned before he was Captain Bell Davies and an RNAS pilot in Word War I. It was he who was responsible for sending a notice to my headmaster about volunteers being wanted for the Fleet Air Arm so I would not have been sitting at his table if it were not for that fact! I did not mention this to him as there was another officer present and it was something I would have preferred to mention in private.

Next morning I spent half an hour trying to start the engine of my Avenger. I could have sworn that it was the booster coil that was not working, but the ground crew assured me that it was OK. I later found that I was correct in my assessment. Anyways the exercise was cancelled owing to the wind being too high for the trials.

Lieutenant David Carter arrived in the afternoon in a Harvard. He missed all the arrester wires but pulled up on his brakes. That is what I wrote in my diary but I wonder now whether the Harvard did in fact have a hook

Back at Crail I received a present from the British Community Council in the Argentine. As I was in the Argentine at the start of the war (during school holidays) I counted as an Argentine Volunteer even though I came back to England under my own steam. Unfortunately the present was cigarettes; I would have preferred food! I did smoke at the time during the war years but only occasionally. Fortunately I gave up smoking a year or two later and have eschewed the wretched weed ever since. When I see the number of friends I have lost through smoking I think that Sir Walter Raleigh has a lot to answer for! And when I notice teenagers taking up the habit I think they must be complete idiots, for they do this despite all the dire warnings that they get.

I flew an Avenger to check out a glide bombing sight. I thought the test a bit ridiculous; I preferred to use the nose of the machine as a sight and any dive bombing with an Avenger was bound to be inaccurate as it could not be dived steeply. Experience and practice was what was required. Despite the fact that the Avengers in the squadron were normally restricted to 200 knots airspeed I was using 220 knots most of the time.

A flight to test a Square Search Computer was postponed as black smoke poured from the exhaust. After the fitter had leaned off the mixture I found during the take-off run that I could get only 2300 rpm instead of 2600, so I had to abort. The fitter said he had probably leaned off the mixture too much.

25 January 1944 I showed David Carter the 'taps' of the Avenger as he had not flown one for some time. A Court of Enquiry was being held in the billiard room regarding a crash near Prestwick. One fact brought out was that the pilot was not in touch either by R/T or W/T. For the first time I learnt that there was an AFO (Admiralty Fleet Order) out to the effect that on a cross country the crew must keep in touch. I had never been in touch during any cross country from Crail.

Just before dinner David Johnson told me that there was an officer on the station who would give us some dancing lessons. We did this in my cabin but as we did not have partners I think any information we acquired could not be put to practical use. Unfortunately Humphries had to go away and there were no further dancing lessons.

On 27 January we learnt that the Argentine had broken off diplomatic relations with the Axis powers. I remarked in my diary that they certainly took their time! The CO went to Farnborough to collect a Mosquito, but it did not arrive at Crail during my time there.

ENSA put on a good play in the evening, it was *Maria Marten, or Murder in the Red Barn*. It was well produced and well acted.

Next day I saw a Lieutenant RN at breakfast that I recognised. Just to make sure I said, 'Were you at school in Berkshire?' He replied in the affirmative and I said, 'Your name is Busbridge, isn't it? Busbridge the runner?' This is what I remembered him for at Bradfield, he always had tremendous stamina and he was in the running VIII. He eventually reached the rank of Captain in the navy.

I was going to fly an Avenger but the pitch control lever got stuck out and the rpm remained the same even when it was in. In other words the propeller was stuck in coarse pitch. However, I flew a Seafire in the afternoon. The weather was not too good as it was cloudy with a few patches of blue. I took the aircraft up to 10,000 feet and did some aerobatics. When I eventually descended through a blue patch I found I was over the water; however, one advantage of having an airfield by the sea is that one has only to steer west (in this case) to hit the coast. I saw some land and then the Isle of May. As mentioned before, the Seafire has a long nose and it is difficult to see ahead on the approach and in this case I found myself over grass instead of runway due to the side wind. I went round again but found that another aircraft was blocking the runway. I was getting a bit worried as low cloud was coming in rapidly. However I managed to land shortly after this.

The following day I again I had trouble with the Avenger pitch control. It shot out on me during the take-off consequently I lost some engine rpm. When it was fixed I did a few ADDLS, they were not my best owing to rough winds.

My next flight in a Seafire went extremely well. I thought my aerobatics were good and my landing was one of my best ever in any aircraft. While at Crail I had started to do wheelie landings instead of three pointers; this involved increasing engine power just prior to touch down and flying level along the runway before letting the main wheels touch.

Afterwards a surprise awaited me. I had a letter from Henri Marchand. I had stayed with him and his family in Paris and then in Brittany when I was trying to improve my French. He had escaped from France across the Spanish border and was now a Sous Lieutenant in the Free French Forces. He was an intelligent man and I always hoped he would make it; his English was good which was in no small way thanks to me because we used to talk English a lot together. I met him for lunch a few months later and had an interesting conversation. At a nearby table was an army officer and when he heard Henri ask me in French how my linguistic ability was progressing I noticed he listened intently to my reply. I just wondered whether if my French had been perfect he might have recruited me as an agent for duties in France! He looked disappointed when my French did not come up to the perfection required for such a job.

826 Squadron started to arrive at Crail, presumably for some working up.

On 1 February I repeated my previous Seafire flight but in a Hurricane this time. As there was 10/10ths cloud over Crail I flew across the estuary to Drem. I eventually came down through a hole in the clouds and once again came down over the sea with no land in sight.

822 Squadron started arriving in the afternoon. I knew several the members – Dick Grimsdale and Crane among others. Also among them was John Burbidge, complete with beard, and we had a few drinks together in the evening. The squadron was equipped with Barracudas and the aircraft were shipped out on a merchant ship to India. In India the aircraft taxied up the main street in line astern to get to their airfield. The slipstream caused havoc with the saris and they were not too popular as a result!

Next day I had to have a night vision test. I got 13 marks. I understood one failed at 12, so I just scraped through.

It was about this time that Bob Kingan, my former TAG, joined the squadron and I spoke to him. He looked very much older and he said he had been very depressed and had been put in a mental home after attempting suicide. He said that this had nearly sent him mad! I flew with him again, the first time for over a year, this time it was in a Stringbag and not an Avenger.

On 5 February something happened that changed my life forever. An Admiralty signal came round asking for volunteers for a helicopter course. My interest in helicopters stemmed from the days when, as a small boy, I read about the exploits of Captain Justice in a comic called *The Adventure*. He had a vessel that was combined submarine, boat and helicopter! Perhaps this first stimulated my interest in helicopters, although no practical vehicle of this sort had yet been flown. Autogiros yes; helicopters no! Note the spelling of 'Autogiro', spelt this way it was Juan de la Cierva's patent although the normal spelling was 'autogyro'. Another name for an autogyro is gyroplane. A toy that first made me think of helicopters was a handgun that had a wind-up spring. One fastened a propeller or rotor to this and when fired the rotor would propel itself into the air relying on the momentum stored in its rotor to give power to the blades. I used to wonder why it would veer off sideways in a wind; it was not until some years later that I realised that it was due to dissymmetry of lift: the blade advancing into the wind obtaining more lift than the retreating one. I was amazed recently to find that the toy is still being made; I spotted a boy using one on television. Another factor influencing my decision to volunteer for this course was something I read while sitting in the middle of the Pacific. An article in one of the aviation magazines described Igor Sikorsky's attempts to build a helicopter. Something about the aircraft fascinated me. Little could I have guessed then that I would be flying helicopters in less than a year and that during the course of my career I would meet Sikorsky three times and even give him a flight in a helicopter!

Anyway, I volunteered for this course and waited to see if the Admiralty would approve of my change.

On 7 February a pupil pranged a Barracuda soon after taking off. Apparently he pulled the aircraft off the deck too soon and stalled. Anyway he ended up near the guardhouse the right way up and crashed into a Dutch barn. He was lucky not to hit to either the guardhouse or the firehouse. I flew the new Commander of the *Pretoria Castle*, Lieutenant-Commander Slee, to Renfrew, near Glasgow, in an Avenger. I called at Donibristle, near Edinburgh, on the way back to pick something up. What a small airfield Donibristle was! And there is a nasty hill in the way if you take off in one particular direction. With a following wind from Donibristle I was back in Crail in 15 minutes.

On 9 February the Fifth Sea Lord, Vice-Admiral Boyd, arrived and spoke to an assembly of officers in the wardroom. He spoke for an hour and a quarter and was most interesting. I remember him remarking how good it was to see young faces. I supposed that after all the old fogies in the Admiralty we were a bit of a contrast! I have the same reaction now that I am no longer in the first flush of youth and meet a lot of fellow old age pensioners. To see young people afterwards is quite stimulating! I remember the Sea Lord saying that he had a transcription on the wall of his office reading, 'Nil illigitimis carborundum' which I gather was dog-Latin for, 'Don't let the bastards get you down'.

On 16 February I had my last flight in a Seafire. Never again would I have the joy of taking a fighter aircraft up to 10,000 feet and 'dance the skies in laughter-silvered wings'. Nor of joining 'the sun-split clouds – and doing a hundred things you'll not have dreamed of – wheeled and soared and swung in sunlit silence'. And nor would I chase 'the shouting wind along through footless halls of air'. Not in a fighter aircraft anyway. The words in quotes are adapted from *High Flight* by John Gillespie Magee.

On the 17th I had the exciting news that my 16-year-old brother Dick had arrived from the Argentine. He was there with me during the summer holidays of 1939. When war was declared I returned home, but he stayed on with our parents. He travelled home in the *Port Wyndham*; by an odd coincidence this was the same shipping line – The Port Line – that we had used coming back from New Zealand in 1931. At that time it was in the *Port Fremantle*. Dick's ship, a cargo vessel of some 10,000 tons displacement, left Buenos Aires, called in at Montevideo to pick up some magnesium and other cargoes and then sailed alone all the way to Liverpool. The passengers they had onboard were mainly Anglo-Argentine volunteers who were being transported to join up. The only slight scare they had during the trip was some phosphorescence that was spotted that might have been the wake of a ship or a submarine or perhaps a whale. By a most amazing coincidence Dick said that an aircraft carrier had followed his ship into the port and it was of Illustrious class. Research proved that this was indeed my old ship HMS *Victorious*.

I spoke to the CO and explained that I had not seen my brother since 1939 and he agreed to give me some time off. Sandy Powell flew me down to York in the back of a Firefly. Conditions were not good owing to low cloud and we both spent the night there. I arrived at Chipstead next afternoon and was greeted by someone who was only eleven years old when I had last seen him. He was now sixteen, his voice had broken, he was taller of course and his face had lengthened. We talked until late in the evening. Dick used to be keen on joining the navy, but his thoughts were now turning towards flying. I suggested he make his mind up after a spell in the JTC at Bradfield. My aunt and uncle went to bed and I remarked that we were bound to have an air raid as we always did when I was at Chipstead. This turned out to be true and we had not been in bed very long before the sirens went. This was all new to Dick and we both got up to see the fun. The searchlights were up and we could hear the noise of planes. Red balls began to drop over London – something I had never seen before – and showers of sparks fell from the sky. We could see that parts of London were on fire and things stayed that way until after the all clear. We had no bangs or bombs near us, and I believe Dick thought things were a bit tame!

Next day I started my motorbike and showed Dick how to do it and also gave him a short ride up Walpole Avenue. I left in the afternoon, catching the night train to Edinburgh. Dick went to my old house, Hillside, at Bradfield. It must have been hard for him arriving at the age of sixteen.

Back at Crail I found I was going to do some more trials on the *Pretoria Castle* with an Avenger. This time they were going to be take-off trials. I flew direct from Crail to the ship, but on arrival found that the dome of the propeller had an oil leak and as there were no facilities for repairs on board had to fly to Renfrew for repairs. We had trouble obtaining the right part and it was getting dark before we found it. I spent the night in Abbotsinch.

The fitters took some time to repair the dome, the main trouble being in getting the old dome off, but we were airborne late morning and had lunch aboard the ship. We started the trials immediately after the meal. On these tests the aircraft was placed on a certain mark so many feet from the bows and I would take off. If the aircraft did not sink after leaving the bows a new mark was placed about ten feet further up the deck. If the aircraft did not lose height then it would be taken down to the hangar deck and extra weight added and tests would start again from similar positions. The extra weight was created by filling droppable tanks with water. The process was repeated again and again while the boffins took figures. Altogether I did 24 landings and take offs in two days plus the two for my two arrivals. These brought my total deck landing sum to 135. Whilst this was a respectable number it was not a patch on the number carried out by Winkle Brown with his figure of over 2,407.

I flew to Abbotsinch with two Admiralty reps in the back. The weather was hazy and I had some trouble finding the place. It was an awful airfield – all grass – and there were crosses on it indicating bad ground. I felt the aircraft would go over on its nose at any moment. I went on to Machrihanish as the weather was not good and anyway I thought that some 832 types might be there. Unfortunately they had left a week earlier; however, the *Victorious* air group was there and I spoke to Lieutenant-Commander Tickler and Lieutenant Jolly. I also met Jack Lee who was on 19 Course St Vincent with me.

I left for Crail next day and went via the Stirling valley. I turned aside to look at Aberfoyle and Loch Chon where Dick and I had spent two very boring school holidays with people who made a living by looking after 'orphans' during their holidays, 'orphans' in this case referring to kids whose parents were abroad.

I flew a Harvard in the afternoon, an aircraft that is very similar to the Yale that I flew in Canada. Those who are old enough to remember the war will recall that the Harvard was an extremely noisy aircraft and instantly recognisable from its sound. I did not enjoy the flight very much as I did not feel too well after the sausage roll I had at lunch!

25 February. Great news! I was told I had been accepted for a helicopter course! I was to report to a Lieutenant-Commander Peat at General Aircraft Ltd, London Air Park, Hanworth, in Middlesex. The geographical location was also good news because it was near London. It could have been in Twatt in the north of the Orkneys or some outlandish place like that; but no it was within a hundred miles of all the places I had spent my youth when in England.

The trouble with my sudden appointment was that with Whatley away there was no Avenger King available for some trials to take place shortly aboard HMS *Atheling*, which was an American-built escort carrier. I can only think that this ship was being used for trials because the *Pretoria Castle* was in dock or employed on other duties. I showed David Adamson around the cockpit of the Avenger, for either he or Gardner would be doing the trials. David took off for a familiarisation flight. He didn't like the aircraft very much; after his experiences on fighter aircraft the Avenger must have felt like a lumbering bus and he found the controls heavy and the constant and necessary use of the trimmers was irritating.

The time came for me to say goodbye to fixed wing flying – apart from some gliding I did, and fortunately there was a Barracuda that had to be taken down to Eastleigh. I thought this would be my last flight in a powered fixed-wing aircraft, but in September when I was at Hanworth I was asked if I would collect a Magister at Brough and take it to Hanworth. I wondered how I would feel flying a fixed-wing aircraft again, but I had no trouble at all and it was as if I had never left it. Like the Haslemere incident where the first thing the recruiting Royal Marine said to me was. 'How do you spell Haslemere?' and my last appointment was to Haslemere, the first fixed-wing aircraft I flew, and the last, was a Magister!

20

HELICOPTER PILOT'S COURSE, HANWORTH

The London Air Park was a small grass airfield surrounded on three sides by houses or the factory of General Aircraft Ltd. In the centre of the field (yes, the centre!) was a hotel, with an acre or two of lawns and trees. The hotel was not operating as such and some of the rooms wore earmarked as our offices, and there was also a small hangar and a plot of ground for the use of the combined RN/RAF Unit. The main activity of General Aircraft was in the construction of Fairey Fireflys, which was ironic for me, for had I stayed in the Service Trials Unit for a few more months I would have undoubtedly added the type to my logbook. As it was, I was obliged to see the aircraft in various stages of construction almost every day for a year.

The whole set-up had a dream-like quality and, indeed, I spent the next twelve months pinching myself to see whether I was alive. Not only was I on the first helicopter course in the country, but to be shot straight from service life to that comparable with a privileged civilian was too good to be true. The contrast could only have been greater if I had come straight from an operational carrier. The spirit of the unit could, on reflection, be compared with that which existed about the time of the First World War, for we had enthusiasm and crude aircraft. There was even a similarity in that while many people expressed their wonder at the things the aircraft could do, those who held the purse strings remained unconvinced and wanted to spend available cash on other things. I remember that a few years after this period someone said that if the government had put as much money into helicopters as it had into the tail of the Brabazon we might have led the world. Even in 1944 we could visualise helicopters that could carry tanks, thus altering the whole concept of battlefield strategy. We thought that helicopters would be in proper airline service in about ten years time, but our ideas ran ahead of practicality in this context.

On arriving at Hanworth I met Lieutenant-Commander Peat, who was the CO of the Unit and who had had a course in the States. He gave me my first flight in the Sikorsky R4 (FT834) on 4 March 1944, thereafter flying but little, spending most of his time on the administrative side. I owed a lot to Igor Sikorsky for he changed my life; some years later I was privileged to meet him no less than three times, the last occasion being when I piloted him in a Widgeon helicopter. He showed an interest in the new system of control that was a great improvement on the controls of the Dragonfly the design upon which the Widgeon was based.

The instructor was Flight Lieutenant 'Jeep' Cable and he was the mainstay of the flying side. He was an ex-Autogiro pilot and had the distinction for many years of being the only man who flew helicopters without having first flown fixed-wing aircraft. He had sound common sense and was so strong that one felt that if he could not get the aircraft to do what he wanted he would get out and lift it into place. He was the kingpin of the unit and we could not have worked so efficiently without him. In August he became CO of the Unit when Lieutenant-Commander Peat was put in charge of the RN/RAF Unit at Floyd Bennett field, New York. The engineer officer was Flight Lieutenant Charles Loder (whom I met again some years later working in some ministry or other). Helping him and liaising with his firm of Sikorsky was Mr Montgomery – 'Monty' to his friends. Monty spent many of his leisure hours touring the English countryside on a bicycle, putting the lie to the idea that Americans never went anywhere except by car. The engineering side was augmented a few days later by Lieutenant 'Robby' Robertson, who was new to helicopters, but quickly found them of absorbing interest. His lectures were enlivened by his artistic skill and many an unusual feature of engineering or flying was enhanced by his drawings. He later emigrated to Australia.

My fellow student on the course was Lieutenant (A) Neil Fuller, RNVR, and my senior as I was only a Sub-Lieutenant. He became a Lieutenant-Commander RN after the war. The remainder of the unit consisted chiefly of naval ratings, for the initial idea of our training was to use the helicopters for convoy protection. To this end the helicopters had been shipped over in flying condition on the deck of a specially converted ship the *Dagestan*. During the voyage the weather had been so inclement that the tests had not been as extensive as had been hoped. Indeed, so rough was the weather that for the next year I was regaled with tales of how high the waves were, what angle the deck had heeled over to, and generally how intrepid everyone had been. If I were to murmur gently, 'When I was in the Home Fleet . . .' or 'When I was in the Arctic . . .' they would look at me as if I was some freak; anyway, wasn't I in the Navy and expected to put up with such things?

1944. An old C30 Autogiro pays a visit to Hanworth. The men facing the camera are, from left to right, Neil Fuller, Robbie Robertson and 'Jeep' Cable.

1944. At Hanworth. Mr Montgomery, the American Advisor, with Mr Taylor and Chas. Loder, the engineering officer.

I am glad to say that the idea of using the R4 against submarines was cancelled – mainly because there were soon to be enough escort carriers to do the job. The mind boggles at the thought of the R4 with a hundred pound depth charge trying to get back to the ship in a fifty knot wind when the maximum speed of the aircraft was only sixty knots.

In discussing the peculiarities of the R4 I must emphasise that although it had severe limitations it did a grand job in showing the world what helicopters could do. With the exercise of only a little imagination one could visualise the future potential of rotary wings. I had a great affection for the R4 and had more fun with it than any other helicopter. Small helicopters are always fun to fly, but this was my first and it provided the novelty and mystique. Additionally there was a certain delight in showing the helicopter to the world; wherever we took the aircraft we caused a sensation, for no one had seen this sort of vehicle before. After all, there were only three helicopters in Britain for a month or two after my arrival at Hanworth; the R4 held the centre of the stage at any gathering, and the pilots could not avoid the limelight.

It must have been about the year 2004 that one of our national newspapers got it into its head that the R4 had been flown by RAF pilots in Burma during the year 1943. I knew this was not possible and the pilots were, in fact, US Army pilots. Since I knew all the British helicopter pilots of that time, or had heard of them, I was able to assure the newspaper that it was not the RAF doing this job in Burma. Did they believe me? No, they did not! My letter was not even published and the false information was even picked up and repeated by someone else.

However, back to the year 1944! After starting the engine on the R4 and warming it up the first unusual control to operate was the combined rotor brake and clutch lever. This was a long vertical lever hinged at the bottom and mounted between the two pilots, who sat side by side. If it was moved forward the rotor brake came on, if it was moved back the clutch would be engaged. Simple, yes, but the clutch was not the centrifugal clutch know today, it was a plate type like the one in motor cars, so very strong springs were used to hold it in the engaged position, consequently, when releasing the rotor brake and engaging the clutch one had to tense one's muscles against a considerable force to prevent the engagement being too fierce. Failure to prevent a quick engagement would result in the shear pins being stripped. These were weak link safety devices fitted in the transmission and in the event of a gear-box seizure the pins would break and allow the rotor to carry on rotating. There was also of course a freewheel clutch similar to the ones we know today, fitted in the transmission.

Unfortunately the pins would shear if the rotor brake were applied too fiercely, and in this case the tail rotor gear-box would be damaged, for the tail-rotor drive shaft would be stopped almost instantaneously. I discovered this the hard way!

The R4 must have been the most underpowered helicopter ever to be put into production. This is probably why, knowing that it was as easy to over-pitch as wink, the designers made the throttle cam profile an exaggerated one so, unfortunately, on raising the collective-pitch lever for the take-off the pilot had to wind *back* the twist grip by copious amounts-to prevent the engine overspeeding. On lowering the lever the converse applied.

In later production models a wooden stop was introduced which prevented the pilot raising the lever above a certain limit, presumably to prevent over-pitching. Whoever thought the idea up could not have appreciated that in the R4 momentary and deliberate over-pitching was necessary in certain manoeuvres. On seeing these stops on new aircraft I would have them removed immediately; they were positively dangerous.

Despite the lack of power in the R4 it is of interest to note that I once managed to reach the height of 8,000 feet, and that this took me twenty minutes.

On the first few aircraft at Hanworth there were two tachometers – two completely separate instruments, one for engine rpm and one for rotor rpm. (I wonder what the pilot of a modern twin-engined helicopter would think if he had three clock faces to scan!) Fortunately this situation did not last long and the new instruments with synchronised superimposed needles were fitted. Additional information was provided by the tachometers: if, when hovering, the engine the rpm commenced to rise and the rotor rpm to fall, it was an indication of clutch slip! Fortunately this was something I experienced only once during a hovering exercise with Jeep and was caused by grease getting on the plates. There was only one red line on the engine tachometer, I believe it was intended as an upper engine rpm limit but, owing to the lack of power, Jeep told me never to let the engine rpm drop *below* this line. I do not know what the rules were in other schools, but the system worked well with us and the Warner Super Scarab engine never seemed to suffer any damage.

Now for the cyclic-pitch stick. Whilst the effect of any stick movement was similar to that of any present-day helicopter, the pilot of the R4 had an additional problem: the stick described an orbit in flight, taking the pilot's hand round in a circle as one flew! This was due to the feed back of forces from the rotor blades which, being crude fabric-covered aerofoils, were virtually impossible to match as a set. True, we had one

1945. The author hovering a Sikorsky R4 at Witley Park, near Haslemere.

aircraft, in which the orbit of the stick was about an inch, but the usual movement was about three inches, consequently one did not ease the *stick* forward, one eased the *orbit* forward; and the hand described a rotary motion for the whole of the flight.

In those early days and for several decades afterwards the tilting of the rotor disc in helicopters was achieved by the flapping of the blades. When the disc was tilted by this method a moment was created about the c.g. (centre of gravity) of the aircraft (the fulcrum being the c.g. and the moment arm being the distance between the rotor head and the c.g.). This meant that not only was there a bit of delay in the response to control movements, but that the controls lacked a certain amount of sensitivity. With the coming of so-called rigid rotors a control movement produced a couple at the rotor head. The rotor would tilt and the fuselage would tilt *with* it, so response and sensitivity were considerably increased.

As for the stick trim, after a month or two enduring the meaningless forces acting on the stick it was quite an advantage for us to fit adjustable pieces of bungee to it so as to relieve some of the muscular strain. The system was taken a stage further in the early WS.51 Dragonfly except that the bungee was hidden from view and was operated by electric motors. Later aircraft used torsion bars. With the coming of powered controls (essential in anything but small helicopters) control forces became negligible and artificial feel and trimmers could be added.

There was only one collective-pitch lever in the R4 and this was situated between the two pilots. In the simplest permutation, if your instructor was trained on the left-hand side then you would be a right-hand seat pilot; your pupils would be left-hand seat pilots and so on. In practice we tried to become ambidextrous, which was easier for the pilots who were trained initially the hard way (i.e. left hand on the stick, right hand on the throttle). On changing seats, from whichever side, a few hours' essential training was required with a safety pilot in the other seat.

Having one central collective-pitch lever simplified the manufacturer's task and for some while pressure was applied by designers of later helicopters on pilots to accept it as the standard. I was always against it and was surprised to find that one or two pilots maintained that two separate levers were unnecessary. The Americans did not appear to have any illusions for very long and even the early Bell model I flew in 1947 had two separate levers. In Britain at least one fatal accident occurred because a pilot believed he could fly on an unfamiliar side without having dual training first.

For dual instruction to be carried out with only one lever there was a slight problem: the twist-grip throttle was not long enough for two hands to be on it at the same time. So the matey situation arose whereby the instructor's hand had to be placed on top of the pupil's, and Jeep's great paw was clamped around my normal-sized hand for two or three hours' dual.

As a right-hand-on-throttle pilot I had an additional difficulty: my mode of ground transport was a motorcycle with a twist-grip throttle! In an emergency in a helicopter one opens the throttle fully; whereas an emergency on a motorcycle generally calls for immediate closing of the throttle. Since, after practice, one's reactions tend to be automatic, I had to ensure that the part of my mind controlling my right hand was fully aware which vehicle I was operating, and this called for extra concentration. Only once did I make a mistake because of this confusion (I made several in the normal course of training due to the throttle not acting in a natural sense, but this was to be expected).

A question often asked by the layman is why the captain of a helicopter sits on the right? It *is* due to two factors: 1. The ancillary switches of the aircraft must be in the centre of the cockpit so as to be available to both pilots. 2. The stick is held in the right hand. Thus the captain does not have to let go of that most important of controls in order to operate the switches. If the poor second pilot wishes to work any of the switches he must, of course, change hands on the stick in order to do so.

Apart from the lack of vertical performance, handling in the hover was normal. Moving forward from the hover into a climb could be tricky, however, especially if there were two crew members, with the extra weight that entailed, and it was a hot calm day. How many present-day pilots have ever tried to move forward from the hover and found that they were over-pitching and were forced to make a landing in order to recover the rpm? None, I expect; but it happened to me on several occasions, especially at the higher altitudes from which I operated after leaving Hanworth. The ground cushion was of greater value than it is today for one would have to maintain it carefully whilst edging forward to gain airspeed, the aim being to exchange it gradually for translational lift. The *ground cushion* or *ground effect* is the increased lift due to the air trapped between the rotor and the ground being at a greater pressure. It was a satisfying feeling when the little hump of a cushion under the front section of the rotor disc would suddenly shoot underneath and dissipate itself rearwards. At the same time the airspeed indicator would give a positive reading. Could the R4 not climb vertically at all, you might ask? Not under the worst conditions. As an example I can mention the time I landed KL113 in the High Street at Wickham (near Lee-on-Solent) for some victory celebrations. In front of the entire population of Wickham, Commodore Halsey climbed aboard for a short flight. The aircraft would go no higher than four feet, and I had no room to move forward to gain translational lift! I had to shout: 'Sorry, sir, I can't get any higher!' He seemed quite content and I landed the aircraft again after a minute's hovering. Without his weight in the aircraft I was able to climb vertically away and then give a short demonstration of the helicopter's capabilities.

In forward flight the aircraft vibrated badly and the maximum airspeed was low. It was ignominious to be overtaken by trains when travelling by 'Bradshaw', but early helicopter pilots became used to it. Even when I was in British European Airways the same humiliating experience would occur with the Bell 47 when the wind was against us. It was also very galling to have to land the R4 whenever there was heavy rain, for we found that the tips of the blades could become damaged if we did not.

The chief difficulty in learning to fly a helicopter is the co-ordination required and this comes with practice. One has to juggle the cyclic and collective controls and the rudder pedals and, *especially*, the throttle.

When automatic rpm control came in some decades later the problems with the throttle were eased somewhat. When flying in autorotation there is an additional skill to be learnt and that is controlling the rotor rpm. However, in a light helicopter like the R4 the problem of the rpm rising above limits if not controlled never occurred at low altitudes. We could do flares and carry out turns in autorotation without bothering about the rotor rpm; indeed we never even knew there was a problem until we started to fly heavier helicopters, so that was one difficulty we, in those pioneering years, never had to face. With heavier helicopters the rotor rpm will tend to rise above the safety margin in any manoeuvres where g is increased; sometimes they can do this with alarming rapidity and the experienced pilot will react almost instinctively and raise the collective pitch lever accordingly – sometimes by quite large amounts. In training, this basic exercise may take quite a bit of time to absorb and one must remember to look after the engine rpm at the same time, although generally they are on the idle mark.

I never carried out any engine-off landings in the R4. The designers had given the aircraft a fairly robust undercarriage, but there was nothing at the forward end to prevent the machine nosing over, and there was a strong feeling that this would occur, especially on grass. In 1945 this belief was proved to be incorrect when many engine-off landings were made at Beaulieu. All the same our opinions had some basis, for it was difficult to taxi forward on grass without the nose of the aircraft pitching down.

Not only did I never carry out any engine-off landings, but for the first thirty hours of training I never flew in autorotation! True, we had discussed autorotation, but with breath slightly bated, and was something we would use only in the event of engine failure, rather than a normal means of descent. The responsibility for this attitude must surely rest with the fact that we had two separate tachometers, which made it difficult to detect what would now be referred to as 'needles split' and 'needles joined'. We were told how to do flare outs, but never practised them at that stage; we just hoped that nothing so awful as engine failure would occur. I was talking to Jeep one day when he said: 'By the way, John, have you tried any autorotations yet?' I blanched: 'G-good God no!' 'I think you ought to try some.' 'T-try some? Well all right, if you say so. What do you want me to do, do I close the throttle and then put the lever down, or put the lever down and then close the throttle?'

He explained what he wanted. Fortunately all the aircraft had the new tachometers by then. I got airborne and climbed to a suitable height and very gingerly lowered the lever, maintaining the rpm at the red line. The lever reached the bottom stop. I said a short prayer and gently closed the throttle. The needles split! I had achieved autorotation! If I had a pound for every occasion I have flown in autorotation since that day I would be a very rich man. Later on, in BEA and at Westland, I trained some 300 pilots to fly helicopters and apart from demonstrating how to do engine-off landings I always got them to do several before flying solo. I would do some more with them after solo. In the Dragonfly and the Bell47-3B-1 I used to carry out engine-off landings for fun, usually trying to land on a designated mark on the airfield. During my helicopter career I must have carried out over 3,000 engine-off landings.

It is worth going into the technique of engine-off landings. Early on we were told that a sharp flare was necessary not only to slow the descent but also to raise the rotor rpm. In 1947 I made my return to helicopters after a gap of over a year and had some dual instruction with Wing Commander Capper of Irvin Bell Helicopter Sales in the Bell47, which British European Airways were to operate. To my surprise he made 'No Flare Landings'. In other words the helicopter was held at a constant airspeed (about 40 knots) during the whole of the approach. The collective-pitch lever was raised just before arrival on the ground. This worked well, but later on I modified it so that a slight flare was made, in a similar way to that of a fixed-wing aircraft; the helicopter then being returned to a level attitude and the lever raised as necessary to make a finely tuned landing. This method is fairly easy for new students to do and will give them confidence.

I thought that this was the final solution to engine-off landings carried out for practice, but any scramble to get into a small space in an emergency would require a different technique and might result in some damage to the aircraft. However I was wrong. It must have been about 1951 when Ken Reed, who was a test pilot at Westland Aircraft prior to my joining the firm, demonstrated to me another technique in the Dragonfly; we knew of it in theory but had never tried it out. After a normal approach a gentle flare was made at about 200 feet altitude and the aircraft was then allowed to descend *vertically*. When all seemed lost and with the aircraft descending rapidly toward the ground the collective-pitch lever was raised fully when the height of about 15 feet was reached. There was sufficient energy in the rotor to completely cushion the landing. I tried this myself and it worked every time, it was just that up to that time we had not appreciated the tremendous energy stored in the rotor. Naturally the manoeuvre is not as straightforward as it might seem by the written word; for example the aircraft might be lighter or heavier which would affect the situation or there might be a wind. Skill is certainly required and if one finds that the helicopter has come to a hover at 10 feet the lever must be lowered to retain as many rotor rpm as possible before cushioning the landing by raising it again. This worked well for the Dragonfly; other aircraft might have different characteristics. Unfortunately Ken told me that the lever must be lowered to the bottom stop immediately after touchdown and I was surprised at the alacrity with which he did this. In fact it would have been better to lower it to just *above* the bottom stop even on normal run-on engine-off landings. I once did an ordinary engine-off landing in a Whirlwind that I was testing. In this particular aircraft the autorotation rpm were too high (because the collective-pitch angle of the blades had been set too low) and what I had not appreciated was that when I put the collective-pitch lever fully down after touchdown the rotor blades would sweep lower than normal. Unfortunately the blades came down and hit the tail boom! Lesson learnt!

My impression of engine-off landings in those early days was that neither we nor the Americans knew much about them and no one had gone into the matter very seriously. In Britain this lapse was rectified by the tests at Beaulieu in 1945. As for the question of who were the first people to do engine-off landings, when doing some research I was surprised to find that both the French in the Breguet-Dorand and the Germans in the Fw61 had carried out some before the war.

On 8 May 1944, Jeep was flying R4 FT835 with the Chief Test Pilot of Boscombe Down, Squadron Leader Hastings, when the cyclic control failed. He autorotated down, fortunately staying the right way up, heaved up the lever at the last moment and both he and his passenger clambered out of the wreckage. The other aircraft were grounded for a few days after that while modifications were carried out to prevent the trouble recurring.

D-Day came and went with absolutely no extra aerial activity; in fact it was all very quiet, most of the action being further south. Later that month Jeep managed to borrow a C.30 Autogiro (K4239) and he gave me two trips in it. I found the most unusual feature of its flying characteristics to be the landing; it felt all wrong to have no collective-pitch lever with which to cushion the touch-down. On reflection, the landings were similar to a powerless landing in a fixed-wing aircraft; one just waited for the speed of the rotor, or the wing, to decay. On the second flight our landing coincided with the arrival of a V1 overhead and we scrambled out of the aircraft and prepared to lie down, but the 'doodlebug' flew on. We had several scares at Hanworth, the worst being when the factory loudspeaker burst forth with, 'Lie down! Lie down!' Naturally we thought that a V1 was diving down on us, but nothing happened and to this day I do not know why the order was given. On reading my diary I find that I had forgotten how much the V1s disturbed our lives. We lost a lot of sleep, had plenty of frights, and on one occasion the paint store at General Aircraft was hit and set on fire. One day I was looking out of a window when a V1 fell nearby; the blast was like a slap in the face.

The most frightening situation that happened to me was when I was in a café just by The Anchor and Kings Head in Shepperton. It was called Len's and was famous for the number of cobwebs that bestrewed the place. Woe betide you if you wanted them moved! The sirens went off – the first we had had for several weeks. We heard one explosion and then heard a doodlebug coming in our direction. I did not want to be caught inside so went outside the door to find that the aircraft was still coming straight for us. The engine coughed and I thought, 'We're for it'. At the same time a searchlight north of our position went out. This was usually a sign that the doodlebug was diving. Then I heard a whistling, which was the first time I had heard such a noise from a flying bomb, but then I had never been so close to one before. The machine sounded just as if it was coming straight for me and I thought, 'After five years of war I've had it!' and, 'Poor old Mum!' My next thought was that I might as well have a look at the wretched thing before I died. I was half kneeling on the ground by then and I looked upwards. The device was going at high speed in a *flat glide* in the direction of Chertsey and at an altitude of about 200 feet. The light in the tail was out as the engine had stopped but the tail was still glowing from the heat. This was the only flying bomb I had ever heard of that did not dive as the engine cut out.

I went back into Len's. Everyone was lying or kneeling down and I said, 'It's all right it's gone over'. No one believed me at first, as they had not heard a bang. I popped into The Anchor where everyone was talking about their experiences. One lady had torn her stockings when lying down and another man had grazed his arm. This was an anticlimax for if the bomb had behaved as all others did they would have been dead. In The King's Head across the way everyone seemed to have made himself or herself scarce. While there I downed a gin, which cost me 2/-.

I kept a map of where flying bombs had landed and which I knew about and it was really surprising to see how many houses got hit. On one occasion I passed a house that had been struck and it was only a few days later that the one next to it was hit. On visiting Chipstead I discovered that all the front windows in my grandmother's house had been blown in by a bomb that landed some hundreds of yards in front of the house. The name of the house was Tepestede, which was the name for Chipstead at the time of the Doomsday Book, indeed above the mantelpiece in the hall was an extract from that work. The name Tepestede had been crossed through which, I was informed, was the custom of the time with place names.

The V2s started to arrive and I remember hearing them coming *after* hearing the explosion of their arrival. I surmised correctly what they were, although at the time the semi-official bulletins stated that they were gas mains exploding (older British readers may recall that, after the war, when a gas main really did explode, some wag at the gas board reported that it was a V2 going off!). The V2s were not so nerve-wracking as the doodle bugs; if you heard a V2 coming you knew that it had missed you.

In case one might think that my time at Hanworth was spent mostly at work – it was not! With only three aircraft and with one or all of them unserviceable or undergoing inspections I had plenty of time off. Indeed, on reading my diary I was amazed at the number of times I was told I was not wanted and I could go off for an afternoon, a day, or even a few days. I spent a lot of time visiting friends and relations. I had digs in a pub in Hampton, The Red Lion, for some months, and as they kept hens I was a given an egg for breakfast every morning, A rare treat! My motorbike came in useful not only to get me from Hampton to Hanworth, but also to travel around the countryside. I eventually sold it and bought my first car, a Ford Popular. An amateur mechanic like me could take it to pieces and reassemble it without too much difficulty, something that would be impossible to do with a modern car.

I took dancing instruction with a studio in Kingston run by the famous Alex Moore. These lessons stood me in good stead when I was able to take up the pastime more seriously in later years. Alex Moore had written a book on dancing in which he had drawn plan views of the positions of one's feet on the floor. He told me that this was the most difficult part of the book to do.

I went up to London several times and during one of those occasions I was introduced to a Wren, Diana Wintersladen, who was stationed at Stanmore, which was an out-station of Bletchley Park. I was not aware of the task she was engaged in at the time and it was only many years later that she was able to tell me or anyone else what she had been doing, in fact she was always scared of letting out the secret by mistake. She married Julian St John Brooks, then a Captain later a Major, to whom I sold my old Ford Popular. I became a friend of the family and a godfather to one of their daughters.

One unusual feature of my trips to London was that I always seemed to come across the CIGS (Chief of the Imperial General Staff) General Sir Alan Brooke (later Field Marshall Lord Alanbrooke) whenever I walked in the Whitehall area. If I passed him I, of course, gave him a salute. He had no guards, which amazed me; he was usually on his own without any protection as far as I could ascertain. It is said that he was the greatest CIGS we have ever had and when I read about the people and decisions he was concerned with I can well believe that fact.

Desmond Whatley from the Service Trials Unit came along to see what I was doing and told me the tragic news that Hutchins and Luke had been killed in a flying accident.

I ran into Alan Lawrence (formerly of 817 Squadron) in London and also met Dick Grimsdale when walking along in Piccadilly. Dick had just come back from Ceylon and gave me news of some of the people I knew. This was the last time I saw Dick for he, too, was killed in 1945 in a flying accident.

Unfortunately during these and later months I heard the sad news that Harold Hawken had been killed when an aircraft landed on top of him while he was waiting to take off. He had great leadership potential and was very pleasant and approachable. Faj Pennington, whose character I've mentioned before, was killed when his aircraft collided with another in the Pacific, he had become a squadron commander by that time. Jeff Jefford was killed when he was in the back of an Avenger and it hit a hill in bad weather. It was not until the end of the war that I heard the Tony Garland, by that time a squadron CO, had been shot down by a Japanese aircraft. After the war, Guy Richardson, who was stroke for the winning eight in the university boat race and who I met a year or two later, was killed when his passenger aircraft crashed at Heathrow.

Reading my diary I came across an interesting list of prices I was charged during those times. Like the cost of living a hundred years previously where you would go up to London to see a show, wine and dine your friends and still have change from £2 – or something like that – my list contained the following:

Newspaper 1d
Bus fare 3d
Train fare 1/6d
Tube fare 2d
Dinner 3/6
Cinema 2/3

I was fairly naïve about the cost of buying food in those days and when I bought a loaf of bread and asked how much it was I was told, 'Two and three', which normally meant 2/3d in those days. I handed the lady half a crown expecting to receive 3d change. However what she had meant was tuppence three farthings!

In August floats were put on F1834 and an unlooked-for bonus was the improvement in stability of the aircraft in forward flight. We carried out some water landings in a nearby quarry and it was great fun landing on water for a change. In twenty-four years of flying helicopters I managed to make water landings on only one other occasion, and that was when carrying out tests with a WS.51 in Southampton water.

The Air Minister, Lord Brabazon, came to visit us. Unfortunately no one had told the gatekeeper to expect him and the great man was kept waiting in his car while enquiries were made. He was not in the best of tempers when he finally saw a demonstration and shook hands with all of us. I met him many years later and reminded him of the incident; surprisingly, he had forgotten it.

Although Neil Fuller and I were on a full-length course, there were several people who came along for courses of varying lengths, depending on their need. Among the first to come was Squadron Leader Alan Marsh. He was a great pilot whose considerable experience covered both fixed and rotary wings, having been CO of an Autogiro squadron. Kind hearted and approachable he nevertheless had plenty of authority when it was needed. Jeep always called him 'Skipper', possibly because he was his former CO. This was the name I always called him by too. After the war both Jeep Cable and Alan Marsh worked for The Saunders Roe Company and they were killed when the Air Horse (a three-rotored helicopter) crashed.

Then there was Major Bill Nelson, who had dropped a rank in order to take the course. And Major Jim Cordes, who was Manager and Chief Test Pilot of No. 8 AAU at Hooten Park. He was responsible for testing the R4s after assembly, and I made several trips up there to pick up aircraft for delivery. Captain Liptrot, who had been a helicopter enthusiast all his life and had actually flown the Asboth 'helicopter' in 1928 (I have used inverted commas because the aircraft used a system of contra-rotating airscrews. It could achieve twelve knots in forward flight, but there was no possibility of flying in autorotation). Squadron Leader Little of Sherburn-in-Elmet; Norman Hill; and L.S. Armandias.

L.S. Armandias was an interesting man. He had dual British and French nationality and after the fall of France he went back to France at considerable risk and rescued some valuable blueprints from a factory. In fact he was a Captain in Army Intelligence and we understood his interest in helicopters was that he thought they could be used to drop agents into France. Possibly the lack of performance of the R4 disabused him of that idea. Anyway, after a course at Hanworth he went on to help with tests at Beaulieu.

After the war Armandias become co-founder of British Messier Limited, thereafter he was involved in many different managerial and consultancy roles, mostly concerned with aeronautical and other military engineering. He was a Fellow of the Royal Aeronautical Society and in 1953 was awarded the Médaille de L'Aéronautique by the French Government for his achievements in aeronautics.

Another frequent caller was Raoul Hafner, who was working on the Rotachute at the time. He occasionally asked us questions as to our preferences for controls and other matters. In the autumn he went to Bristol and started work on the design of the Sycamore.

In the late summer of 1944 some of the pilots who had been trained on a parallel course in the USA started to call in. Among them were 'Sox' Hosegood, Ken Reed, Peter Albeury, Dick Bradbury, Basil Arkell – and a promising young (i.e. junior to me) officer named Alan Bristow. In 1945 he had the misfortune to be sent to Twatt in the north of the Orkneys for radar calibration work, which proves that not all of us were lucky enough to be appointed to congenial parts of the world at that time. He later became a test pilot with Westland Aircraft. The rest of his career is history for after whale hunting in the Antarctic and rescue work for the French in Vietnam (for which he received the Croix de Guerre) he formed his own firm Bristow Helicopters, which is known throughout the helicopter world.

Also returning from America were Major Richardson and Wing Commander Brie. The latter had come over earlier in the year in the *Daghestan*, but had returned almost immediately to the States. He later became my boss in the BEA Helicopter Unit.

The year at Hanworth was not spent entirely on training, in fact this was completed in a month or so, any delays being due to having no aircraft to fly. There were other jobs to do, notably ferrying aircraft round the countryside to their new bases. On one joyous occasion I flew round the jumps at Sandown Park!

One particular ferry job involved four helicopters and these had to be brought from Hooten Park to the RAF at Andover, where a school was starting up. So, for the first time in England four helicopters flew in formation. We flew from Hooten Park to Andover stopping at Cosford, Morton in the Marsh and Little Rissington to refuel on the way. The other pilots were Wing Commander Brie, Sox Hosegood, and Dick Bradbury. The largest formation I ever flew in was a decade of so later when over one hundred helicopters flew in line astern at the Paris Air Show.

To think of building a civil airport in the middle of a war I thought to be a bold step, and while at Hanworth we could see from the air the progress made in the creation of Heathrow Airport. At that time the runways were being made and great swathes of land were being carved out. There were few buildings apart from temporary ones. I thought I might try to be the first person to land there by making out that my cap had flown out of the window and then landing to pick it up. Looking back I regret that I did not carry out this idea!

21

ADMIRALTY SIGNALS ESTABLISHMENT, HASLEMERE

After a year at Hanworth I was appointed to the ASE (Admiralty Signals Establishment) at Haslemere. I had digs in Chiddingfold, a village nearby, but later moved to Cranleigh. So far as organisation went the Helicopter Unit had a curious existence: for pay and flying maintenance we were supported by Worthy Down; for discipline and control we were managed by Lythe Hill, Haslemere; the Helicopter Unit itself was based at Witley Park, a private estate near Haslemere. There were just two pilots: Neil Fuller and myself, and we worked from a caravan. There were a dozen ratings who did the maintenance in a canvas hangar. The whole set-up was pleasant enough in summer, but a bit frigid in winter.

It was about this time that my logbook entries change because the Admiralty decided to call the R4 the Gadfly. The RAF, on the other hand, called the aircraft the Hoverfly I. Our main task was radar calibration, for which purpose we would hover over the experimental area at Witley at an altitude of a few hundred feet, usually at full power, while tests and trials were made with new designs. How the aircraft held together under these conditions I do not know, but they did, and the radar people must have been thankful for having such a fine system for calibrating their systems. By far the greatest amount of work seemed to be for the Type 262. I did not know anything about it then, and it has remained a closed book to me since, but years later I mentioned the magic number 262 to a radar expert and his eyes lit up; he knew it well! So all our hovering had not been in vain.

Other tasks consisted of transporting personnel and goods (such as cathode ray tubes) round the country, and once I flew all the way to Drem for some forty five minutes hovering for some radar calibration. I was told that those few minutes had saved weeks of work. On this flight I had as a passenger Bill Thomson who was in 832 Squadron with me, what he was doing at Drem I do not remember. I met Bill several times after the war and was in contact with him until he died in Dunedin.

I once flew a naval officer down to Plymouth and landed in the Naval Barracks, this was the first time they had seen a helicopter down that way. This officer had his cap blown out of the window during the flight and we had to land in a field to pick it up!

I also managed to make a landing at Bradfield. It was, of course, the first time the boys had seen a helicopter. And for good measure I landed at my Grandfather's place at Awbridge.

Readers will notice that I have called the two main controls of the helicopter the *collective-pitch lever* and the *cyclic-pitch stick*. They were abbreviated to *lever* and *stick* during my training and I used these names when I subsequently trained some three hundred pupils. However the modern tendency is to refer to these controls as the *collective* and the *cyclic*. Reluctant as I am to convert adjectives to nouns I now go along with these appellations.

Germany was defeated. Then the atom bomb finished Japan. I was demobilised in January 1946 and did not touch a helicopter again for twenty months.

POSTSCRIPT

Now, when I reflect on the war there is no denying that I had an extremely cushy life during it. One reads about life in stormy weather in destroyers in the Atlantic for example, or the life of a soldier knee deep in mud or in a fox hole and being fired on by machine guns or mortar, or the Merchant Navy crews forever fearing a torpedo would come through the ship's side at any minute; the prisoners of war, especially those in the Far East; the millions in concentration camps. Countless numbers of people had an extremely hard time compared with that which I had and I'm sure many would have given their right arms to exchange places with me. For most of the war I had a decent bed to sleep in, unlike soldiers in the field.

I was lucky. During my time in the Navy I escaped death by some near collisions in the air; I crossed the Atlantic five times by sea without experiencing a submarine attack; I was in the Home Fleet covering Russian convoys; I was in Operation Pedestal, surely the most vital Malta convoy of the war. In that operation a bomb dropped on the deck of my ship only about twenty yards away from me and did not explode, another dropped near me into the sea and I got splashed. I operated by night in a lone biplane over the English Channel and got shot at. I went to the Pacific and back in HMS *Victorious* without seeing a Jap – that is, if you can discount the two Japanese prisoners of war we carried on board back to the States! On the ground I narrowly missed being chopped into pieces by a runaway Avenger. Back in Britain I had my face slapped by the blast from a V1. Another one flew low over my head in a flat glide rather than diving as they usually did. And in the Coral Sea I was upside down under water in my aircraft. I also had an engine failure when testing an aircraft and crashed in a field; and I had another engine failure, which if it had happened a minute earlier would have forced me to ditch in the sea instead of landing at the airfield almost below me. And due to my own carelessness I nearly ended up in bits on the Isle of Arran. Yes, I was indeed lucky. Again, when I started life with helicopters in 1944 I was living the life of a glorified civilian and yet was still in uniform – and it was an exceedingly interesting time to be in the helicopter world.

I'm afraid that most of my contemporaries in the Fleet Air Arm have gone to that great aircraft carrier in the sky and there are few of us left who were in 19 Course St Vincent. Hence the remark when I met a Fleet Air Arm man and he heard that I was in 19 Course, *'19 Course?* You should be dead!'

INDEX AND GLOSSARY

Note. It is not always practical to mention the ranks of service personnel. That which is accurate one day might be inaccurate a week later and changed yet again shortly afterwards. Indeed, the author knew of a flight controller at Manston who was a Pilot Officer one day and a Squadron Leader the next! In the majority of cases the ranks are omitted.

Page numbers in italics denote an illustration.

Brown L, shot down, 93

Browne, Bill, 73; finds *Tirpitz*, *92*; fatal accident, 150–151

Browning machine gun, 23

Burke, Geoff, 11

Burma, R4 operations in, 219

Burr, Lt, fatal accident, 206

Burbidge, John, foreword; in Norway operation, 89; at Manston, 121, *180*, at Tontouta 188; at San Diego, *187*; in 822 Squadron, 211

Busbridge, K.F. Lt RN, later Captain, 210

C.30 Autogiro, *218*; flight in, 226

Cable, 'Jeep', 217: accident in R4, 226: fatal accident in Air Horse, 230

Campbeltown, 208

Capability Brown, 21

Cap bands, *38*

Capper W/Cdr, 225

Captain Justice, 212

Captain's seating position in helicopter, reasons, 222

Carley floats, save lives, 100

Carpenter, Sid, *28*; helped with essay, 34; at Niagara, *43*; fatal accident and funeral, 63

Carter, David, 209

CASU = Carrier Air Service Unit

Charger, USS, deck landings on, 139; bad day for Martlets, 139

Chaser, HMS, 203

Chesapeake Bay, 139

Child, Gerry, lands on Icelandic beach, 80; in crash, 81; at Manston, 121; Channel operation, 124

Chipstead, 4 *et seq.*

Christmas day in Atlantic, 1942, 131

Cierva, Juan de la, 212

CIGS = Chief of the Imperial General Staff, 228

CINCPAC = Commander in Chief Pacific

Clams, Italian revenge, 191

Clockwork Mice, 63

Cloud cover, 211: Ten tenths is total cloud cover. The tenths were changed to eighths after the war and often referred to as 'Octas'

Clutch in R4, 219; clutch slip, 220

Clyde, sailing from, 33, 130

Coffman starter, 72

'Collective': pilots' abbreviation for collective-pitch lever.

Collective-pitch changes in a helicopter rotor: the rotor blades change pitch by equal amounts and in the same direction. Contrast with *cyclic pitch*.

Collective-pitch lever in side-by-side seating, 222

Compass platform, 74; personnel on, 74

Connolley, Gerry, in night operation, 88; depth charges whale, 119, 202

Convicts at Kingston, Ontario, 47

Convoys, *see* Malta and Russian

Coral Sea, 1–3, 180–184

Cordes, Major Jim, 230

Cork, Dickie, aboard Vic, 114

Corsair, in mid-air collision, 164, 191

Couple (statics), 221 (def: a pair of equal forces acting on the same body in opposite and parallel directions)

Cox, Gordon, 22

Crail, (RNAS), Ch. 81; after Malta convoy 119; appointment to 198

Cramp, Jack, 60, *62*

Cranfield, forced landing near, 26

Cristobal, arrive and remove projecting guns, 143, 145; on way to UK, 189

Croydon School, NZ, 205

Cuba, in sight, 143

Cuban officer, 191

Cullen, deck-landing crash, 193

Cumberland, HMS, 104

Cutlery, RAF system, 32, 40, 51

CW List Illustrated, 46

'Cyclic': pilots' abbreviation for cyclic-pitch stick.

Cyclic pitch changes in a helicopter rotor: The variation in pitch of the rotor blades as they rotate, depending on the position of the pilot's control. Blades diametrically opposite each other change pitch in opposite directions. Contrast with *collective pitch*.

Dagistan, Atlantic crossing, 217

Dancing lessons, 210, 228

Dash, Sergeant Major, 22

Randall, John, in 771 Squadron, 66; deck
 landing crash, 134; *169*, at Tontouta,
 177; song about crash, 185
Rangitane, intercepted by German raider,
 12
Ravager, HMS, 202
Ready Room, 92
Reardon RAF, fatal accident, 47
Reed, Ken, returns to UK from USA, 231;
 demonstrates vertical engine-off
 landing, 225
Reggiane 2001, attacks *Victorious*, 116
Reid, 'Black smoke Reid', 189
Renown, HMS, NZ reminiscences, 81–82;
 joins Home Fleet, 81; ALT on, 85;
 Russian convoy, 91
Repulse, HMS, news of sinking, 68
Reykjavik, RAF camp near, 49; Hugill flies
 to, 80
Richardson, Guy, in New York, 141; in San
 Diego, 187, 188; died in Heathrow
 crash, 229
Richardson, Major, 231
Richardson, Ray, 141
Rigid rotors, 221
RNAS = Royal Naval Air Station. Until
 1918 Royal Naval Air Service
Robertson L/A TAG, 93
Robertson, Robbie, engineer at Hanworth,
 217, *218*
Robin USS, pseudonym for HMS *Victorious*
 in Pacific
Roc, Blackburn, 65; differences from Skua,
 66; flight characteristics, 67
Rocket defence at Manston, 128
Rockettes, 141, 190
Rodney, HMS 76, Malta convoy Ch.12, out
 of control, 118
Roscoe, Third Officer WRNS, 203
Ross Cdr later Capt., joins *Victorious* as
 commander, 130, letter from, 182
Ross rifle, 14
Rosser, Petty Officer later CPO, 203
Rosyth, *Victorious* refits at, 96
Rotachute, Hafner designs, 231
Rotherham G.A. Cdr, finds *Bismarck* berth
 empty, 66
Rotor blades, advancing and retreating,
 212

Roundels, changed to US, types, 157
Royal Hotel, Thurso, 208
RPM = Revolutions Per Minute.
Russian convoys, 91, 95, 99, 105
Russian officers at Norfolk, 192
Rutherford 'Mac', foreword; at Manston,
 122, 125, 126

San Diego, 157, 186–188, *187*
Santa Maria convoy, *see* Operation
 Pedestal
Saratoga USS, 1; wardroom compared, 71;
 size, 171; 173, visit to, 172; engines,
 172; embarked aboard, 178; near
 collision, 183; turning circle, 178;
 living quarters, 183; letter from
 Captain, 183; letter from Admiral, 184
SBD (Dauntless dive bomber), 1; accident,
 161
Sardinian airfields attacked, 113
Saunders, Hugh, joins 832 Squadron, 138,
 192; ditches, 202
Scapa Flow, natural harbour in the
 Orkneys, base for the Home Fleet in
 WWII
Schonfeldt, 201
Sea Flight by Hugh Popham, 10, 22, 114
Seafire, first flight in, 206; evaluation, 206;
 last flight in, 213
Searchlights, evasion practice, 128; cause
 nuisance in Hawaii, 162
Selby L/A, 199
Send Her Victorious, by Mike Apps, 130
Service Trials unit, Ch.19, 198–215
SFTS (Service Flying Training School), Ch.
 5
Shackleton Group Capt., CO RAF
 Kingston, dies, 44
Shagbat, nickname for Walrus
Shaw, Artie, band leader aboard USS
 Washington, 174
Shaw, Brian, Squadron Staff Officer, 70, *83*
Shaw, F.A. 'Tubby' CO of 882 Squadron,
 165
Shear pins in R4 helicopter, description,
 219–220
Sheffield, HMS, 81
Shepherd, Dick, deck landing crashes, 81;
 shot down 93